AF716666

A DATAFIED MIND

The fast-paced evolution of emotion technology and neurotechnology, along with their commercial potential, raises concerns about the adequacy of existing legal frameworks. International organisations have begun addressing these technologies in policy papers, and initial legislative responses are underway. This book offers a comprehensive legal analysis of EU legislation regulating these technologies. It examines four key use cases frequently discussed in media, civil society, and policy debates: mental health and well-being, commercial advertising, political advertising, and workplace monitoring. The book assesses current legal frameworks, highlighting the gaps and challenges involved. Building on this analysis, it presents potential policy responses, exploring a range of legal instruments to address emerging issues. Ultimately, the book aims to offer valuable insights for legal scholars, policymakers, and other stakeholders, contributing to ongoing governance debates and fostering the responsible development of these technologies.

Elisabeth Steindl is a legal scholar with an interdisciplinary background. Holding doctorates in both law and comparative literature, she brings a multidimensional approach to complex legal questions. Her research, focused on the regulatory and ethical implications of digital technologies and innovation, is guided by a global outlook and a commitment to fresh perspectives on the rapidly evolving landscape of emerging technologies.

A Datafied Mind

UNTANGLING EU REGULATION OF EMOTION TECHNOLOGY AND NEUROTECHNOLOGY

ELISABETH STEINDL

CAMBRIDGE
UNIVERSITY PRESS

CAMBRIDGE
UNIVERSITY PRESS

Shaftesbury Road, Cambridge CB2 8EA, United Kingdom

One Liberty Plaza, 20th Floor, New York, NY 10006, USA

477 Williamstown Road, Port Melbourne, VIC 3207, Australia

314–321, 3rd Floor, Plot 3, Splendor Forum, Jasola District Centre, New Delhi – 110025, India

103 Penang Road, #05–06/07, Visioncrest Commercial, Singapore 238467

Cambridge University Press is part of Cambridge University Press & Assessment, a department of the University of Cambridge.

We share the University's mission to contribute to society through the pursuit of education, learning and research at the highest international levels of excellence.

www.cambridge.org
Information on this title: www.cambridge.org/9781009671620

DOI: 10.1017/9781009671644

© Elisabeth Steindl 2025

This publication is in copyright. Subject to statutory exception and to the provisions of relevant collective licensing agreements, no reproduction of any part may take place without the written permission of Cambridge University Press & Assessment.

When citing this work, please include a reference to the DOI 10.1017/9781009671644

First published 2025

Cover image: BlackJack3D / Getty Images

A catalogue record for this publication is available from the British Library

A Cataloging-in-Publication data record for this book is available from the Library of Congress

ISBN 978-1-009-67162-0 Hardback
ISBN 978-1-009-67165-1 Paperback

Cambridge University Press & Assessment has no responsibility for the persistence or accuracy of URLs for external or third-party internet websites referred to in this publication and does not guarantee that any content on such websites is, or will remain, accurate or appropriate.

For EU product safety concerns, contact us at Calle de José Abascal, 56, 1°, 28003 Madrid, Spain, or email eugpsr@cambridge.org

Thought – to call it by a prouder name than it deserved – had let its line down into the stream. It swayed, minute after minute, hither and thither among the reflections and the weeds, letting the water lift it and sink it, until – you know the little tug – the sudden conglomeration of an idea at the end of one's line: and then the cautious hauling of it in, and the careful laying of it out?

Virginia Woolf, *A Room of One's Own*

Contents

List of Abbreviations — *page* ix

Introduction — 1

1 **Setting the Scene** — 5

2 **The Classification of Mind Data under the GDPR** — 13
- 2.1 Is Mind Data Considered Sensitive? — 15
- 2.2 Should Mind Data Be a Sui Generis Special Category? — 29
- 2.3 How Could the New Special Category Be Defined? — 35

3 **The New Regulatory Approach under the AIA** — 39
- 3.1 Emotion Recognition Systems — 41
- 3.2 Classification as Personal Data Remains Central — 54
- 3.3 General-Purpose AI, Generative AI — 55

4 **Use Case 1: Mental Health and Well-Being** — 59
Is My Data Safe and Are the Devices Efficient?
- 4.1 GDPR: Robust in Theory but Lacking in Practice — 60
- 4.2 MDR: Classification Rules Result in Avoidance of Certification — 70
- 4.3 AIA: High Standards for Medium- to High-Risk Medical Devices — 80
- 4.4 EHDS: Controversial Integration of Wellness Apps — 82

5 **Use Case 2: Commercial Advertising** — 89
May Commercial Companies Use Mind Data for Targeted Advertising?
- 5.1 GDPR: When All Else Fails, Consent Prevails — 91
- 5.2 UCPD: Great Potential, Amendments Needed — 106
- 5.3 AVMSD: Ads Using Subliminal Techniques Are Prohibited — 116

6 **Use Case 3: Political Advertising** — 119
Is There a Higher Bar for Political Advertisers?

6.1 GDPR: Consent Remains Prevalent 122
6.2 UCPD: Commercial Fairness Is No Criterion for Political Ads 127
6.3 TTPA: Limited Practical Effect 128
6.4 DSA: Difficulties in Meeting the High Expectations 133
6.5 AIA: Prohibition of Subliminal, Manipulative, or Deceptive Techniques 149

7 **Use Case 4: Employment Monitoring** 158
Is My Boss Allowed to Spy on My Mind?
7.1 GDPR: Fragmented Protection in the Employment Context 160
7.2 Equality Acquis: An Extra Layer of Protection 176
7.3 PWD: Prototype for an Employment-Specific Data Protection Law 180
7.4 AIA: Regulation Remains Fragmented 185

Concluding Remarks 190

Bibliography 195
Index 215

Abbreviations

AI	Artificial Intelligence
AIA	Artificial Intelligence Act
AVMSD	Audiovisual Media Services Directive
BCI	Brain–Computer Interface
CFR	Charter of Fundamental Rights
CJEU	Court of Justice of the European Union
DMA	Digital Markets Act
DPD	Data Protection Directive
DPIA	Data Protection Impact Assessment
DPO	Data Protection Officer
DSA	Digital Services Act
ECHR	European Convention on Human Rights
ECtHR	European Court of Human Rights
EDPB	European Data Protection Board
EDPS	European Data Protection Supervisor
EED	Employment Equality Directive
EEG	Electroencephalogram
EHDS	European Health Data Space
ERS	Emotion Recognition System
EU	European Union
FRIA	Fundamental Rights Impact Assessment
GDPR	General Data Protection Regulation
GPAI	General-Purpose AI
GPSD	General Product Safety Directive
GPSR	General Product Safety Regulation
MDCG	Medical Device Coordination Group
MDD	Medical Devices Directive
MDR	Medical Devices Regulation
MDTs	Mind Datafying Technologies
NLP	Natural Language Processing

PWD	Platform Work Directive
TFEU	Treaty on the Functioning of the European Union
TTPA	Regulation on the Transparency and Targeting of Political Advertising
UCPD	Unfair Commercial Practices Directive
VLOPs	Very Large Online Platforms
VLOSEs	Very Large Online Search Engines
WP29	Article 29 Data Protection Working Party

Introduction

Advances in digital technologies, particularly in data analytics and artificial intelligence (AI), have enabled significant progress in datafying the human mind. Two technologies that stand out for their ability to translate – accurately or not – mental faculties, states, and processes into data are emotion technology and neurotechnology. Collectively coined as 'Mind Datafying Technologies' (MDTs) in this book, both technologies are increasingly being deployed beyond their traditional applications in the medical field. Driven by leading technology companies, MDTs are being rapidly adopted and commercialised, expanding into sectors such as lifestyle and well-being, marketing, advertising, gaming, smart products, employment, and education. Additionally, law enforcement and the military have shown growing interest in MDTs.

The fast-paced evolution of both technologies, coupled with their likelihood of commercial growth and success, sparks concerns about the adequacy of our legal frameworks. International organisations and advisory bodies have started addressing the risks associated with MDTs in their policy papers, with initial recommendations underway. Neuroscientists, ethicists, legal scholars and policymakers are actively debating the implementation of new governance instruments, including potential new rights related to neurotechnology, often referred to as 'neurorights'.

A key feature of this book is its approach to viewing the governance of neurotechnology and emotion technology not as separate independent issues, but as two sides of the same coin. While traditional approaches have often considered the challenges related to neurotechnology as an isolated and unique phenomenon, this book argues for a more integrated perspective, specifically beyond the distinct medical sector. It suggests that regulatory efforts towards both fields should be seen as interconnected challenges, requiring a comprehensive, multifaceted response. This approach is beginning to be reflected in emerging policy trends for neurotechnology governance.[1]

1 For example, the United Nations Educational, Scientific and Cultural Organization (UNESCO), Outcome Document of the First Meeting of the AHEG First Draft of a Recommendation on the

Complementing ongoing debates on international governance instruments and the adequacy of existing human rights catalogues, this book deliberately focuses on the exploration of EU secondary law, positioning itself within a multilevel governance framework. Recognising the procedural complexities of adopting new primary law, the study highlights how existing secondary law may offer agile and flexible instruments to address some of the concerns frequently associated with MDTs.[2] Current developments in EU secondary law underscore the timeliness and relevance of this approach. During the most recent legislative period, EU legislators adopted major general legislation with the intention of substantially shaping the regulatory digital landscape in Europe. In addition to strengthening the general legal framework, they also introduced important sector-specific laws. Several of these new laws are expected to have a profound impact on how MDTs are regulated. Drawing on established legislation, this book places particular emphasis on examining the effects of these newly adopted EU laws.

Delving into the legal analysis, it becomes evident that the General Data Protection Regulation (GDPR) and the Artificial Intelligence Act (AIA) stand out as foundational pieces of legislation, each warranting separate and focused attention before addressing specific domains. The GDPR establishes a distinct regulatory framework for personal data, serving as a cornerstone and constant reference point for all subsequent digital legislation. The restrictive association of emotion technology and neurotechnology with biometric data under the GDPR is discussed in the initial part of the book, highlighting the fundamental complexities this poses for regulating MDTs. The AIA, in turn, provides a groundbreaking regulatory framework for Emotion Recognition Systems (ERS). As a novel legal instrument, it holds significant implications for the regulation of MDTs, both within the EU and on a global scale. Its specificity and recent adoption make it a critical focus of the book's broader analysis. Together, the GDPR and the AIA establish a foundational basis for sector-specific applications, which are then explored in detail through four selected use cases.

Ethics of Neurotechnology (First Version), SHS/BIO/AHEG-Neuro/2024/1 (9 May 2024) aimed to introduce a new category called 'cognitive biometric data', intended to encompass neural data alongside data collected by non-neural biometric technologies that are processed to infer mental states. (<https://unesdoc.unesco.org/ark:/48223/pf0000389768?posInSet=1&queryId=cfc56e24-7a88-4b19-90e7-63bcfc4e556b> accessed 4 May 2025).

The Unesco Draft Text of the Recommendation on the Ethics of Neurotechnology, SHS/IGM-NEURO/2025/MAY/3 (9 April 2025), does not reiterate the introduction of such a category. Instead, it includes 'non-neural data allowing cognitive states inferences', stating that 'several sensor technologies collect biometric data indirectly informing about neural activity.' (<https://unesdoc.unesco.org/ark:/48223/pf0000393395> accessed 19 June 2025).

2 A recent study for the European Parliamentary Research Service, Scientific Foresight Unit (STOA), supports the option of exploring EU secondary law in the context of neurotechnology: Guilherme Maia de Oliveira Wood and others, 'The Protection of Mental Privacy in the Area of Neuroscience – Societal, Legal and Ethical Challenges', (2024) European Parliament, Directorate-General for Parliamentary Research Services <https://data.europa.eu/doi/10.2861/869928> (accessed 8 January 2025).

The four selected use cases in Chapters 4–7 represent topics frequently spotlighted in media, civil society, and policy debates. They include examples from the fields of mental health and well-being, commercial and political advertising, as well as workplace monitoring. Domains deliberately not included are the deployment of MDTs by law enforcement and the military. While these applications have garnered significant attention, the legal frameworks governing the domains differ substantially from all other use cases. Addressing these areas would require a thorough analysis beyond the scope of this book. Building upon the legal analysis of the four use cases de lege lata, the book explores a diverse array of available legal instruments de lege ferenda.

Arguably, the in-depth exploration of both established and emerging laws, crucial for understanding and navigating the legal landscape of MDTs, can be daunting – especially for those less familiar with the complexities of EU law and its constant evolution. To address this challenge, the book employs semi-fictional vignettes as a narrative technique, guiding readers through the intricate legal landscape. These vignettes not only bring abstract legal provisions to life but also aim to make them relatable and accessible, helping readers envision their real-world implications.

At the core of the book's methodological approach lies a use case-based technique. This approach draws inspiration from disciplines such as computer science, business analysis, and systems engineering – fields that frequently analyse complex systems, model interactions and workflows, and optimise system functionalities. When adapted to the legal field, it becomes a valuable tool for analysing complex legal systems, clarifying the interplay both within individual provisions and between different legal elements, and presenting developments in a tangible, comprehensible, and stakeholder-focused manner. This approach is used in the book to sketch a comprehensive picture of the secondary law landscape governing MDTs in selected fields. By examining a substantial body of laws, analysing the intricate interactions among legal components, and delving into critical pain points, the approach provides a detailed and layered understanding of the regulatory environment. The illustrative nature of the technique offers a nuanced perspective on the practical implications of the legal provisions, highlighting gaps, inconsistencies, and ambiguities. Insights derived from the detailed exploration of the legal framework form the foundation for crafting potential policy responses. Hence, this approach bridges the gap between abstract legal analysis and pragmatic policymaking, enabling policymakers and stakeholders to better envision the impact of various policy options.

In keeping with its practical approach, the book does not delve into the philosophical aspects surrounding MDTs, nor does it address broader questions such as the nature of the mind, the mind-body problem, or the metaphysical debates on cognition and consciousness. While these considerations are undoubtedly important, they require a more theoretical exploration, which contrasts with the book's chosen approach. Similarly, the book does not engage with the societal benefits or harms of MDTs, nor does it examine whether these technologies can accurately identify or infer the states of the mind – an issue often contested by experts, particularly in contexts outside of the medical field.[3] Acknowledging that MDTs continue to be developed and adopted by the market despite fierce criticism of their scientific validity, the book adopts a distinctly pragmatic perspective. It focuses solely on the regulatory landscape for MDTs and the available instruments to regulate them. In doing so, the book seeks to contribute to ongoing policy debates by providing an additional perspective and resource for balanced decision-making, with the hope of encouraging further discussion on thoughtful governance and effective regulation for MDTs.

3 See, for instance, Lisa Feldman Barrett and others, 'Emotional Expressions Reconsidered: Challenges to Inferring Emotion from Human Facial Movements', (2019) 20 *Psychological Science in the Public Interest*, 1–68.

1

Setting the Scene

Before delving into the legal implications, it is helpful to briefly review the current state of the debate and establish the context for the ensuing discussion. Both emotion technology and neurotechnology remain in their formative stages, with their definitions, boundaries, and applications evolving rapidly. As these technologies progress, policymakers, legislators, and legal scholars have become increasingly aware of the regulatory challenges they present. The key developments in this area will be summarised in a general overview before the detailed legal analysis begins.

The term 'neurotechnology' has yet to be definitively defined.[1] Typically, it refers to technologies designed to interact directly with the brain or the nervous system, allowing for the monitoring, recording, or modulating of neural activities. Most relevant for this book are Brain–Computer Interfaces (BCIs), which are increasingly utilised not only in the distinct medical but also in various other markets. BCIs link the brain to an external computer and come in various forms. They can either be implanted directly into the brain, known as 'invasive BCIs', or worn externally, referred to as 'non-invasive BCIs'.[2]

[1] The OECD Recommendation of the Council on Responsible Innovation in Neurotechnology, (2019), describes neurotechnology as 'devices and procedures used to access, monitor, investigate, assess, manipulate, and/or emulate the structure and function of the neural systems of natural persons' (section II). (<https://legalinstruments.oecd.org/en/instruments/OECD-LEGAL-0457> accessed 29 April 2025).

The UNESCO Draft Text of the Recommendation on the Ethics of Neurotechnology, SHS/IGM-NEURO/2025/MAY/3 (9 April 2025), proposes the following definition: 'Neurotechnology refers currently to devices, systems, and procedures – encompassing both hardware and software – that directly measure, access, monitor, analyze, predict or modulate the nervous system to understand, influence, restore, or anticipate its structure, activity, function, (speech, motor). Neurotechnology combines elements of neuroscience, engineering, material science, and computing, among others' (section I para 2).

[2] For a more granular understanding of the types and functioning of BCIs, see Chang S. Nam and others (eds.), *Brain–Computer Interfaces Handbook: Technological and Theoretical Advances* (CRC Press 2018).

Discussions concerning the legitimacy and ethics of neurotechnology have been a topic of interest in scholarly research for a considerable time.[3] Over the past few decades, a legal subfield known as 'neurolaw' has emerged, originating from reflections on the potential influence of neurotechnology on criminal justice and the judiciary system.[4] Ever since, scholars have been engaged in vivid debates surrounding both traditional and novel legal concepts with regard to neurotechnology.[5]

Traditional neurolaw research focuses on questions related to violations of fundamental rights and their implications.[6] Indeed, emerging neurotechnologies bring a number of fundamental rights considerations to the forefront.[7] Of particular significance is the impact on the right to freedom of thought, the right to respect for private and family life, the right to physical and mental integrity, the right to the protection of personal data, the right to freedom from discrimination, the right to a fair trial, and the *nemo tenetur* principle against self-incrimination. Ultimately, all build upon the right to human dignity, which may be at stake when facing technologies that have the potential to alter a person's identity, autonomy, and agency and invade their innermost privacy.

In the early 2000s, a concept known as 'cognitive liberty' surfaced from the intersection between neuroethical and neurolegal considerations.[8] It initiated a rights-based approach to neurotechnology that is ongoing.[9] The concept of cognitive liberty was introduced as an intended update to the traditional freedom of thought, meant to protect every person's fundamental right to think independently and to have sole jurisdiction over the control of one's own electrochemical brain state and

[3] For a detailed exploration of the notion of neuroexceptionalism and whether a call for new rights can be drawn from it, see Dara Hallinan and others, 'Legal Neuroexceptionalism: Framing a Concept', (2023) 14(2) *European Journal of Law and Technology* <www.ejlt.org/index.php/ejlt/article/view/902> accessed 8 January 2025.

[4] See J. S. Taylor and others, 'Neuropsychologists and Neurolawyers', (1991) 5 *Neuropsychology*, 293 <https://doi.org/10.1037/0894-4105.5.4.293>.

[5] For recent examples, see Tade Matthias Spranger (ed.), *International Neurolaw: A Comparative Analysis* (Springer 2012); Eugenio Picozza (ed.), *Neurolaw: An Introduction* (Springer 2016); Antonio D'Aloia and Maria Chiara Errigo (eds.), *Neuroscience and Law: Complicated Crossings and New Perspectives* (Springer 2020); Sjors Ligthart and others (eds.), *Neurolaw: Advances in Neuroscience, Justice & Security* (Springer 2021); Pablo López-Silva and Luca Valera (eds.), *Protecting the Mind: Challenges in Law, Neuroprotection, and Neurorights* (Springer Cham 2022).

[6] For a brief history on neurolaw/neurorights, see, e.g., Marcello Ienca, 'On Neurorights', (24 September 2021) *Frontiers in Human Neuroscience* <https://doi.org/10.3389/fnhum.2021.701258>.

[7] Sjors Ligthart and others, 'Minding Rights: Mapping Ethical and Legal Foundations of "Neurorights"', (2023) 32(4) *Cambridge Quarterly of Healthcare Ethics*, 461–481 <https://doi.org/10.1017/S0963180123000245>.

[8] See R. G. Boire, 'On Cognitive Liberty I', (1999) 1 *Journal of Cognitive Liberties*, 7–13; R. G. Boire, 'On Cognitive Liberty II', (2000) 2(2) *Journal of Cognitive Liberties*, 7–20; R. G. Boire, 'On Cognitive Liberty III', (2001) 2(1) *Journal of Cognitive Liberties*, 7–22.

[9] For an overview on attempts to implement neurorights, see Elisa Moreu Carbonell, 'The Regulation of Neuro-Rights', (2021) 2(2) *European Review of Digital Administration & Law – Erdal*, 149–162 <https://doi.org/10.53136/979125994752914>.

mental processes.[10] The concept of cognitive liberty as a right to self-determination of one's own mental processes and the protection of one's mental privacy was then further developed to include not only the protection of individuals against the coercive and unconsented use of neurotechnology but also the freedom of individuals to use them and to enhance one's cognitive abilities.[11]

In recent years, the rapid advancement of neurotechnology and its expanding presence in the consumer market, driven by substantial investments from major tech companies,[12] has sparked a wave of proposals to revise the existing catalogue of fundamental rights. The call for a right to cognitive liberty was complemented by a list of further neuro-specific rights, such as the right to mental privacy, the right to mental integrity, and the right to psychological continuity.[13] Advocacy groups are pushing for even more neuro-specific rights to be introduced and implemented.[14] At the same time, there appears to be a return towards a more refined focus on the concept of cognitive liberty.[15]

International organisations have started paying considerable attention to neurotechnology, with policy initiatives in this area gaining momentum. In 2019, the Organization for Economic Cooperation and Development (OECD) has adopted a 'Recommendation on responsible innovation in Neurotechnology' as a first standard of its kind.[16] In the Recommendation, the OECD calls on members and nonmembers to enable the capacity of oversight and advisory bodies to address novel issues in neurotechnology. The section on safeguarding personal brain data and other information gained through neurotechnology is in close alignment with the European data protection framework.[17] However, considering that the thirty-eight

[10] Wyre Sententia, 'Neuroethical Considerations: Cognitive Liberty and Converging Technologies for Improving Human Cognition' (2004) 1013 *Annals of the New York Academy of Sciences*, 221–228 <https://doi.org/10.1196/annals.1305.014>.

[11] Jan Christoph Bublitz, 'Cognitive Liberty or the International Human Right to Freedom of Thought', in J. Clausen and N. Levy (eds.), *Handbook of Neuroethics* (Springer 2015), 1309–1333 <https://doi.org/10.1007/978-94-007-4707-4_166>.

[12] Elisabeth Steindl, 'Consumer Neuro Devices within EU Product Safety Law: Are We Prepared for Big Tech Ante Portas?', (2024) 52 *Computer, Law & Security Review*, 105945 <https://doi.org/10.1016/j.clsr.2024.105945>.

[13] Marcello Ienca and Roberto Andorno, 'Towards New Human Rights in the Age of Neuroscience and Neurotechnology', (2017) 13(5) *Life Sciences, Society and Policy* <https://doi.org/10.1186/s40504-017-0050-1>.

[14] The Neurorights Foundation, for example, is calling for five neurorights: the right to mental privacy, the right to personal identity, the right to free will, the right to fair access to mental augmentation, the right to protection from bias. See <https://plum-conch-dwsc.squarespace.com/> accessed 8 January 2025.

[15] Nita Farahany, *The Battle for Your Brain: Defending the Right to Think Freely in the Age of Neurotechnology* (St. Martin's Press 2023).

[16] OECD, Recommendation of the Council on Responsible Innovation in Neurotechnology, (2019) <https://legalinstruments.oecd.org/en/instruments/OECD-LEGAL-0457> 8 January 2025.

[17] OECD, Recommendation of the Council on Responsible Innovation in Neurotechnology, section III, point 7.

OECD Member States go far beyond EU territory and span jurisdictions ranging from New Zealand and Australia to Costa Rica, Canada, and the US, to name but a few non-EU Member States, it becomes evident that the recommendations regarding safeguards for brain data are essential and should not be underestimated in their (albeit rather symbolic) value.

Following the OECD Recommendation, other international organisations have also begun to examine the implications of neurotechnology. The Council of Europe has initiated a strategic action plan on the ethics of biomedicine (2020–2025), including a chapter on applications of neurotechnology.[18] The Secretary General of the UN stressed in his 2021 report that there is an evident need to update or clarify 'our application of human rights frameworks and standards to address frontier issues and prevent harms in the digital or technology spaces, including in relation to [...] neuro-technology'.[19] UNESCO has published a report on the ethical issues of neurotechnology,[20] and a document on the risks and challenges of neurotechnology for human rights.[21]

In 2024, international initiatives addressing neurotechnology have accelerated further. In April 2024, the OECD complemented their Recommendation with a neurotechnology toolkit to support policymakers in implementing it.[22] In May 2024, UNESCO published a first draft of their Recommendation on the Ethics of Neurotechnology.[23] In August 2024, the UN Human Rights Council Advisory Committee issued its report, 'Impact, Opportunities and Challenges of Neurotechnology with Regard to the Promotion and Protection of All Human Rights'.[24]

In addition to these developments on the international level, there are noteworthy regulatory initiatives occurring on national or state law levels. Latin America appears to be leading the way, with significant legislative efforts in countries such as Chile, Mexico, Brazil, and others, aimed at introducing rights specifically

18 Council of Europe, Strategic Action Plan on Human Rights and Technologies in Biomedicine <www.coe.int/en/web/bioethics/strategic-action-plan> accessed 27 January 2025.

19 UN, Our Common Agenda – Report of the Secretary-General, (2021), section 35 <www.un.org/en/content/common-agenda-report/assets/pdf/Common_Agenda_Report_English.pdf> accessed 8 January 2025.

20 UNESCO, Ethical Issues of Neurotechnology: Report, Adopted in December 2021, (2022) <https://doi.org/10.54678/QNKB6229>.

21 UNESCO, The Risks and Challenges of Neurotechnologies for Human Rights, (2023) <https://doi.org/10.54678/POGS7778>.

22 OECD, Neurotechnology Toolkit to support policymakers in implementing the OECD Recommendation on Responsible Innovation in Neurotechnology, (2024).

23 UNESCO, First Version of a Draft Text of a Recommendation on the Ethics of Neurotechnology, SHS/BIO/AHEG-Neuro/2024/1 (Paris, 9 May 2024) <https://unesdoc.unesco.org/ark:/48223/pf0000389768?posInSet=1&queryId=cfc56e24-7a88-4b19-90e7-63bcfc4e556b> 8 January 2025.

24 UN Human Rights Council Advisory Committee, 'Impact, Opportunities and Challenges of Neurotechnology with Regard to the Promotion and Protection of All Human Rights' (A/HRC/57/61) (2024) <https://documents.un.org/doc/undoc/gen/g24/133/28/pdf/g2413328.pdf> accessed 20 January 2025.

addressing neurotechnology or neurodata.[25] In the US, states like Colorado, Minnesota, and California are advancing privacy protection for neurodata/neuroal data.[26]

In the EU, the regulatory focus concerning neurotechnology currently revolves around soft-law instruments. Spain is addressing neurotechnology in its 'Charter of Digital Rights' (2021), outlining fundamental digital rights specifically concerning the use of neurotechnology.[27] In France, a charter for the responsible development of neurotechnologies has been presented by the Ministère de l'Enseignement supérieur et de la Recherche (Ministry for Higher Education and Research, 2022).[28] On the EU level, the telecommunications and digital ministers have launched the León Declaration on European Neurotechnology.[29]

The newfound awareness among policymakers regarding neurotechnology is not without its share of serious dissenting opinions. Legal scholars criticise a possibly overhasty implementation of new 'neurorights'.[30] They recommend conducting a thorough doctrinal assessment of existing laws and carefully identifying any potential shortcomings before introducing new rights.

While the governance of neurotechnology has been a longstanding topic of debate, the regulation of emotion technology has only recently emerged as a subject of discussion. Emotion technology is still a nascent field, with no definitive consensus on the precise terminology used to describe it yet. Terms such as 'affective

25 For an overview on the initiatives in Latin America, see Future of Privacy Forum, 'Privacy and the Rise of "Neurorights" in Latin America' (20 March 2024) <https://fpf.org/blog/privacy-and-the-rise-of-neurorights-in-latin-america/> accessed 8 January 2025. For the Mexican Digital Rights Charter, addressing Neurorights, see Carta de derechos de la persona en el entorno digital código de buenas práticas <www.infocdmx.org.mx/images/biblioteca/2022/Carta_Derechos_Persona_EntornoDigital_Digital.pdf> accessed 8 January 2025.

26 Skye Witley, 'Brain-Scanning Technology Spurs State Moves on Neural Privacy' (13 February 2024) <https://news.bloomberglaw.com/privacy-and-data-security/brain-scanning-technology-spurs-state-moves-on-neural-privacy> accessed 8 January 2025.

27 Carta de los derechos digitales, chapter XXVI <www.lamoncloa.gob.es/presidente/actividades/Documents/2021/140721-Carta_Derechos_Digitales_RedEs.pdf> accessed 8 January 2025.

28 Ministère de l'Enseignement supérieur et de la Recherche, Charte de développement responsable des neurotechnologies (17 November 2022) <www.enseignementsup-recherche.gouv.fr/fr/charte-de-developpement-responsable-des-neurotechnologies-87964> accessed 8 January 2025.

29 EU Léon Declaration on European Neurotechnology: A Human Centric and Rights-Oriented Approach (2023). Previously accessible at <https://spanish-presidency.consilium.europa.eu/media/04rh53jr/le%C3%B3n-declaration.pdf>. Note: This document appears to have been removed from the Internet.

30 For critical discussions, see, for instance, Diego Borbón and Luisa Borbón, 'A Critical Perspective on NeuroRights: Comments Regarding Ethics and Law', *Frontiers in Human Neuroscience* (25 October 2021) <https://doi.org/10.3389/fnhum.2021.703121>; Jan Christoph Bublitz, 'Novel Neurorights: From Nonsense to Substance', (2022) 15(7) *Neuroethics* <https://doi.org/10.1007/s12152-022-09481-3>; Sjors Ligthart and others, 'Minding Rights'; Jan Christoph Bublitz, 'Neurotechnologies and Human Rights: Restating and Reaffirming the Multi-layered Protection of the Person', (2024) 28(5) *International Journal of Human Rights*, 782–807 <https://doi.org/10.1080/13642987.2024.2310830>; Maia de Oliveira Wood and others, 'The Protection of Mental Privacy'.

computing', 'affect technology', 'emotion AI', 'emotional AI', 'emotion recognition', 'emotion detection', 'emotion analysis', 'emotional analytics', 'sentiment analysis', or 'sentiment detection' are often used interchangeably in the media and in policy discussions. These terms generally refer to technologies that are designed to analyse and interpret human emotions/affects through different modalities, such as audio, video, or text.[31] Due to the close conceptual overlap between these terms, this book adopts 'emotion technology' as an umbrella term to encompass the various approaches and applications within this emerging field, providing a unified framework for discussion. The common denominator of all these different approaches is that they make inferences about individuals' affective states by sensing and measuring data points, using both passive and active data collection. The accuracy of emotion technology remains a topic of considerable debate, particularly when applied outside the medical field.[32]

The body of legal scholarship examining aspects related to the governance and regulation of emotion technology is gradually expanding.[33] Considering that the technology itself is a relatively recent development, the corresponding body of scholarly work is however still in its early stages and evolving. The current literature is not yet sufficiently developed to reliably discern major trends akin to those identified in the field of neurotechnology. Recurring topics include, however, privacy and data protection concerns, coupled with questions surrounding the classification of data and the technology's scientific validity.

International advisory bodies have slowly started to address emotion technology. In comparison to the dimension of the policy discussions surrounding the governance of neurotechnology, the attention devoted to emotion technology is

[31] The emotional AI Lab describes emotional AI as 'technologies that use affective computing and artificial intelligence techniques to sense, learn about and interact with human emotional life. It is a weak form of AI in that these technologies aim to read and react to emotions through text, voice, computer vision, biometric sensing and, potentially, information about a person's context' (Emotional AI Lab, 'What Is Emotional AI' <https://emotionalai.org/so-what-is-emotional-ai/> accessed 8 January 2025).

[32] See, for instance, Lisa Feldman Barrett and others, 'Emotional Expressions Reconsidered'.

[33] See, for instance, Andrew McStay and L. Urquhart, '"This Time with Feeling?" Assessing EU Data Governance Implications of Out of Home Appraisal Based Emotional AI', (2019) 24 First Monday 10 <https://doi.org/10.5210/fm.v24i10.9457>; Gretchen Greene, 'The Ethics of AI and Emotional Intelligence: Data Sources, Applications, and Questions for Evaluating Ethics Risk', Partnership on AI (2020) <https://partnershiponai.org/paper/the-ethics-of-ai-and-emotional-intelligence/> accessed 8 January 2025; Peggy Valcke and others, 'Constitutional Challenges in the Emotional AI Era', in H.-W. Micklitz and others (eds.), *Constitutional Challenges in the Algorithmic Society* (Cambridge University Press 2021), 57–77; Andreas Häuselmann, 'Fit for Purpose? Affective Computing Meets EU Data Protection Law', (August 2021) 11(3) *International Data Privacy Law*, 245–256 <https://doi.org/10.1093/idpl/ipab008>; Elisabeth Steindl, 'Does the European Data Protection Framework Adequately Protect our Emotions?', (2022) 8 (2) *European Data Protection Law Review*, 311–319. <https://doi.org/10.21552/edpl/2022/2/20>. Jubin Dejam, *Gefühlsdatenschutz. Eine Untersuchung der datenschutzrechtlichen Rahmenbedingungen von Datenverarbeitungen mittels Affective Computing*, Frankfurter Studien zum Datenschutz 69 (Nomos 2023) <https://doi.org/10.5771/9783748917953>; A. Häuselmann and others, 'EU Law and Emotion Data' (11th International Conference on Affective Computing and Intelligent Interaction ACII, Cambridge, MA, USA, 2023), 1–8 <https://doi.org/10.1109/ACII59096.2023.10388181>; Damian Clifford, *Data Protection Law and Emotion* (Oxford University Press 2024).

considerably more limited, both in terms of quantity and quality. Noteworthy examples, however, illustrate the growing significance of the topic and underscore its increasing prominence on the agenda. In highlighting some of the examples, the Council of Europe Consultative Committee of the Convention for the protection of individuals with regard to automatic processing of personal data (Convention 108) recommends, in its Guidelines on Facial Recognition (2021), prohibiting 'affection recognition' – defined as the use of technology to identify or classify human emotions – in certain sensitive areas such as education, insurance, and workplaces.[34] The UN Committee on the Rights of the Child, in their General Comment No. 25 (2021) on children's rights in relation to the digital environment, recommends that practices relying on neuromarketing or emotional analytics used to promote products, applications, and services be prohibited from engagement directly or indirectly with children.[35] Moreover, the UN Committee calls upon States to introduce and update, de lege ferenda, data protection regulation and prohibit practices 'that manipulate or interfere with children's right to freedom of thought and belief in the digital environment, for example by emotional analytics or inference'.[36]

Regulatory authorities in the EU, including the European Data Protection Board (EDPB) and the European Data Protection Supervisor (EDPS), have also begun to focus on emotion technology. This is reflected, for instance, in the EDPB Guidelines 8/2020,[37] which address the targeting of social media users, and in the EDPB/EDPS Joint Opinion 05/2021 on the proposed AIA.[38] In their Joint Opinion 05/2021, they recommend a full ban of Emotion Recognition Systems under the AIA.

EU legislators have not endorsed the call for a complete prohibition. Instead, they have responded to the ongoing debate in a more nuanced manner, introducing the first comprehensive, multilayered regime for the regulation of Emotion Recognition Systems under the AIA.[39]

The decision to address the regulation of neurotechnology and emotion technology together in this book, coining the term 'Mind Datafying Technologies' (MDTs)

[34] Council of Europe, Consultative Committee of the Convention for the Protection of Individuals with Regard to Automatic Processing of Personal Data (Convention 108), Guidelines on Facial Recognition (2021), 8 <https://edoc.coe.int/en/artificial-intelligence/9753-guidelines-on-facial-recognition.html> accessed 8 January 2025.

[35] UN Committee on the Rights of the Child, General Comment No. 25 (2021) on Children's Rights in Relation to the Digital Environment, section 42 <https://digitallibrary.un.org/record/3906061> accessed 8 January.

[36] UN Committee on the Rights of the Child, General Comment No. 25, section 62.

[37] EDPB, Guidelines 8/2020 on the Targeting of Social Media Users, Version 2.0, Adopted on 13 April 2021.

[38] EDPB–EDPS, Joint Opinion 05/2021 on the Proposal for a Regulation of the European Parliament and of the Council Laying Down Harmonized Rules on Artificial Intelligence (Artificial Intelligence Act) (18 June 2021).

[39] A general legal analysis of the framework governing Emotion Recognition Systems under the AIA will be provided in Chapter 3, titled 'The New Regulatory Approach under the AIA.' This will be further complemented by a detailed legal analysis within each of the four use cases, Chapters 4–7.

to encompass both fields due to their shared ability to translate mental faculties, processes, and states into data, is a fundamental one. It forms the foundation for the legal analysis that follows, providing a cohesive framework to tackle the regulatory challenges these technologies present. It is a deliberate choice that, in the author's view, offers a fresh perspective with the capacity to enrich the broader discourse and inform ongoing policy debates.

The legal analysis begins by exploring the legal nature of the data processed by MDTs under the GDPR. It then evaluates the implications of regulating Emotion Recognition Systems within the framework of the newly adopted AIA. Building on these general considerations that are applicable across all domains, the book explores the regulation of MDTs within specific contexts in four selected use cases of Chapters 4–7 as illustrative examples. The analysis examines the impact of both established EU laws and emerging EU legislation. Throughout the book, the findings will serve as a basis for formulating potential policy responses de lege ferenda, applying a variety of legal instruments.

2

The Classification of Mind Data under the GDPR

The entire operation of MDTs hinges upon the processing of data. Therefore, the existing data protection framework builds the first legal reference governing their deployment. Compared to other jurisdictions, the EU has a long-standing and robust data protection regime. Article 16 of the Treaty on the Functioning of the European Union (TFEU) and Article 8 of the Charter of Fundamental Rights (CFR) enshrine the protection of personal data at primary law level.[1] An increasingly elaborate framework of regulations and directives is shaping Europe's policy approach to data protection and data governance at secondary law level.[2]

The General Data Protection Regulation (GDPR) serves as the primary point of contact for practitioners, laying down core principles for the processing of personal data and providing a set of rights for the data subjects. Following the Data Protection Directive 95/46/EC (DPD), the GDPR was proposed in 2012 and became applicable in 2018. Being the first regulation of its kind on a global scale, the GDPR has introduced cornerstone principles and fundamental concepts into the protection and classification of personal data, which several similar legislations have subsequently adopted.[3]

Among the fundamental concepts of the EU data protection framework are the distinctly different legal regimes for personal data and non-personal data. Within the realm of personal data, an additional distinction exists between the regime for special category data (also referred to as 'sensitive' data) and that for normal

1 Consolidated versions of the Treaty on European Union and the Treaty on the Functioning of the European Union 2012/C 326/01; Charter of Fundamental Rights of the European Union 2012/C 326/02.

2 For a normative discussion of EU data protection law within the broader regulatory framework, see Orla Lynskey, *The Foundations of EU Data Protection Law* (Oxford University Press 2015); Raphaël Gellert, *The Risk-Based Approach to Data Protection* (Oxford University Press 2020).

3 Regulation (EU) 2016/679 of the European Parliament and of the Council of 27 April 2016 on the Protection of Natural Persons with Regard to the Processing of Personal Data and on the Free Movement of Such Data, and Repealing Directive 95/46/EC (General Data Protection Regulation), OJ 2016 L 119/1.

personal data.[4] Due to advancements in AI and data analytics, both concepts are increasingly coming under scrutiny. Nonetheless, the protection of data processed by MDTs continues to be governed by this binary approach.

The territorial scope of the GDPR is remarkably wide. The GDPR applies to any processing of a controller or a processor established in the Union, regardless of whether the processing takes place in the Union, as well as to the processing of personal data by any controller or processor not established in the Union, provided the processing relates to the offering of goods or services within the Union or the monitoring of the behaviour of data subjects therein.[5] Thus, the principles and concepts of the regulation are not restricted to data subjects, processors, and controllers within the EU, but their impact goes far beyond European borders by sheer market power and market mechanisms.[6]

Arguably, the primary innovators and major tech firms driving the development and commodification of MDTs are based outside Europe, with many of them being US companies. However, these companies and their devices are still subject to European data protection requirements if they intend to operate in the European internal market and do business with European customers. This means that the regulation of MDTs by the European data protection framework de lege lata holds significant economic and practical importance not only for Europeans but also for a wider global audience.

As regards the material scope, the GDPR applies solely to the processing of personal data. Generally, the GDPR and its respective case law follow a broad notion of personal data.[7] The data processed by MDTs in the use cases discussed in this book, Chapters 4–7, namely in the context of mental health and well-being, personalised advertising for commercial or political purposes, and employee monitoring, is typically associated with a user profile. Such a user profile usually contains parameters such as a name or an IP (Internet Protocol) address, which are then linked to the data set.[8] The data in these scenarios is therefore relating to an identified or identifiable natural person. Thus, the processed data in the examined

4 The GDPR itself uses the term 'sensitive data' only in Recital 10 GDPR: 'This Regulation also provides a margin of manoeuvre for Member States to specify its rules, including for the processing of special categories of personal data ("sensitive data").'

5 Article 3 GDPR.

6 See Anu Bradford, *The Brussels Effect: How the European Union Rules the World* (New York, 2020; online edn, Oxford Academic, 19 December 2019) <https://doi.org/10.1093/oso/9780190088583.001.0001>.

7 Article 4(1) GDPR defines personal data as 'any information relating to an identified or identifiable natural person ("data subject")'. For a list of relevant case law, see, for instance, Lee A. Bygrave and Luca Tosoni, Article 4(1) in Christopher Kuner and others, *The EU General Data Protection Regulation (GDPR), A Commentary* (print publication date: 2020; published to Oxford Scholarship Online 2021), <https://doi.org/10.1093/oso/9780198826491.001.0001>.

8 Recital 30 GDPR specifies that: '[n]atural persons may be associated with online identifiers provided by their devices, applications, tools and protocols, such as internet protocol addresses'.

contexts commonly qualifies as personal data, and the processing lies within the material scope of the GDPR.[9]

2.1 IS MIND DATA CONSIDERED SENSITIVE?

One of the most consequential doctrinal decisions enshrined in the GDPR is the distinction between special category versus normal personal data, and the differing legal regimes following thereof. The more rigid legal regime for special category data reflects the higher risks of misuse, which can result in widespread human rights abuses and detrimental effects for individuals, such as unfair discrimination.

Notably, the strict distinction between sensitive and non-sensitive data is relevant not only for compliance with the GDPR. It bears consequences for the entirety of digital law and all its related norms, as it remains a constant point of reference for all legal pieces addressing personal data, directly or indirectly.

Sarah, a psychology student, and her friend Drew, a computer scientist, plan to co-found a company. Both are intrigued by the potential of MDTs. They consider developing software that utilises emotion technology or designing a BCI. They are committed to complying with all relevant laws. While they are not experts in data protection, they have heard about GDPR and personal data, understanding that some but not all personal data is considered sensitive. They are wondering whether the data processed by their future software would be classified as sensitive and if such classification would have any consequences for the development of their software.

Whether the data processed by MDTs can and will be classified as sensitive, initiating the regime for special category data, is crucial to all parties. It impacts all roles outlined in the GDPR: the controller and the processor, from a professional data governance and data management point of view, as well as the data subject, from a data protection and privacy perspective. Safeguards for the protection of special category data should already be implemented in the design and be part of the functioning of a device or software. Therefore, it is a question that should be considered from the outset of the development phase. Sarah and Drew are rightly posing the question of whether the data processed by their software is going to be classified as sensitive and what requirements they need to consider at the very early stages of development.

The GDPR imposes a general prohibition on the processing of sensitive data in Article 9(1) GDPR, with exemptions to this prohibition to be found in Article 9(2) GDPR. The number of these exemptions is exhaustive, and they are to be

[9] For applications where the nature of the processed data as personal data is put in question, see Section 2.1.4 'Personal Data or Not'.

applied restrictively. The classification of data as sensitive initiates a regime of special requirements. These requirements are not understood as a separate regime in isolation from the already existing regime for the processing of normal personal data. Rather, they are intended to enhance the latter with respect to the increased risks to fundamental rights and freedoms.[10] Following prevailing opinion, the processing of special category data necessitates an exemption for processing according to Article 9(2) GDPR, in addition to (not replacing) the requirement for a valid legal basis according to Article 6(1) GDPR.[11] Further, the bundle of requirements for sensitive data processing includes the appointment of a Data Protection Officer (DPO)[12] and the performance of a Data Protection Impact Assessment (DPIA)[13] where the processing of special categories of data is on a large scale.[14] The processing of sensitive data has to be taken into account by data controllers when deciding whether data may be processed for another purpose.[15] Moreover, the GDPR has limited automated decision-making to cases where explicit consent has been obtained or for reasons of substantial public interest under EU or national law.[16]

Article 9 GDPR encompasses several opening clauses that allow for national deviations.[17] For example, Article 9(4) GDPR allows Member States to adopt even stricter provisions concerning the processing of genetic data, biometric data, or data concerning health. The latter two categories are particularly relevant for data processed by MDTs.

While in the common understanding the data processed by MDTs – information about our emotions, thoughts, intentions, and psychological states – is perceived as very intimate, its classification as sensitive data according to data protection law is not self-evident.[18] When Sarah and Drew check the GDPR for terms such as 'emotion data', 'affective data', 'cognitive data', 'neuro data', 'neural data', 'brain

10 Argumentum: 'In addition to the specific requirements for such processing, the general principles and other rules of this Regulation should apply' (Recital 51 GDPR).

11 Established literature supports this view, inter alia, with recourse to Recital 51 GDPR. The CJEU confirmed this opinion verbatim in C-667/21 *ZQ versus Medizinischer Dienst der Krankenversicherung Nordrhein, Körperschaft des öffentlichen Rechts* [2023], section 71–79.

12 Article 37(1)(c) GDPR.

13 Article 35(3)(b) GDPR.

14 While the GDPR does not define large-scale processing, Recital 91 GDPR offers some indicators. For regulatory guidance on the matter, see Article 29 Data Protection Working Party, Guidelines on Data Protection Officers (DPOs), WP 243 Rev.01, As Last Revised and Adopted on 5 April 2017, 7–8; Article 29 Data Protection Working Party, Guidelines Data Protection Impact Assessment (DPIA) and Determining Whether Processing Is 'Likely to Result in a High Risk' for the Purposes of Regulation 2016/679, WP 248 rev.01, As Last Revised and Adopted on 4 October 2017, 10.

15 Article 6(4)(c) GDPR.

16 Article 22(4) GDPR.

17 Article 9(2)(a)–(b), (2)(g)–(j), (3), and (4) GDPR.

18 See also Marcello Ienca and Gianclaudio Malgieri, 'Mental Data Protection and the GDPR', (2022) 9(1) *Journal of Law and the Biosciences*, 1–19 <https://doi.org/10.1093/jlb/lsac006>.

data', or 'mental data' – terms used frequently in the media or by policymakers and scholars in the context of MDTs – their search does not yield any results. These and similar terms are not familiar to the GDPR; they are not among the listed categories in Article 9(1) GDPR or elsewhere to be found.

For data processed by MDTs to be classified as special category data, it must fall within one of the categories listed in Article 9(1) GDPR. Article 9(1) GDPR defines an exhaustive list of data types that are considered special category. The list comprises 'data revealing racial or ethnic origin, political opinions, religious or philosophical beliefs, or trade union membership, and the processing of genetic data, biometric data for the purpose of uniquely identifying a natural person, data concerning health or data concerning a natural person's sex life or sexual orientation'.[19] This list is exhaustive. However, it is important to note that the listed categories are not mutually exclusive and may, in fact, overlap. Data can therefore be classified in more than one of the categories at the same time.

2.1.1 *The Biometric Dilemma*

The techniques employed by MDTs are predominantly linked to the category of biometric data. Alas, the classification of data processed by MDTs as special category biometric data according to the GDPR is remarkably complex.[20]

As early as 2003, the Article 29 Data Protection Working Party (hereinafter referred to as 'WP29')[21] issued a working document on biometrics[22] in response to the expanding use of biometric techniques. Therein, the WP29 distinguishes two categories of biometric techniques:

> Firstly, there are physical and physiological-based techniques which measure the physiological characteristics of a person and include: fingerprint verification, finger

[19] Article 9(1) GDPR.

[20] For a comprehensive outline of the challenges of biometric data for data protection, see Nancy Yue Liu, *Bio-Privacy: Privacy Regulations and the Challenge of Biometrics* (Routledge 2011) <https://doi.org/10.4324/9780203804087>. Els J. Kindt, *Privacy and Data Protection Issues of Biometric Applications: A Comparative Legal Analysis* (Springer 2013).

[21] The Article 29 Data Protection Working Party (WP29) served as the regulatory data protection body until 25 May 2018, when it was replaced by the European Data Protection Board (EDPB). Arguably, the guidelines and documents by the WP29 were adopted before the GDPR became applicable. However, these guidelines and documents have significantly informed the legislative process of the GDPR and remain relevant insofar as the EDPB has not adopted new documents on the topic and/or they are compatible with the GDPR. The EDPB itself often builds upon them. For a list of the WP29 Guidelines that the EDPB has explicitly endorsed, see: <www.edpb.europa.eu/our-work-tools/general-guidance/endorsed-wp29-guidelines_en> accessed 8 January 2025.

[22] The WP29 and the EDPS use the term 'biometrics' mainly as a synonym of 'biometric data'. For the nuances between these two terms and their legal and technical notions, see Catherine A. Jasserand, 'Avoiding Terminological Confusion between the Notions of "Biometrics" and "Biometric Data": An Investigation into the Meanings of the Terms from a European Data Protection and a Scientific Perspective', (2016) 6(1) *International Data Privacy Law*, 63–76 <https://doi.org/10.1093/idpl/ipv020>.

> image analysis, iris recognition, retina analysis, face recognition, outline of hand patterns, ear shape recognition, body odour detection, voice recognition, DNA pattern analysis and sweat pore analysis, etc.
>
> Secondly there are behavioural-based techniques, which measure the behaviour of a person and include hand-written signature verification, keystroke analysis, gait analysis, etc.[23]

Moreover, the WP29 describes three main characteristics for biometric data, namely that it is:

- universal (the biometric element exists in all persons)
- unique (the biometric element must be distinctive to each person) and
- permanent (the property of the biometric element remains permanent over time for each person).[24]

These characteristics – universal, unique, or at least sufficiently distinctive to allow separating two individuals, and permanent – remain relevant to this day. They are further elaborated in scholarly literature,[25] and they are referred to in commentaries stating that biometric data is '*in principle*, shared across most if not all of the human population, stable at least for considerable periods of a human's life, and distinctive if not unique for each individual'.[26]

In 2012, the WP29 revisited the topic in an Opinion on developments in biometric technologies. The description of biometric data there is both broad and narrow at the same time. Accordingly, biometric data may encompass 'biological properties, behavioural aspects, physiological characteristics, living traits or repeatable actions' – an immensely open wording – but then the WP29 significantly narrows the definition to include only data 'where those features and/or actions are both unique to that individual and measurable, even if the patterns used in practice to technically measure them involve a certain degree of probability'.[27] Already then, in 2012, the WP29 highlighted that biometric data changes irrevocably the relation between body and identity, as biometric data can make bodily characteristics 'machine-readable' and thus subject to further use.[28] MDTs take this a step further – they aim to not only make the human body but also the human mind machine-readable and subject to further use.

Determining whether the data processed by MDTs will be considered biometric data under the GDPR and, if so, whether it will be classified as special category data

[23] Article 29 Data Protection Working Party, Working Document on Biometrics (WP80), Adopted on 1 August 2003, 3.

[24] WP 80, 3.

[25] See, e.g., Kindt, *Privacy and Data Protection Issues*, part I, chapter 2.

[26] See Lee A. Bygrave and Luca Tosoni, Article 4(14) in Kuner and others, *The EU General Data Protection Regulation (GDPR)*, original emphasis.

[27] Article 29 Data Protection Working Party, Opinion 3/2012 on Developments in Biometric Technologies (WP 193), Adopted on 27th April 2012, 3–4.

[28] WP 193, 4.

gives rise to several uncertainties. In essence, the complexities circle around three key questions:

- Is the data uniquely identifying and thus biometric data in the narrow sense of the GDPR or not?
- Is the data used for the purpose of identification and thus considered special category data or not?
- Does the data even qualify as personal data, or, if not, does it fall outside the scope of the GDPR?

Sarah and Drew explore various options for their future software. These include:

Scenario (a): *a personal mood tracker using face and voice recognition;*
Scenario (b): *a recruitment software employing gesture dynamics and (non-identifying) voice analytics (e.g. trembling and volume) to evaluate whether a candidate is responding truthfully or not;*
Scenario (c): *a chatbot for customer service utilising natural language processing (NLP) to infer emotions from clients' written complaints;*
Scenario (d): *a non-invasive BCI using in-ear electroencephalogram (EEG) for user authentication.*

Sarah and Drew try to understand whether the processed data would be classified as biometric data under the GDPR and, if so, whether it qualifies as sensitive.

2.1.2 *Uniquely Identifying or Not*

The GDPR refers to biometrics in several of its provisions. Article 4(14) GDPR defines biometric data as 'personal data resulting from specific technical processing relating to the physical, physiological or behavioural characteristics of a natural person, which allow or confirm the unique identification of that natural person, such as facial images or dactyloscopic data'.[29] Considering the rather broad notion of personal data in general, the definition of biometric data in the GDPR is strikingly limited in that biometric data has to 'allow or confirm the unique identification' of a data subject.[30] By restricting the definition of biometric data to only such data that has uniquely identifying qualities, the GDPR continues the line of reasoning introduced earlier by the WP29.

[29] Recital 51 GDPR adds that the definition of biometric data covers the processing of photographs only 'when processed through a specific technical means allowing the unique identification or authentication of a natural person'.

[30] See also Paul Quinn and Giancarlo Malgieri, 'The Difficulty of Defining Sensitive Data: The Concept of Sensitive Data in the EU Data Protection Framework', (2021) 22 *German Law Journal*, 1583–1612 <https://doi.org/10.1017/glj.2021.79>. For further discussion on biometrics as universal unique identifiers, see, e.g., Kindt, *Privacy and Data Protection Issues*, part II, chapter 4.

Biometrics which rely on uniquely identifying characteristics are also known as first generation biometrics; this can be traced back to the nineteenth century, when fingerprinting first emerged in law enforcement.[31] The decisive elements for qualifying biometric data as uniquely identifying are typically its distinctiveness and permanence. More recently, however, second generation and even generation 2.5 or 3 biometrics, as well as so-called weak or soft biometrics, have entered the market.[32] These newer forms are increasingly used for the classification or categorisation of natural persons and have become essential components of the technological portfolio that companies can choose from. The scientific community has not yet agreed upon an exact terminology to distinguish the respective categories. Weak biometric data is sometimes described as less unique or less stable (e.g. body shape, behavioural patterns, voice, body sounds), whereas soft biometrics are considered to be more generic in nature (e.g. gender or age). Other descriptions distinguish hard biometrics relating to physiological modalities, such as fingerprints, ear patterns, or vasal analysis, that do not change over time versus soft biometrics relating to physiological and psychological aspects of a person, such as behaviours and emotions, that do shift depending on time or circumstance, or both, such as gait and facial analysis.[33]

The data processed by Sarah and Drew's future software in scenario (a), the personal mood tracker using face together with voice recognition, relates to distinctive physical, physiological, or behavioural characteristics of a natural person. Both face and voice contain features and patterns which are unique to each person. The data processed by scenario (a) can thus be considered biometric data according to Article 4(14) GDPR.

The same holds true for scenario (d), the non-invasive BCI.[34] Identifying individuals solely based on data collected from their brain may seem challenging; however, reports suggest its feasibility in laboratory settings with a minimum of thirty seconds' worth of data.[35] This aligns also with the OECD's Recommendation of the Council on Responsible Innovation in Neurotechnology, which states that personal brain data is 'data relating to the functioning or structure of the human brain of an identified or identifiable individual that includes unique information about their

[31] ICO, Biometrics: Insight, Version 1.0 (2022), 5 <https://ico.org.uk/media/4021972/biometrics-insight-report.pdf> accessed 8 January 2025.

[32] K. Nandakumar and A. K. Jain, 'Soft Biometrics', in S. Z. Li and A. K. Jain (eds.), *Encyclopedia of Biometrics* (2009) <https://doi.org/10.1007/978-0-387-73003-5_225>; ICO, Biometrics: Insight, Version 1.0 (2022).

[33] See ICO, Biometrics: Insight, Version 1.0 (2022), 6.

[34] The legal nature of the data processed by BCIs has been put in question, particularly in the pre-GDPR era. See, for example, Dara Hallinan and others, 'Neurodata and Neuroprivacy: Data Protection Outdated?', (2014) 12(1) *Surveillance & Society*, 55–72 <https://doi.org/10.24908/ss.v12i1.4500>.

[35] See Future of Privacy Forum, 'Privacy and the Connected Mind'. In the same vein, the EDPS stipulates that brain waves are unique to each individual (EDPS, Arturo Brazal, and others, 'TechDispatch – Neurodata', TechDispatch 2024-1 <https://doi.org/10.2804/411725>).

physiology, health, or mental states'.[36] Brain recordings therefore can, in general, be considered biometric identifiers.[37] Therefore, the data processed by Sarah and Drew's non-invasive BCI in scenario (d) qualifies as biometric data according to Article 4(14) GDPR as well.

Scenario (b), the recruitment software using gesture dynamics and the trembling and volume of a candidate's voice to draw inferences about the truthfulness of their responses, raises instead doubts whether the data can be classified as biometric data according to the GDPR in sensu stricto. The processed data does relate to the physical, physiological, or behavioural characteristics of a natural person, and it does qualify as biometric data in a broader sense. However, data such as gesture dynamics and the trembling or volume of the voice is not permanent. It is not even stable for a considerable period of time. The literature acknowledges that certain biometric characteristics may require some flexibility regarding their permanence, as they are more susceptible to changes compared to others.[38] For instance, the face of a person can change due to gain or loss of weight or due to ageing. Nonetheless, the data in scenario (b) fluctuates continuously. Moreover, gesture dynamics and voice characteristics such as trembling, volume, or pauses, or similar non-identifiable features, do not sufficiently differentiate any two individuals to allow or confirm unique identification in the sense of singling them out or distinguishing one person from another. Therefore, data processed by MDTs like the recruitment software described in scenario (b) does not meet the criteria of biometric data within the strict confines of Article 4(14) GDPR.

In practice, modern biometric techniques, using soft or weak or generation 2.5 or 3 biometrics, are often merged with traditional biometric techniques to create what is known as multimodal biometrics.[39] In such cases, the entire data set would be classified as biometric data in the strict sense of the GDPR, given the inclusion of traditional biometrics in the set, provided the data sets are inextricably linked.

Finally, text-based data is not considered biometric data at all. The text-based chatbot data for customer service in scenario (c) will therefore not be classified as biometric data under the GDPR. It will result as normal personal data (unless it is considered special category data for other reasons). Given the recent surge in interest in Large Language Models, sparked by the breakthrough launch of ChatGPT to the public, this may result in a growing regulatory loophole for text-based deployments of MDTs.

36 OECD, Recommendation of the Council on Responsible Innovation in Neurotechnology (2020) <https://legalinstruments.oecd.org/en/instruments/OECD-LEGAL-0457> accessed 8 January 2025.

37 See also Stephen Rainey and others, 'Is the European Data Protection Regulation Sufficient to Deal with Emerging Data Concerns Relating to Neurotechnology?', (2020) 7(1) *Journal of Law and the Biosciences*, 1–19 <https://doi.org/10.1093/jlb/lsaa051>.

38 See Kindt, *Privacy and Data Protection Issues*, 21.

39 See also WP 193, 6.

At an interim stage, it can be concluded that not all of the data processed by MDTs qualifies as biometric data. Even if it does, it may qualify as biometric data only in a broader sense but not in the narrow sense of the GDPR.

In the next step, Sarah and Drew need to establish whether the data actually qualifying as biometric data under the GDPR matches the specific type of biometric data that is protected as special category data.

2.1.3 *Identification or Verification/Authentication*

Biometric data as a special category has been introduced to data protection law relatively recently compared to longer established categories.[40] The previous DPD did not include biometric data in its (then non-exhaustive) list of special category data.[41] Unlike other special categories, which are considered special category solely due to their sensitive nature in relation to the fundamental rights and freedoms, the classification of biometric data as special category data depends significantly on the purpose of processing.

In their Opinion 2012, the WP29 distinguished several purposes for the processing of biometric systems:

> *Biometric identification*: The identification of an individual by a biometric system is typically the process of comparing biometric data of an individual (acquired at the time of the identification) to a number of biometric templates stored in a database (i.e. a one-to-many matching process).
>
> *Biometric verification/authentication*: The verification of an individual by a biometric system is typically the process of comparing the biometric data of an individual (acquired at the time of the verification) to a single biometric template stored in a device (i.e. a one-to-one matching process).
>
> *Biometric categorisation/segregation*: The categorisation/segregation of an individual by a biometric system is typically the process of establishing whether the biometric data of an individual belongs to a group with some predefined characteristic in order to take a specific action. In this case, it is not important to identify or verify the individual but to assign him/her automatically to a certain category. For instance an advertising display may show different adverts depending on the individual that is looking at it based on the age or gender.[42]

The legal definition of biometric data in Article 4(14) GDPR seems to be open to the purposes of identification as well as authentication/verification of a natural person. According to the definition in Article 4(14) GDPR, biometric data 'means personal data resulting from specific technical processing relating to the physical,

[40] See also Section 2.2.

[41] For a description of how the notion of biometric data was incorporated into the EU data protection context, see Jasserand, 'Legal Nature of Biometric Data'.

[42] WP 193, 5–6.

physiological or behavioural characteristics of a natural person, which allow or confirm the unique identification'. Biometric identification would thus be covered by allowing the unique identification, whereas biometric verification would be covered by confirming the unique identification.[43] Recital 51 indicates a similar understanding by linking the definition of biometric data to 'processing through a specific technical means allowing the unique identification or authentication'.

In contrast, Article 9(1) GDPR specifies that only 'biometric data *for the purpose of uniquely identifying a natural person*' (emphasis added) will be classified as special category data. In other words, not all biometric data 'which allow or confirm the unique identification' (Article 4(14) GDPR) but solely biometric data that is indeed processed 'for the purpose of uniquely identifying' (Article 9(1) GDPR) a data subject is considered sensitive by the GDPR. If all biometric data, as defined per Article 4(14) GDPR, were to be considered special category data, Article 9(1) GDPR could simply include 'biometric data' among the listed categories without further explanation. Yet, Article 9(1) GDPR is very distinct in referring to biometric data specifically 'for the purpose of uniquely identifying a natural person'. Recital 91 GDPR supports this interpretation further, distinguishing between 'special categories of personal data' and 'biometric data'.[44]

The definitional discrepancies between Article 4(14) and 9(1) GDPR have spurred numerous debates among scholars. Parts of the scholarship emphasise the evident disparity in wording between Article 9(1) and Article 4(14) GDPR, bolstering their argument by referencing comments made by the Council during the trilogue negotiations on the GDPR, which suggest a similar interpretation.[45] Other scholars dispute this interpretation, considering the entirety of data according to Article 4(14) GDPR sensitive.[46] Upon closer examination, Recital 51 GDPR appears to exacerbate the complexity surrounding the interpretation of sensitive/non-sensitive biometric data rather than offering guidance and clarity. While it does in fact address both the purpose of unique identification and authentication of a natural person related to the definition of biometric data, it does so in the context of sensitive data.

Ultimately, the definitional disparities between Article 4(14) and Article 9(1) GDPR persist as a fact, presenting a challenge for any legal practitioner that neither regulatory guidance nor scholarly discourse has fully resolved. Moreover, this disparity extends to every piece of legislation that cites the GDPR as the determining legal framework for the processing of personal data.

[43] See Jasserand, 'Legal Nature of Biometric Data', 309.

[44] Recital 91, Sentence 2 GDPR reads:

> 'A data protection impact assessment should also be made where personal data are processed for taking decisions regarding specific natural persons following any systematic and extensive evaluation of personal aspects relating to natural persons based on profiling those data or following the processing of special categories of personal data, biometric data, or data on criminal convictions and offences or related security measures.'

[45] See Bygrave and Tosoni, Article 4(14) in Kuner and others, *The EU General Data Protection Regulation (GDPR)*.

[46] See Jasserand, 'Legal Nature of Biometric Data'.

Applying an interpretation in sensu stricto, Article 9(1) GDPR and thus the legal regime for special category data applies only to biometric data that is used for the purpose of identification, but not for other purposes (including authentication/verification). This stance is underscored by the EDPB in their Guidelines on automated decision-making. Therein, the EDPB stresses that for considering a processing to be processing of special category, the biometric data has to be processed 'for the purpose of uniquely identifying a natural person'.[47]

One rationale behind this decision by the legislator may have been that identification systems are likely to pose a higher risk to the fundamental rights and freedoms of data subjects compared to verification systems.[48] Identification involves the process of comparing biometric data of an individual to a number of biometric templates stored in a database (1:n matching process), according to the definition by the WP29 previously mentioned. In contrast, verification processes do not necessarily involve the storage of personal data in a centralised database and usually require processing data for fewer individuals.[49]

Depending on the exact purpose but also functioning of Sarah and Drew's specific software, it will either be subject to the regime for special category or not. The data in scenarios (a) and (d) have been classified before in Section 2.1.2 as biometric data according to the GDPR, they are therefore eligible for being considered special category biometric data. Scenario (a) is a personal mood tracker using face and voice recognition. Provided the specific mood tracker does indeed compare biometric data of the data subject to biometric templates in a database (1:n matching process) for the purpose of identification, the data will qualify as special category biometric data according to Article 9(1) GDPR.[50] However, scholars are noting that, in practice, this may often not be the case.[51]

Scenario (d) is a BCI using an in-ear EEG (e.g. via earbuds) for customer authentication. The BCI thus replaces traditional forms of authentication, such as PIN codes, fingerprints or iris-scans. Considering that the purpose of the device is

47 EDPB, Guidelines 3/2019 on Processing of Personal Data through Video Devices, Version 2.0, Adopted on 29 January 2020, 18 and 19.

48 See Bygrave and Tosoni, Article 4(14) in Kuner and others, *The EU General Data Protection Regulation (GDPR)*.

49 See WP 80, 4.

50 The term 'special category biometric data' is also used by the ICO to distinguish between normal and sensitive biometric data: 'Article 9 of the UK GDPR singles out some types of personal information as more sensitive and gives them extra protection. These include biometric data when used for the purpose of uniquely identifying someone. In this guidance, we use the term "special category biometric data" to refer to this.' (ICO, 'Key Data Protection Concepts: What Is Special Category Biometric Data?' <https://ico.org.uk/for-organisations/uk-gdpr-guidance-and-resources/lawful-basis/biometric-data-guidance-biometric-recognition/key-data-protection-concepts/#whatisspecial> accessed 8 January 2025.)

51 See Häuselmann and others, 'EU Law and Emotion Data'; Tereza Duchoňová, 'Voice As the Window to the Soul: Analysis of the Level of Protection Granted by the GDPR to Emotions Inferred from One's Voice', (2024) 3/2023 *CompLex*. <www.jus.uio.no/ifp/forskning/om/publikasjoner/complex/2023/complex_voice_as_the_window_to_the_soul_analysis-.html> accessed 8 January 2025.

authentication rather than identification, scenario (d) would not meet the criteria for special category biometric data.

The data in scenario (b), the recruitment software, falls under the broader definition of biometric data but does not meet the narrow criteria specified by the GDPR. Therefore, it is not eligible for classification as special category biometric data.

The data processed by the NLP-based chatbot in scenario (c) is not classified as biometric data at all.

As demonstrated in the analysis, classifying the data processed by MDTs as special category biometric data is a highly challenging task, involving both legal and technical complexities. Scenario (a) requires a case-by-case assessment, carefully evaluating the exact technical functioning and purpose for processing. In practice, it is questionable whether many devices would allow for a classification of the processed data as special category biometric data. The data processed in scenarios (b), (c), and (d) does not meet the criteria for special category biometric data, either. Unless the processed data qualifies for another special category listed in Article 9(1) GDPR – for instance, by association with another characteristic in the list of special category data, such as data concerning health or political opinion or similar – it will be classified as normal personal data.[52] The GDPR will still be applicable, however only the legal requirements for normal personal data have to be met. Despite the intimate nature of the information and the significant potential for harm to the fundamental rights of the data subject, the processing would only need to adhere to the requirements for normal personal data. Sarah and Drew would not have to implement enhanced safeguards to protect the data.

The British data protection authority, the Information Commissioner's Office (ICO), comes to a similar conclusion regarding emotion technology and the classification of data under the UK GDPR:

> Potentially high risk data processed via related modalities may not be considered special category biometric data or even biometric data under the UK GDPR. This is because in many cases it is not used for the purpose of or even allow for uniquely identifying a person. Not being classified as special category data reduces the legal safeguards and restrictions around its processing.[53]

2.1.4 *Personal Data or Not*

The third type of biometric systems described by the WP29, biometric categorisation systems, points to yet another dilemma related to biometrics and the deployment of MDTs: When biometrics are processed for the purpose of categorisation, there is a risk that the data may not be considered personal data at all. In these instances, the data falls entirely outside the scope of GDPR protection.

[52] For an analysis regarding the classification as data concerning health or data revealing political opinion, see the respective use cases 1 and 3 in Chapters 4 and 6.

[53] ICO, Biometrics: Foresight, Version 1.0, (2022), 11.

Systems for biometric categorisation or segregation have been defined by the WP29 as systems that aim to establish whether the biometric data of an individual belongs to a group with certain characteristics in order to initiate a specific action. Identification or verification/authentication are not the objectives of these categorisation/classification systems. Their goal is to automatically assign individuals to a specific category or to detect whether the present group shares certain characteristics, prompting an action.[54] The ICO has defined the purpose of classification as 'categorising aspects of a person, whether physical or behavioural, often via inferences', adding that this 'may or may not be personal data depending on how (and if) it is linked to a known person'.[55]

In the context of MDTs, there are applications where biometric categorisation systems are used to infer emotions. A well-known case is the advertising board in Piccadilly Circus in London, which, for a certain period, reportedly detected not only features such as gender and age but also the mood of passers-by through a facial detection system, optimising ads accordingly.[56] The company owning the billboard was eager to state that the technology of the screen 'does not collect or store any personal data and is unable to record images or audio'.[57] Alas, if the data processed by such systems is indeed not classified as personal data, it creates the paradoxical situation where people's inner state is inferred but the information is not recognised as being personal data. As a result, such data is not covered by the protection provided under the legal regime for personal data.

Sarah and Drew are exploring another potential application:

> ***Scenario (e)**: a biometric system that infers customers' moods in a shopping mall using video cameras. Based on the emotions detected, the lights in the mall could be adjusted (e.g. dimmed/brightened) or a specific scent dispersed to enhance people's inclination to purchase products.*

They ponder how the data processed by such a system would be classified under existing data protection law.

---

54 The level of protection for data processed by categorisation systems and the privacy of data subjects, understood not as individuals but as a member of a specific group or category, have been consistent points of critique regarding the prevailing data protection laws. Calls to address 'group privacy' proactively have been voiced before, see, e.g., Luciano Floridi, 'Open Data, Data Protection, and Group Privacy', (2014) 27 *Philosophy Technology*, 1–3 <https://doi.org/10.1007/s13347-014-0157-8>; Luciano Floridi, 'Group Privacy: A Defence and an Interpretation', in L. Taylor and others (eds.), *Group Privacy: New Challenges of Data Technologies* (Springer 2016), 83–100.

55 ICO, Biometrics: Insight, Version 1.0 (2022), 6.

56 According to the Archived Privacy Policy Piccadilly Lights, the data collection ended in September 2018. (See Peggy Valcke and others, 'Constitutional Challenges in the Emotional AI Era', in Micklitz and others (eds.), *Constitutional Challenges*, 57–77 n. 37.)

57 Landsec, 'London's Iconic Piccadilly Lights Are Switched Back On' (Press Release 26 October 2017) <https://landsec.com/media/press-releases/2017/londons-iconic-piccadilly-lights-are-switched-back> accessed 24 January 2025.

The question of whether biometrics can be classified as non-personal data at all relates to a long-lasting dispute among data protection scholars. The general assumption that biometrics are '*usually* personal data' underpins the vast majority of biometric schemes.[58] However, there are exceptions to this norm. The WP29 noted in their working document in 2003 that it 'appears' that 'biometric data can always be considered as "information relating to a natural person" as it concerns data, which provides, by its very nature, information about a given person'.[59] Notably, the use of the word 'appears' leaves a window for interpretational discretion whether or not indeed all biometric data is to be considered personal data. In 2012, the WP29 reiterated in an Opinion that 'biometric data, by their very nature, are directly linked to an individual' – but then the WP29 qualifies this statement a few pages later by adding that biometric data is 'in most cases' personal data.[60]

Discussions on the personal nature of biometric data are particularly intense regarding detection systems employing momentary processing. These detection systems do not aim to identify or even authenticate an individual; instead, they process data for only a very short duration to prompt an action and do not store the data afterward. Given the inherently 'ephemeral' or 'transient' nature of the processing, the controversies primarily revolve around whether the data subject is identifiable, which is a key criterion for classifying the data as personal data according to EU data protection law.[61]

Within the EU legal framework, biometric data is defined as a subcategory of personal data in the GDPR. Applying the GDPR to any kind of data set requires determining whether the data set falls under the territorial and material scope of the legislation. Only if it does this, can compliance be requested. With regard to the material scope of the GDPR, the data must meet the definition of personal data in Article 4(1) GDPR, further elaborated in Recital 26 GDPR, before it can be classified as biometric data according to Article 4(14) GDPR.[62] Additionally, Article 4(14) GDPR itself defines that 'biometric data means *personal data* resulting from specific technical processing' (emphasis added). Therefore, the data must first be classified as personal data – otherwise, its processing falls outside the scope of the GDPR, and the GDPR (including all rights and principles enshrined therein) will not be applicable.

58 Bygrave and Tosoni, Article 4(14) in Kuner and others, *The EU General Data Protection Regulation (GDPR)*.

59 WP 80, 5.

60 WP 193, 2 and 7.

61 Peter A. E. Davis, 'Facial Detection and Smart Billboards: Analysing the "Identified" Criterion of Personal Data in the GDPR', (2020) 6(3) *European Data Protection Law Review* <https://doi.org/10.21552/edpl/2020/3/7>; Damian George and others, 'GDPR Bypass by Design? Transient Processing of Data under the GDPR', (2019) 9(4), *International Data Privacy Law*, 285–298 <https://doi.org/10.1093/idpl/ipz017>; see also Christiane Wendehorst, Article 3, Margin Number 350 Subsequential, in Mario Martini and Christiane Wendehorst (eds.), *KI-VO. Künstliche Intelligenz-Verordnung* (C. H. Beck 2024).

62 See also Bygrave and Tosoni, Article 4(14) in Kuner and others, *The EU General Data Protection Regulation (GDPR)*.

Regulatory authorities in the EU seemingly struggle to reach a unanimous approach on the matter. In 2017, the Irish Data Protection Commissioner (DPC) published a press release concerning the use of digital advertisement screens in public spaces and their use of facial detection technology to determine the advertisements and images to be displayed to individuals. In the press release, the DPC stated that, following their assessment, 'the technology used involves the use of facial detection technology only, with advertising display images being determined during the period while the individual is within the range of the camera, but do not involve the use of facial recognition technology; that is, the technology used does not involve the recording, analysis, matching, profiling or storage of personally identifiable data'.[63] In the same vein, the Bavarian Data Protection Supervisory Authority concluded in 2017 that the detection of a data subject's gender and age for an advertisement board in a supermarket did not relate to the processing of personal data. According to the Authority, the extremely limited time of storage of 150 milliseconds involved only the transfer of metadata instead of personal data.[64]

In contrast, the Italian Data Protection Authority (DPA), the Garante Per La Protezione Dei Dati (GDPD), reached a conclusion in 2017 that the recording of images of individuals for only a few tenths of a second in the random-access memory of an electronic device did constitute processing of personal data.[65] In 2021, the British ICO argued in an opinion on live facial recognition systems that controllers are processing personal data every time the system captures a facial image – even if it is processed only momentarily.[66]

Additional parameters discussed in this context include whether the data subject is identifiable solely because and as long as they are in the vicinity of the sensor or camera collecting the data, and whether this processing has any concrete effect on

63 Statement cited here: 'Ireland: DPC Releases Statement on Use of Facial Detection Technology in Advertising' (16 May 2017) <www.dataguidance.com/news/ireland-dpc-releases-statement-use-facial-detection> accessed 13 August 2024. See also Nadehzda Purtova, 'The Law of Everything: Broad Concept of Personal Data and Future of EU Data Protection Law', (2018) 10 *Law, Innovation and Technology*, 40–81, n. 200 <https://doi.org/10.1080/17579961.2018.1452176>.

64 Heike Anger, 'Gesichtsscan im Supermarkt ist unbedenklich', *Handelsblatt* (12 June 2017) <www.handelsblatt.com/politik/deutschland/datenschuetzer-zu-real-werbebildschirm-gesichtsscan-im-supermarkt-ist-unbedenklich/19921456.html?ticket=ST-143784-Qpdthm7uM2VsokkEhOHW-ap5> accessed 8 January 2025.

65 'Alla luce di quanto rappresentato da Grandi Stazioni Retail S.p.A. e sulla base della documentazione prodotta, risulta […] che seppur per un breve lasso di tempo, pari a qualche decimo di secondo, il sistema installato dalla Società comporta un trattamento di dati personali, consistenti nelle immagini del volto degli interessati, finalizzato a desumere dall'immagine del viso una serie di informazioni utilizzate per effettuare analisi dell'audience pubblicitaria.' Garante per la protezione dei dati personali, 'Installazione di apparati promozionali del tipo 'digital signage' (definiti anche Totem) presso una stazione ferroviaria – 21 dicembre 2017 [7496252]. <www.garanteprivacy.it/web/guest/home/docweb/-/docweb-display/docweb/7496252> accessed 8 January 2025.

66 ICO, Information Commissioner's Opinion: The Use of Live Facial Recognition Technology in Public Places, 18 June 2021, 27 <https://ico.org.uk/media/2619985/ico-opinion-the-use-of-lfr-in-public-places-20210618.pdf> accessed 8 January 2025.

the data subject.[67] When the German Constitutional Court in Karlsruhe ruled on the potential infringement of the fundamental right to personal data protection in a case involving license plate recognition by authorities, it concluded that no such infringement occurs if the data is incidentally collected in an untargeted manner solely due to technical reasons. However, the data must be immediately separated in a technically anonymous and traceless manner without any interest or knowledge.[68]

Overall, it is a set of criteria and circumstances that should be considered to determine whether the data subject is identifiable, with duration of processing and storage playing a key role. In Sarah and Drew's scenario (e), their intention is not to identify any individuals. Instead, they aim to process the data for only a minimal period – mere split seconds – without storing any of it. Moreover, their system will not customise outcomes (such as adjusted lights or a dispersed scent in the shopping mall) based on the data of a single individual but based on the aggregated data of all customers collectively. The effect will similarly be directed towards all customers collectively rather than any one person individually. Given these circumstances, they believe it is unlikely the customer data processed by their emotion detection system in scenario (e) would be classified as personal data. The processing of non-personal data falls beyond the scope of the GDPR and does not require any safeguards for the protection of personal data.

2.2 SHOULD MIND DATA BE A SUI GENERIS SPECIAL CATEGORY?

The special category MDTs are most commonly associated with is that of biometric data. As demonstrated in the scenarios above, determining whether data processed by MDTs qualifies as special category biometric data can be a lengthy and inherently complex process. Whether the data will indeed be considered special category biometric data under the GDPR depends on multiple factors and requires comprehensive expertise; some grey areas remain unresolved. The extensive domain of text-based MDTs falls entirely outside the definition of biometric data. The data protection level for such data is only that afforded to all normal personal data. Alternatively, the data may fall within the scope of a different special category, such as health or political opinion, depending on the specific purpose and context of processing.

Within the EU data protection framework, a systematic approach tailored for data processed by MDTs is currently lacking. As a result, the data protection level related to MDTs is fragmented, leaving substantial parts of the data with only basic protection. This issue not only applies under the GDPR but also extends to any other legal act referencing the GDPR as the predominant legislation for the processing

[67] Wendehorst, Article 3, Margin Number 351 in Martini and Wendehorst, *KI-VO*.

[68] Bundesverfassungsgericht Beschluss vom 18. Dezember 2018, 1 BvR 142/15, section 43 <www.bundesverfassungsgericht.de/SharedDocs/Entscheidungen/DE/2018/12/rs20181218_1bvr014215.html> accessed 8 January 2025.

of personal data. Beyond considerations surrounding the complexities of the legislative procedure involved, it is therefore both legitimate and prudent to explore further options within the GDPR, such as the establishment a new sui generis special category.

2.2.1 *The Concept of Special Category Data*

The concept of special categories,[69] on an international scale, was first introduced in 1980 by the OECD Guidelines on the Protection of Privacy and Transborder Flows of Personal Data.[70] These guidelines are a non-binding recommendation to OECD Member States. Therein, the OECD deems different degrees of sensitivity for data appropriate.[71] However, despite discussing a number of sensitivity criteria, the expert group was unable to reach a consensus on a defined set of universally recognised sensitive data.[72] Notably, the one sensitivity criterion explicitly mentioned in the OECD guidelines is the risk of discrimination.

The Council of Europe's Convention for the Protection of Individuals with Regard to Automatic Processing of Personal Data (1981) was the next important signifier.[73] Article 6 of the Convention listed 'personal data revealing racial origin, political opinions or religious or other beliefs, as well as personal data concerning health or sexual life' as special categories of data. The list itself was not intended to be exhaustive. On the contrary, signatory states were free to add further categories of sensitive data in their national laws.

Similarly, the EU Data Protection Directive 95/46/EC (1995) did not contain an exhaustive list. Article 8(1) DPD lists 'personal data revealing racial or ethnic origin, political opinions, religious or philosophical beliefs, trade-union membership, and the processing of data concerning health or sex life' as special categories. Member States could incorporate additional categories in the legal transposition under national law.

In their Advice paper on special categories of data (2011), the WP29 confirmed that there were certain categories of personal data 'distinct from all other personal data', which would require extra protection and should be processed only for

69 For a brief history of special category data, see Quinn and Malgieri, 'The Difficulty of Defining Sensitive Data'.

70 OECD Guidelines on the Protection of Privacy and Transborder Flows of Personal Data (OECD Publishing 2002) <https://doi.org/10.1787/9789264196391-en>. (On national and state-law level, the concept of special category data had already been adopted in Sweden and in the German state of Hessen before the OECD Guidelines.)

71 OECD Guidelines on the Protection of Privacy and Transborder Flows of Personal Data, para 3.

72 OECD Guidelines on the Protection of Privacy and Transborder Flows of Personal Data, para 7, section 51.

73 Council of Europe, Convention for the Protection of Individuals with Regard to Automatic Processing of Personal Data, European Treaty Series No. 108 (1981) <https://rm.coe.int/1680078b37> accessed 8 January 2025.

specific purposes and under special conditions.[74] The WP29 clearly expressed that the reason for incorporating the concept of sensitive data was the 'presumption that misuse of these data could have more severe consequences on the individual's fundamental rights, such as the right to privacy and non-discrimination, than misuse of other, "normal" personal data'.[75]

Compared to the DPD, the GDPR expands the list of special category data by adding three more data types: the category of genetic data, biometric data for the purpose of uniquely identifying a natural person, and data concerning a natural person's [...] sexual orientation (Article 9(1) GDPR). Contrary to the former Directive, Article 9(1) GDPR is considered to be a closed list. Member States can therefore no longer add further special categories. According to Article 9(4) GDPR, Member States may introduce further conditions, including limitations, for the processing of genetic data, biometric data, or data concerning health – however, they cannot implement further categories. Furthermore, the GDPR has broadened the exceptions to the general prohibition for processing special category data, now encompassing substantial public interest (Article 9(2)(g) GDPR), preventive or occupational medicine (Article 9(2)(h) GDPR), public health (Article 9(2)(i) GDPR), and research or archiving (Article 9(2)(j) GDPR).

Recital 51 GDPR elaborates on the considerations underlying special categories in data protection law, stating that '[p]ersonal data which are, by their nature, particularly sensitive in relation to fundamental rights and freedoms merit specific protection as the context of their processing could create significant risks to the fundamental rights and freedoms'.

2.2.2 *Mind Data Meets the Criteria*

Around the time of the GDPR's adoption, the EU Commission began considering whether information about emotions should be subject to a higher level of protection, given the potential harm its disclosure could cause. In the 2017 proposed draft of the e-Privacy Regulation,[76] Recital 2 states that: '[t]he content of electronic communications may reveal *highly sensitive information about the natural persons* involved in the communication, from personal experiences and *emotions* to medical conditions, sexual preferences and political views, the disclosure of which could result in personal and social harm, economic loss or embarrassment' (emphasis

74 Article 29 Data Protection Working Party, Advice Paper on Special Categories of Data ('Sensitive Data') (2011), 4.

75 Article 29 Data Protection Working Party, Advice Paper on Special Categories of Data ('Sensitive Data'), 4.

76 Proposal for a Regulation of the European Parliament and of the Council Concerning the Respect for Private Life and the Protection of Personal Data in Electronic Communications and Repealing Directive 2002/58/EC (Regulation on Privacy and Electronic Communications) COM/2017/010 final – 2017/03 (COD).

added). Recital 20 explicitly urges that information revealing details of an individual's emotional, political, or social complexities merits 'enhanced privacy protection'. Hence, in contrast to the GDPR, which was proposed in 2012 and contains no such passage or provision, the EU Commission seemingly began recognising the need for heightened legal protection for emotions and emotional complexities in the 2017 draft e-Privacy Regulation.[77]

Key considerations for including data in the list of special category under the GDPR revolve around the inherently sensitive nature of the data, which requires special protection, as the context of its processing could create significant risks to fundamental rights and freedoms.[78] The fundamental rights most evidently at risk in the context of MDTs include the right to privacy and the right to data protection, which are persistently infringed upon by current practices that apply automated processing to identify and infer insights from individuals' minds without their awareness and consent. Both will serve as consistent focal points throughout the book.

Furthermore, there is a noticeable increase in scholarly interest in the right to freedom of thought, particularly within the context of neurotechnology.[79] The original scope of the fundamental right to freedom of thought, conscience and religion is closely connected with the choice of religion and belief. However, the wider scope of protection can cover as much as the 'internal and private realm of the individual',[80] including the so-called forum internum, the inner space where personal thought, conscience, and religion are held, developed, refined and changed.[81] In the 2021 report by the UN Special Rapporteur on freedom of religion or belief,

77 It is worth noting, however, that both relevant sections are not part of the legally binding Provisions but part of the Recitals and that the Regulation has not been adopted.

78 Recital 51 GDPR.

79 Jan Christoph Bublitz, 'Freedom of Thought in the Age of Neuroscience: A Plea and a Proposal for the Renaissance of a Forgotten Fundamental Right', (2014) 100(1) *ARSP: Archiv Für Rechts- Und Sozialphilosophie / Archives for Philosophy of Law and Social Philosophy*, 1–25 <www.jstor.org/stable/24756752> accessed 8 January 2025; Susie Alegre, 'Rethinking Freedom of Thought for the 21st Century', (2017) (3) *European Human Rights Law Review*, 221–233 <https://susiealegre.com/wp-content/uploads/2020/04/Alegre%20from%202017_EHRLR_Issue_3_Print_final_0806%5B6745%5D.pdf> accessed 8 January 2025; Sjors Ligthart, 'Freedom of Thought in Europe: Do Advances in "Brain-Reading" Technology Call for Revision?', (2020) 7(1) *Journal of Law and the Biosciences* <https://doi.org/10.1093/jlb/lsaa048>; Jan Christoph Bublitz, 'Freedom of Thought as an International Human Right: Elements of a Theory of a Living Right', in M. J. Blitz and J. C. Bublitz (eds.), *The Law and Ethics of Freedom of Thought*, Vol. 1, Palgrave Studies in Law, Neuroscience, and Human Behavior (Palgrave Macmillan 2021) <https://doi.org/10.1007/978-3-030-84494-3_3>; Sjors Ligthart and others, 'Rethinking the Right to Freedom of Thought: A Multidisciplinary Analysis' (2022) 22(4) *Human Rights Law Review* <https://doi.org/10.1093/hrlr/ngac028>.

80 Paul M. Taylor, *Freedom of Religion: UN and European Human Rights Law and Practice* (Cambridge University Press 2005), 115 <https://doi.org/10.1017/CBO9780511616129>.

81 Jim Murdoch, *Protecting the Right to Freedom of Thought, Conscience and Religion under the European Convention on Human Right* (Council of Europe Human Rights Handbook 2012), 18; Sue Anne Teo, 'How to Think about Freedom of Thought (and Opinion) in the Age of AI', (2024) 53 *Computer Law & Security Review* <https://doi.org/10.1016/j.clsr.2024.105969>.

the forum internum is described as 'a person's inner sanctum (mind) where mental faculties are'.[82] Reflecting on the developments in digital technology, neuroscience, and cognitive psychology, along with their potential to enable access to our thoughts and influence how we think, feel, and behave, the UN Special Rapporteur notes that 'the advancing design and increasingly widespread use of these technologies raise pertinent questions for policymakers, among others, about how to protect forum internum rights, including freedom of thought'.[83] In the context of data processing by MDTs, the entire concept of this forum internum is compromised by the notion that third parties have unrestricted and/or unauthorised digital access to people's minds. Notably, the right to freedom of thought is one of the very few human rights deemed unconditional and absolute.[84]

Moreover, the right to mental integrity, intended to protect the autonomy of the mind against actions that negatively affect the mind (its mental states, processes, functions, abilities), could be infringed upon by unethical employments of MDTs.[85]

The information identified or inferred by MDTs through automated processing – insights about individuals' inner states – is intrinsically intertwined with their personality. It constitutes a fundamental aspect of human identity and mental personhood and is thus inextricably linked with the right to human dignity. In *Schwarz*, the Advocate General asserts that using biometrics is never an insignificant choice as they 'change irrevocably the relation between body and identity, in that they make the characteristics of the human body "machine-readable" and subject to further use'.[86] The same line of reasoning can be applied in the context of MDTs as they make the characteristics of the human mind 'machine-readable' and subject to further use.

Humans naturally identify and infer emotions and related concepts – whether accurately or not – as part of reciprocal social interaction. Yet the dynamics change fundamentally when similar tasks are performed through automated processing.

82 Interim Report of the Special Rapporteur on Freedom of Religion or Belief, Ahmed Shaheed: 'Freedom of Thought', published on 05 October 2021 (A/76/380), 3 <www.ohchr.org/en/documents/thematic-reports/a76380-interim-report-special-rapporteur-freedom-religion-or-belief> accessed 8 January 2025.

83 Interim Report of the Special Rapporteur on Freedom of Religion or Belief, Ahmed Shaheed: 'Freedom of Thought', 4.

84 In the context of the absolute nature of the fundamental right to freedom of thought, scholarly debates have arisen on whether a distinction should be made between thoughts that reach a certain threshold of seriousness and importance, and more trivial thoughts, with only the former deserving full protection (Ligthart and others, 'Rethinking the Right to Freedom of Thought'). Conversely, scholars are questioning this standpoint, given today's computational abilities to infer intimate information from the most innocuous data points (Teo, 'How to Think about Freedom of Thought').

85 Jan Christoph Bublitz, 'Neurotechnologies and Human Rights: Restating and Reaffirming the Multi-layered Protection of the Person', (2024) 28(5) *The International Journal of Human Rights*, 782–807, 788 <https://doi.org/10.1080/13642987.2024.2310830>.

86 Opinion of Advocate General Megozzi delivered on 13 June 2013 Case C-291/12 *Michael Schwarz* v *Stadt Bochum*, section I para 1.

The identification and inference of individuals' inner states through automated processing, whether accurate or not, is not part of a reciprocal social interaction in which signals are exchanged between two or more parties on an equal footing. Rather, it is a one-sided process. Individuals' minds are datafied and scanned for information, which is then made subject to further use. More often than not, the inferred information serves institutional or corporate interests, such as in targeted advertising, behavioural profiling, or surveillance, fostering an environment where individuals' inner states are commodified, manipulated, or used to make decisions without their consent or understanding.

Unlike human perception, automated processing operates at an unprecedented scale and persistence, enabling the identification and inference of the inner state of mind of individuals in ways far beyond human capability. This grants access to information that would otherwise remain hidden, exacerbating the imbalance of power. The massive-scale processing significantly amplifies the risks associated with biases or misinterpretations, exponentially increasing the potential for discrimination. EU legislators themselves stressed in the Artificial Intelligence Act that 'AI systems identifying or inferring emotions or intentions of natural persons on the basis of their biometric data may lead to discriminatory outcomes and can be intrusive to the rights and freedoms of the concerned persons.'[87] False assumptions and judgements about individuals' inner state, as well as inaccurate inferences and predictions about their dispositions, can result in discrimination based on known characteristics, such as gender, age, or race.[88] For instance, it has been observed that darker-skinned faces may be interpreted as angrier or as having more negative emotions than white faces, regardless of their actual expression.[89] This bias could result in discriminatory effects across various contexts, such as security screenings, employment decisions, or university admissions. Additionally, the British ICO points out that even new forms of discrimination may emerge relating to neurotechnology. Examples given by the ICO include the risk of discrimination against neurodivergent people from inaccurate systems and databases trained on neuro-normative patterns, and the possibility of unfair treatment in the workplace or by services offered based on individuals' emotional states.[90]

In summary, the data that is identified and inferred by MDTs through automated processing is inherently sensitive in relation to the fundamental rights and freedoms of natural persons. Given that the data protection framework de lege lata does not guarantee an appropriate level of protection for this type of data, the introduction

87 Recital 44 AIA.

88 Practical examples of possible discriminatory effects caused by MDTs will be discussed in use case 4 in Chapter 7 in the context of work.

89 See Lauren Rhue, 'Racial Influence on Automated Perceptions of Emotions', (2018) <https://papers.ssrn.com/sol3/papers.cfm?abstract_id=3281765> accessed 8 January 2025.

90 ICO, ICO Tech Futures: Neurotechnology (2023), 19 <https://ico.org.uk/about-the-ico/research-and-reports/ico-tech-futures-neurotechnology/> accessed 8 January 2025.

of a sui generis special category for data processed by MDTs should be proactively considered de lege ferenda. Importantly, the decision to designate data as special category would have a lasting impact on every piece of legislation building on the GDPR's regulatory regime.

The fact that some data may incidentally be associated with existing special categories does not present a sustainable argument against introducing a sui generis special category. Already today, data protection law recognises overlapping special categories like data concerning health, biometric data, and genetic data. Despite this, legislators have not refrained from adding the latter two categories to the list of special categories in the GDPR. On the contrary, establishing a sui generis special category could emphasise the role and significance that this type of data holds for data subjects in relation to their fundamental rights and freedoms. Furthermore, it would resolve current doubts or misunderstandings regarding classification and address legal loopholes that allow circumventing the enhanced legal regime for special category data. Sarah and Drew would have clear understanding of the legal nature of the data and could take appropriate action.

2.3 HOW COULD THE NEW SPECIAL CATEGORY BE DEFINED?

Current approaches to governing MDTs are predominantly focused on the types of data or technologies that are used for revealing insights about the inner state of mind of individuals. The EU, for instance, has tied the definition of Emotion Recognition Systems (ERS) under the AIA to systems that use biometric data for identifying or inferring emotions or intentions.[91] However, restricting the scope of the new sui generis category exclusively to a biophysical basis excludes data derived from other origins, such as text. Conversely, establishing a new special category for data processed by a specific technology, such as neurotechnology, would contradict one of the basic principles of the legislation. The GDPR is a technology-neutral law. As stated in Recital 15 GDPR, the protection of natural persons should remain technologically neutral in order to prevent risks of circumvention. This means that the GDPR does not show favouritism or discrimination towards any particular technology. Rather, the GDPR's focus lies in safeguarding the information pertaining to a natural person and protecting their rights and freedoms.

Following this rationale, this book advocates for a fundamental shift in perspective. Instead of continuing to debate the precise technological or biophysical parameters that render our minds datafiable and may reveal sensitive information, the debate should centre on safeguarding what truly matters: the sensitive information itself. People are less concerned with the specific technology or biophysical

[91] Article 3(39) AIA defines an Emotion Recognition System as 'an AI system for the purpose of identifying or inferring emotions or intentions of natural persons on the basis of their biometric data'.

characteristic used to reveal their inner state of mind; what matters to them is that this information is exploited and instrumentalised without their awareness, leaving them vulnerable to manipulation and increasing the risks to their fundamental rights and freedoms. Whether the information is obtained through text-based datamining, neurotechnology, or other tools, by analysing their brain, face, voice, gestures, or written messages is secondary to them. Rather, this book advocates for strengthening safeguards for the information itself that is sensitive in relation to the fundamental rights and freedoms.

Crafting a precise definition for such a new sui generis special category is inherently complex, as there is a risk that an overly broad definition could render the category unenforceable. An initial definition could be formulated as follows:

> **Article 4(27) GDPR new:** 'mind data' means personal data resulting from automated processing for the purpose of identifying or inferring emotions, thoughts, intentions or psychological states of a natural person.

The umbrella term 'mind data' for the new sui generis special category builds on the European Parliament's reference to 'states of mind' in its draft definition of Emotion Recognition Systems.[92] Limiting the scope to personal data 'resulting from automated processing for the purpose of identifying or inferring' seeks to confine the scope to information that genuinely requires additional safeguards. The purpose-based approach aligns closely with the rationale applied by the legislators in defining ERS under the AIA. Moreover, such a purpose-based approach is not new to defining special category data within data protection law; legislators have already adopted it when defining special category biometric data in Article 9(1) GDPR, which refers to 'biometric data for the purpose of uniquely identifying a natural person'.[93]

To maximise coherence within the legal framework, the proposed definition brings together concepts related to the mind that have already been incorporated into existing legislation, though they are currently dispersed across various laws. The AIA has explicitly introduced the concepts 'emotions' and 'intentions' while the Platform Work Directive has incorporated the concept 'psychological states' into hard law.[94] Unfortunately, none of these legal pieces provide precise definitions for these concepts. However, over time, legal practice is expected to give them substance as the laws take effect, aided by regulatory guidance, judicial interpretation, or both. This process will inevitably bring greater clarity, also supporting the proposed definition.

Additionally, this book advocates for integrating the term 'thoughts'. The line between emotions and thoughts is already difficult to draw, making it challenging

92 For a detailed comparison of the different definitions for Emotion Recognition Systems proposed during the legislative process, see Section 3.1.

93 See also Quinn and Malgieri, 'The Difficulty of Defining Sensitive Data'.

94 Article 3(39) AIA and Article 7 Platform Work Directive. Both laws will be discussed in detail further on.

to establish clear distinctions between the two. In his 2021 report on the freedom of thought, the UN Special Rapporteur notes:

> What constitutes 'thought' not only lacks legal precision, but also scientific and philosophical consensus. Neuroscientists generally agree that thoughts are created when billions of neurons (nerve cells) in the brain – connected by trillions of synapses – fire together. But the consensus ends there. Some neuroscientists distinguish 'thought' from other cognitive processes, including emotion, based on the primary part of the brain engaged. Others emphasize the complex, highly interrelated nature of anatomical aspects of the brain that support cognitive functions, comparing efforts to 'trace a thought from beginning to end' to 'asking where the forest begins'. Many stakeholders treat 'thought' as an individual process and/or product of thinking. [...] Others reject this conceptual distinction, asserting that emotions are an integral part of thought processes, by making a mind more inclined to think one thing over another.[95]

The suggestion to integrate the concept of 'thoughts' also draws on the considerations of the European Parliament during the drafting process of the AIA (as evident in the definition of ERS in the draft version by the Parliament) and supporting scholarly work.[96] Moreover, incorporating 'thoughts' would strengthen the definition's future resilience by anticipating potential advancements in neurotechnology.

In clarifying the scope further, the proposed definition does not encompass personal data resulting from automated processing for the purpose of identifying or inferring mere physical aspects or states. Within the EU data protection framework, this type of data can be covered by existing categories, such as data concerning health and/or biometric data/special category biometric data.[97] The proposed distinction aligns with the legislators' approach to ERS, as evidenced by Recital 18 AIA, which excludes physical states from the notion of ERS.[98] Guidance from regulatory authorities and case law on the distinguishing lines for ERS under the AIA will provide additional clarity and strengthen the suggested approach.

Based on the proposed definition, the sui generis category could be included in the list of special category data according to Article 9(1) GDPR.

95 Interim Report of the Special Rapporteur on Freedom of Religion or Belief, Ahmed Shaheed: 'Freedom of Thought', 5–6.

96 See Christiane Wendehorst and Yannic Duller, 'Biometric Recognition and Behavioural Detection: Assessing the Ethical Aspects of Biometric Recognition and Behavioural Detection Techniques with a Focus on Their Current and Future Use in Public Spaces', Study Requested by the European Parliament's Committee on Legal Affairs and Petitions' (JURI and PETI committees) (2021), 70–71 <www.europarl.europa.eu/RegData/etudes/STUD/2021/696968/IPOL_STU(2021)696968_EN.pdf> accessed 8 January 2025.

97 A detailed discussion on the classification of data concerning health will be provided in use case 1, Chapter 4.

98 For a detailed discussion, see Section 3.1, 'Emotion Recognition Systems'.

> **Article 9(1) GDPR new:** Processing of personal data revealing racial or ethnic origin, political opinions, religious or philosophical beliefs, or trade union membership, and the processing of genetic data, biometric data for the purpose of uniquely identifying a natural person, data concerning health, or data concerning a natural person's sex life or sexual orientation, or mind data shall be prohibited.

Alternatively, legislators could take a more nuanced approach. Drawing on the definitional discrepancies between normal biometric data and special category biometric data, legislators could intentionally create a similar framework for mind data. This approach would involve a broader definition of normal mind data while significantly narrowing the scope of special category mind data. By adopting such a two-tier approach, the legal regime for normal mind data would remain that of normal personal data while the stricter regime would only apply to special category mind data, owing to its heightened risks to fundamental rights and freedoms.

3

The New Regulatory Approach under the AIA

A main focus of the EU's strategy towards regulating AI has been to establish a framework that would promote trustworthy and human-centred AI, blending cutting-edge technology with ethical standards.[1] To guide these efforts, the Commission appointed a High Level Expert Group on Artificial Intelligence (AI HLEG), which produced key documents such as the Ethics Guidelines for Trustworthy AI (2019),[2] and the Assessment List for Trustworthy AI (ALTAI) (2020).[3] In 2021, the EU Commission presented its AI Package, including a Communication on fostering a European approach to AI,[4] and the Proposal for a Regulation on Artificial Intelligence (hereinafter referred to as 'Commission Proposal').[5]

Subsequently, the Council of the EU adopted their Common Position in December 2022 (hereinafter referred to as 'Council Position'),[6] followed by the EU Parliament's Amendments, adopted in June 2023 (hereinafter referred to as

1 EU Commission, 'Artificial Intelligence: Commission Kicks off Work on Marrying Cutting-Edge Technology and Ethical Standards' (Press Release 8 March 2018) <https://ec.europa.eu/commission/presscorner/detail/en/IP_18_1381> accessed 8 January 2025.

2 EU Commission: Independent HLEG on Artificial Intelligence, Ethics Guidelines for Trustworthy AI (2019) <https://digital-strategy.ec.europa.eu/en/library/ethics-guidelines-trustworthy-ai> accessed 8 January 2025.

3 EU Commission: Independent HLEG, Assessment List for Trustworthy Artificial Intelligence (ALTAI) for Self-Assessment (2020) <https://digital-strategy.ec.europa.eu/en/library/assessment-list-trustworthy-artificial-intelligence-altai-self-assessment> accessed 8 January 2025.

4 EU Commission, Communication from the Commission to the European Parliament, the Council, the European Economic and Social Committee of the Regions Fostering a European Approach to Artificial Intelligence (COM/2021/205 final) <https://eur-lex.europa.eu/legal-content/EN/TXT/?uri=celex:52021DC0205> accessed 30 January 2025.

5 Proposal for a Regulation of the European Parliament and of the Council Laying Down Harmonized Rules on Artificial Intelligence (Artificial Intelligence Act) and Amending Certain Union legislative Acts (COM/2021/206 final).

6 Proposal for a Regulation of the European Parliament and of the Council Laying Down Harmonised Rules on Artificial Intelligence (Artificial Intelligence Act) and Amending Certain Union Legislative Acts – General Approach, Institutional File 2021/0106(COD).

'Parliament Amendments').[7] After extensive negotiations, a political agreement was reached in December 2023, marking the conclusion of the trilogue process amidst substantial media attention. The finally adopted Act (hereinafter referred to as 'AIA') was published in the Official Journal of the EU in July 2024, entering into force on 1 August 2024.[8]

The original design of the AIA, rooted in a conventional product safety law approach, faced significant scrutiny with the emergence of Open AI's famous Large Language Modell, ChatGPT, in November 2022.[9] By that time, both the Commission Proposal and the Council Position were already in motion, leaving the bulk of the discussion on how to regulate emerging forms of AI, particularly General Purpose AI and Generative AI, to the Parliament Amendments and the subsequent trilogue negotiations. Moreover, scholars and civil rights organisations pressed for the integration of more robust fundamental rights elements into the AIA.[10] This led to the introduction of a fundamental rights impact assessment into what was initially conceived as a conventional product safety law, along with provisions to ensure environmental protection, democracy, and the rule of law.[11]

The territorial scope of the AIA is similarly broad as the GDPR's scope, expanding to providers and deployers from third countries where the output produced by their AI system is used in the Union.[12] Provided the MDTs use an AI system meeting the definition of AI under the AIA and lie within the scope of the Regulation, they have to comply with its requirements.[13]

7 Amendments Adopted by the European Parliament on 14 June 2023 on the Proposal for a Regulation of the European Parliament and of the Council on Laying Down Harmonised Rules on Artificial Intelligence (Artificial Intelligence Act) and Amending Certain Union Legislative Acts (COM(2021)0206 – C9-0146/2021–2021/0106(COD)).

8 Regulation (EU) 2024/1689 of the European Parliament and of the Council of 13 June 2024 Laying Down Harmonised Rules on Artificial Intelligence and Amending Regulations (EC) No 300/2008, (EU) No 167/2013, (EU) No 168/2013, (EU) 2018/858, (EU) 2018/1139 and (EU) 2019/2144 and Directives 2014/90/EU, (EU) 2016/797 and (EU) 2020/1828 (Artificial Intelligence Act). OJ L.

9 See, for instance, Kai Zenner, 'A Law for Foundation Models: the EU AI Act Can Improve Regulation for Fairer Competition', *OECD.AI Policy Observer* (23 July 2023) <https://oecd.ai/en/wonk/foundation-models-eu-ai-act-fairer-competition> accessed 8 January 2025.

10 VUB Brussels Privacy Hub, 'More than 150 university professors from all over Europe and beyond are calling on the European institutions to include a fundamental rights impact assessment in the future regulation on artificial intelligence', (12 September 2023) <https://brusselsprivacyhub.com/2023/09/12/brussels-privacy-hub-and-other-academic-institutions-ask-to-approve-a-fundamental-rights-impact-assessment-in-the-eu-artificial-intelligence-act/> accessed 8 January 2025; 'Civil Society Urges European Parliament to Protect People's Rights in the AI Act', (19 April 2023) <https://edri.org/our-work/civil-society-urges-european-parliament-to-protect-peoples-rights-in-the-ai-act/> accessed 8 January 2025; 'Open letter to EU AI Act Negotiators: Do Not Trade Away Our Rights!' (8 December 2023) <https://edri.org/wp-content/uploads/2023/12/Open-letter-to-EU-AI-Act-negotiators_Do-not-trade-away-our-rights-8-December-2023.pdf> accessed 8 January 2025.

11 Article 1 AIA and Recital 1 AIA.

12 Article 2 AIA.

13 Article 3(1) AIA defines an AI system as: 'a machine-based system that is designed to operate with varying levels of autonomy and that may exhibit adaptiveness after deployment, and that, for explicit or

3.1 EMOTION RECOGNITION SYSTEMS

The AIA is the first piece of EU legislation that pro-actively addresses emotion recognition systems (ERS).[14] The definition and classification of ERS have sparked heated debates during the legislative process and the trilogue negotiations. It is therefore essential to examine the different proposals by the Commission, the Council, and Parliament to gain a better understanding of the rationale behind the version that was finally adopted.

Notably, ERS have been directly linked to biometric data in all draft versions, and this remains the case in the adopted Act. Text-based MDTs are therefore not eligible for consideration as ERS under the AIA.

From a legal point of view, the Parliament Amendments offered the most innovative definition. The Parliament introduced new legal mechanisms to address some of the issues outlined in the preceding section, particularly the lack of protection for individuals as members of a group under the GDPR and the challenges surrounding the definition of biometric data and special category biometric data. Aiming to enhance the privacy of individuals as members of a group, the Parliament proposed to link the definition of ERS not only to systems that identify or infer emotions and so on of individuals but also to those that identify or infer emotions of groups. Seeking to address the intricacies concerning biometric data under the GDPR, the Parliament retained the existing GDPR-definition of biometric data unchanged but introduced an entirely new category – biometric-based data – incorporating both into the definition of ERS. The Parliament Amendments thus tried to resolve the biometric dilemma in the GDPR by keeping the original GDPR-definition of biometric data and complementing it with another category, specifically addressing newer forms of biometric data (soft, weak, generation 2.5 or 3 biometric data).

The adopted Act does not reflect these innovations. Rather, the adopted version represents a combination of the Commission Proposal and the Council Proposal. The Council, also being aware of the complexities concerning biometric data and techniques under the GDPR, proposed to detach the definition of biometric data under the AIA from the definition of biometric data under the GDPR. The Council deleted the problematic passage 'which allow or confirm the unique identification' from the original GDPR provision. The adopted version hence defines biometric data as 'personal data resulting from specific technical processing relating to the

implicit objectives, infers, from the input it receives, how to generate outputs such as predictions, content, recommendations, or decisions that can influence physical or virtual environments'. Arguably, this definition leaves some room for interpretative speculation. For illustrative reasons, the examples discussed in this book will be considered meeting the criteria and falling within the scope of the AIA.

14 For the sake of clarity, it is worth recalling that the deployment of MDTs for law enforcement and military purposes has been deliberately excluded from the scope of this book, as it requires a separate analysis and thorough contextualisation. Consequently, the regulation of ERS in these domains also falls beyond the scope of this work and will not be discussed in detail.

	Commission proposal	Council position	Parliament Amendments	Adopted Act
Emotion Recognition System	means an AI system for the purpose of identifying or inferring *emotions or intentions* of natural persons on the basis of their *biometric data*; Article 3(34)	means an AI system for the purpose of identifying or inferring *psychological states, emotions or intentions* of natural persons on the basis of their *biometric data*; Article 3(34)	means an AI system for the purpose of identifying or inferring *emotions, thoughts, states of mind or intentions* of individuals or *groups* on the basis of their *biometric and biometric-based data*; Article 3(34)	means an AI system for the purpose of identifying or inferring *emotions or intentions* of natural persons on the basis of their *biometric data*; Article 3(39)
Biometric data	means personal data resulting from specific technical processing relating to the physical, physiological or behavioural characteristics of a natural person, *which allow or confirm the unique identification* of that natural person, such as facial images or dactyloscopic data; Article 3(33)	means personal data resulting from specific technical processing relating to the physical, physiological or behavioural characteristics of a natural person, such as facial images or dactyloscopic data; Article 3(33)	means biometric data *as defined in* Article 4, point (14) of *Regulation (EU) 2016/679*; Article 3(33)	means personal data resulting from specific technical processing relating to the physical, physiological or behavioural characteristics of a natural person, such as facial images or dactyloscopic data; Article 3(34)
Biometric-based data			means data resulting from specific technical processing relating to physical, physiological or behavioural *signals* of a natural person; Article 3(33a)	

Definitions of 'emotion recognition system' and 'biometric'/'biometric-based data' across different versions of the AIA (emphasis added).

physical, physiological or behavioural characteristics of a natural person, such as facial images or dactyloscopic data' (Article 3(34) AIA).

In full, the AIA now defines an ERS as 'an AI system for the purpose of identifying or inferring emotions or intentions of natural persons on the basis of their biometric data' (Article 3(39) AIA). Additionally, Recital 14 AIA states that:

> [t]he notion of 'biometric data' used in this Regulation should be interpreted in light of the notion of biometric data as defined in Article 4, point (14) of Regulation (EU) 2016/679, Article 3, point (18) of Regulation (EU) 2018/1725 and Article 3, point (13) of Directive (EU) 2016/680. *Biometric data can allow for the authentication, identification or categorisation of natural persons and for the recognition of emotions of natural persons.*[15]

Recalling Sarah and Drew's scenarios from the previous section:

Scenario (a): *a personal mood tracker using face and voice recognition;*
Scenario (b): *a recruitment software employing gesture dynamics and (non-identifying) voice analytics to evaluate whether a candidate responds truthfully or not;*
Scenario (c): *a chatbot for customer service utilising natural language processing to infer emotions from clients' written complaints;*
Scenario (d): *a non-invasive BCI using in-ear EEG for user authentication.*

Sarah and Drew's scenarios (a) is a personal mood tracker. The mood tracker identifies or infers the user's mood using face and voice recognition. Scenario (a) relies on biometric data. Whether the biometric technique used in scenario (a) is for identification purposes or not is irrelevant under the AIA. Scenario (a) can be classified as ERS under the AIA.

Sarah and Drew's scenario (b) is a software employing gesture dynamics and (non-identifying) voice analytics (e.g. trembling and volume) to infer whether a candidate responds truthfully. Applying a strict interpretation of the GDPR-definition of biometric data, characteristics like gesture dynamics or voice characteristics that do not possess uniquely identifying qualities are not considered biometric data. Under the AIA-definition of biometric data, the problematic passage ('which allow or confirm the unique identification') has been deleted. Additionally, Recital 18 AIA clarifies specifically that the detection of gestures or movement, such as the movement of hands, arms, or head, and characteristics like a raised voice or whispering are within the scope of ERS, if 'used for identifying or inferring emotions'.[16] Therefore, the AI system in scenario (b) is eligible for classification as ERS under the AIA.

[15] Recital 14 AIA, emphasis added.
[16] See also EU Commission, Annex to the Communication to the Commission, Approval of the Content of the Draft Communication from the Commission – Commission Guidelines on Prohibited Artificial Intelligence Practices Established by Regulation (EU) 2024/1689 (AI Act), C(2025) 884

The AIA definition of biometric data, distinct from that of the GDPR, offers a possible path forward in resolving some of the intricacies concerning biometric data we met in Sections 2.1.1–2.1.3. First, under the AIA, the specific purpose of processing, whether it be for identification, authentication/verification, or categorisation, is irrelevant. The assumed distinction between normal biometric and special category biometric data under the GDPR is no longer decisive for ERS under the AIA. Second, unlike the GDPR, the AIA does not require biometric data to be able to uniquely identify a natural person. This adaptation includes modern biometrics currently failing to meet the GDPR's stringent criteria to 'allow or confirm the unique identification'. The Commission Guidelines on prohibited AI practices confirm that the AIA definition of biometric data is broad, including any biometric data used for emotion recognition.[17]

From a pragmatic point of view, breaking away from the original GDPR definition of biometric data represents the least disruptive solution to overcome evident legislative shortcomings. No doubt this approach will positively affect the regulation of MDTs. From a doctrinal perspective and considering the wide-ranging implications of the GDPR as a cornerstone of EU data protection legislation and firm point of reference for a sheer endless number of related acts, it would however be preferable to address the biometric dilemma also within the GDPR, considering that the new definition of biometric data in the AIA:

- cannot resolve the definitional disparities within the data protection framework;
- has no impact on the regulation of MDTs falling outside the scope of the AIA; and
- fails to address other legal acts referencing the GDPR as primary legal framework for personal data processing.

Therefore, the biometric dilemma will persist until revisited and resolved within the original source, the GDPR.

A more complex issue is whether the system in scenario (b) meets the requirement of identifying or inferring emotions or intentions. The terminological ambiguities surrounding states and processes of the mind are evident in the definitions of ERS across the different versions of the AIA. The Commission proposed 'emotions or intentions', the Council added 'psychological states' to the definition, the Parliament refined the term more comprehensively and in finer detail, including 'emotions, thoughts, states of mind or intentions'. Ultimately, EU legislators opted in the adopted version for 'emotions or intentions' as continuous parameters.

final, section 269. <https://digital-strategy.ec.europa.eu/en/library/commission-publishes-guidelines-prohibited-artificial-intelligence-ai-practices-defined-ai-act> accessed 6 February 2025. Note that the Commission has approved and published the draft guidelines, but not formally adopted them.

17 EU Commission, Annex to the Communication to the Commission, Approval of the Content of the Draft Communication from the Commission – Commission Guidelines on Prohibited Artificial Intelligence Practices, section 252.

Recital 18 AIA aims to provide further guidance on the matter:

> The notion of 'emotion recognition system' referred to in this Regulation should be defined as an AI system for the purpose of identifying or inferring emotions or intentions of natural persons on the basis of their biometric data. The notion refers to emotions or intentions such as happiness, sadness, anger, surprise, disgust, embarrassment, excitement, shame, contempt, satisfaction and amusement. It does not include physical states, such as pain or fatigue, including, for example, systems used in detecting the state of fatigue of professional pilots or drivers for the purpose of preventing accidents. This does also not include the mere detection of readily apparent expressions, gestures or movements, unless they are used for identifying or inferring emotions. Those expressions can be basic facial expressions, such as a frown or a smile, or gestures such as the movement of hands, arms or head, or characteristics of a person's voice, such as a raised voice or whispering.[18]

The non-exhaustive list in Recital 18 AIA includes emotions or intentions such as happiness, sadness, anger, surprise, disgust, embarrassment, excitement, shame, contempt, satisfaction, and amusement.[19] The Commission Guidelines on prohibited AI practices stipulate that the 'concept of emotions or intentions should be understood in a wide sense and not interpreted restrictively'.[20] Sarah and Drew's scenario (b) is designed to infer whether a candidate responds truthfully or deceptively. Their software may look for indicators like nervousness, fear, excitement, shame, satisfaction, happiness, or comparable emotions to evaluate whether a candidate is telling the truth or not. If so, their system can be classified as ERS.

The explanations provided by Recital 18 AIA are surprisingly lengthy, yet the guidance it offers raises some questions. Recital 18 AIA explicitly excludes 'physical states, such as pain or fatigue, including, for example, systems used in detecting the state of fatigue of professional pilots or drivers for the purpose of preventing accidents' from the notion of ERS. At first glance, this exemption of physical states appears confusing. The AIA defines ERS as AI systems 'for the purpose of identifying or inferring emotions or intentions'. Since physical states are not within the scope of this definition, they would not need to be excluded. Nevertheless, legislators deemed it necessary to specify in Recital 18 AIA that physical states are not included within the notion of ERS.

The exemption of physical states from the notion of ERS in Recital 18 AIA is rooted in the close entanglement of emotions and physical states, especially when the processing is based on biometric data. The entire field of affective computing essentially

18 Recital 18 AIA.

19 The emotions listed in Recital 18 AIA show significant overlaps with Paul Ekman's theory of seven universal facial expressions, including fear, contempt, disgust, sadness, anger, happiness, and surprise (see <www.paulekman.com/resources/universal-facial-expressions/> accessed 8 January 2025).

20 EU Commission, Annex to the Communication to the Commission, Approval of the Content of the Draft Communication from the Commission – Commission Guidelines on Prohibited Artificial Intelligence Practices, section 247.

relies on the assumption that emotions are not purely mental states but a combination of cognitive and physical aspects, with only these physiological changes in the body being measurable and quantifiable.[21] In a White Paper on voice assistants, the French DPA, the Commission Nationale de l'Informatique et des Libertés (CNIL), described how emotions are encoded by observing bodily or physiological changes that accompany specific emotions.[22] For instance, fear typically results in an increased pulse rate, higher blood pressure, and a dry mouth, leading to a louder, higher-pitched voice and quicker speech. In contrast, emotions like boredom or sadness are associated with a lower heart rate and manifest in a softer, lower-pitched voice and slower speech. Already minor changes in a speaker's mental state trigger physiological changes, such as changes in the nervous system or variations in respiration and muscle tension.[23]

Given that observed bodily or physiological changes can allow inferences about both physical and emotional states, blurring the lines between the two, particular emphasis must be placed on accurately determining the system's true purpose. The AIA defines ERS as AI systems *for the purpose of identifying or inferring emotions or intentions*. In the context of prohibited AI practices, the Commission clarifies that:

> 'Identification' occurs where the processing of the biometric data (for example, of the voice or a facial expression) of a natural person allows to directly compare and identify an emotion with one that has been previously programmed in the emotion recognition system. 'Inferring' is done by deducing information generated by analytical and other processes by the system itself. In such a case, the information about the emotion is not solely based on data collected on the natural person, but it is inferred from other data, including machine learning approaches that learn from data how to detect emotions.[24]

If the purpose of an AI system is not the identification or inference of emotions or intentions, then such a system should not be classified as an ERS. Arguably, this grants deployers remarkable discretion in determining whether their AI system falls within the scope of ERS or not, potentially resulting in borderline uses and complicating enforcement. Practitioners would benefit from further clarification of the concept of ERS, for instance through a code of practice issued by the AI Office, including diverse practical examples and delineating its boundaries.

[21] Rosalind W. Picard, *Affective Computing* (The MIT Press 2000), chapter 1, in particular at 22.

[22] Martin Biéri and others, 'On the Record: Exploring the Ethical, Technical and Legal Issues of Voice Assistants', White Paper Collection No 1. (2020), 9 <www.cnil.fr/sites/cnil/files/atoms/files/cnil_white-paper-on_the_record.pdf> accessed 8 January 2025.

[23] Jacob Leon Kröger and others, 'Privacy Implications of Voice and Speech Analysis – Information Disclosure by Inference', in M. Friedewald and others (eds.), *Privacy and Identity Management: Data for Better Living: AI and Privacy*, Privacy and Identity 2019, IFIP Advances in Information and Communication Technology, Vol. 576 (Springer, 2020) <https://doi.org/10.1007/978-3-030-42504-3_16>.

[24] EU Commission, Annex to the Communication to the Commission, Approval of the Content of the Draft Communication from the Commission – Commission Guidelines on Prohibited Artificial Intelligence Practices, section 246.

An alternative course of action to the one taken by the legislators would have been to decouple the definition of ERS from biometric data and expand it to encompass a broader notion than just emotions or intentions. This deviation would not have relied on maintaining two distinct definitions of biometric data – one in the GDPR and another in the AIA. Furthermore, this approach would have facilitated the inclusion of text-based ERS within the definition.

Summarising the analysis of Sarah and Drew's scenarios against the definition of ERS under the AIA: Both scenarios (a) and (b) meet the definition of ERS and have to comply with the requirements for ERS set out in the AIA. The text-based application in scenario (c) is not classified as ERS because it is not based on biometric data. The EEG-based application in scenario (d) is designed for authentication purposes. Provided its purpose is not to identify or infer emotions or intentions during this process, scenario (d) does not meet the definition of ERS.

3.1.1 *Limited Risk*

Intense debates during the legislative process have focused not only on the exact definition of ERS in the AIA but also on their regulation. The AIA, originally following the model of conventional product safety laws, applies a risk-based approach,[25] primarily distinguishing three different risk categories that affect ERS: limited risk, high risk, and unacceptable risk. While the Commission Proposal suggested mainly including ERS in the limited risk category (Article 52(2) Commission Proposal), with additional references in the high-risk category for law enforcement, migration, asylum, and border control management, the finally adopted AIA outlines a more nuanced regulatory framework for ERS.

The limited risk category is regulated in Chapter 4 AIA. Deployers of ERS,[26] accordingly, will be bound by the requirements for limited risk AI systems as outlined in Article 50(3) AIA.[27] These requirements, situated at the low end of all possible requirements, primarily centre around transparency. Deployers of ERS 'shall inform the natural persons exposed thereto of the operation of the system, and shall process the personal data in accordance with Regulations (EU) 2016/679 and (EU) 2018/1725 and Directive (EU) 2016/680, as applicable'.[28]

[25] Product safety is considered one of the earliest examples of risk-based approach to regulation in the EU. See Jukka Ruohonen, 'A Review of Product Safety Regulations in the European Union', (2022) 3 *International Cybersecurity Law Review*, 345–366 <https://doi.org/10.1365/s43439-022-00057-8>.

[26] Deployers are defined by the AIA as a 'natural or legal person, public authority, agency or other body using an AI system under its authority except where the AI system is used in the course of a personal non-professional activity' (Article 3(4) AIA).

[27] Recital 132 AIA reiterates the biometric nature of ERS ('Moreover, natural persons should be notified when they are exposed to AI systems that, *by processing their biometric data*, can identify or infer the emotions or intentions of those persons or assign them to specific categories.' Emphasis added).

[28] Article 50(3) AIA.

Deployers of the software developed by Sarah and Drew in scenario (a) therefore have to implement mechanisms to ensure that users exposed to these systems are aware of their operation. The reference to processing in accordance with the GDPR at this point rekindles the complexities previously discussed regarding normal versus special category biometric data; however, it does not exacerbate them.

Additionally, Chapter 4 AIA also regulates Sarah and Drew's scenario (c), not as an ERS but as an AI system intended to directly interact with a natural person. Article 50(1) AIA stipulates that providers of AI systems intended to interact directly with natural persons need to ensure that these systems are designed and developed in a way that the natural persons are informed about the fact that they are interacting with an AI system. Therefore, chatbots like the one in scenario (c), used here by a customer service, must make the clients aware they are engaging with an algorithm rather than a human customer service agent, unless this is evident for a reasonably well-informed client based on the circumstances and the context of use. Paragraph 5 adds that the information must be given in a clear and distinguishable manner at the time of the first exposure or interaction, conforming to the applicable accessibility requirements. Paragraph 6 provides that the requirements do not affect the requirements of Chapter 3 concerning high-risk AI systems. These risk classes are therefore not mutually exclusive and both can be applicable at the same time.[29]

3.1 2 *High Risk*

The high-risk category is regulated in Chapter 3 AIA. According to Article 6(1) AIA, AI systems covered by Union harmonisation regulation listed in Annex I AIA (para a) and required to undergo third-party conformity assessment (para b) are considered high-risk AI systems; both clauses have to be met cumulatively. Additionally, Article 6(2) AIA stipulates that AI systems referred to in Annex III are considered high risk.[30] In essence, Annex III encompasses domains where the use of AI systems is likely to pose severe risks, including critical infrastructure, education, employment, essential private and public services, law enforcement, migration, asylum and border control management, and administration of justice and democratic processes. Annex III section 1(c) AIA lists 'AI systems intended to be used for emotion recognition'. ERS are thus considered high-risk AI systems according to Article 6(2) in conjunction with Annex III section 1(c) AIA.

[29] Strictly interpreted, Article 50 suggests that para 5 and para 6 are limited to para 1 (certain AI systems intended to interact directly with natural persons) and 4 (AI systems that generate or manipulate image, audio, or video content). However, the inclusion of ERS in Annex III AIA illustrates that ERS, too, can fall into different risk categories simultaneously.

[30] The Commission is empowered to amend, modify or remove high-risk AI systems from Annex III (Article 7 AIA).

The breadth and depth of the requirements for high-risk AI systems are significant. In response to concerns raised by stakeholders regarding the inclusion of AI systems in Annex III, which may not necessarily pose a high risk but are classified as such merely due to the sector of use, both the Council Position and the Parliament Amendments introduced an additional safety layer. According to Article 6(3) AIA, Annex III high-risk AI systems shall not be classified high-risk AI systems where they do not pose 'a significant risk of harm to the health, safety or fundamental rights of natural persons, including by not materially influencing the outcome of decision making'.[31]

ERS are unlikely to be affected by the exemption in Article 6(3) AIA. As previously established in the context of the GDPR, the risk to the fundamental rights of natural persons is inherent to ERS (what may still require further guidance or judicial precedents is the threshold of 'significant risk'). Moreover, the last sentence in Article 6(3) AIA clarifies that an 'AI system referred to in Annex III shall always be considered to be high-risk where the AI system performs profiling of natural persons'.[32] Since ERS typically rely on profiling, they are not subject to this exemption.

The requirements for high-risk AI systems, as outlined in Chapter 3 AIA, are indeed substantial. Section 2 of Chapter 3 AIA lists the requirements for high-risk AI systems, Section 3 of Chapter 3 AIA outlines the obligations for providers and deployers of high-risk AI systems and other parties. Essentially, the requirements for high-risk AI systems aim to translate the ethical principles and key requirements outlined in the Ethics Guidelines for trustworthy AI into hard law.[33] Legislators have put great emphasis on transparency measures (e.g. through logging of activity, detailed documentation, record-keeping, information to deployers), risk assessment and mitigation systems, high quality of datasets, human oversight, technical robustness, and security. In addition, deployers that are bodies governed by public law or private entities providing public services shall perform a fundamental rights impact assessment (FRIA) for high-risk systems. As a legal instrument in EU digital law, such a FRIA is relatively young. An initial version can be found in the Digital Services Act.[34] First

31 The implementation of this risk filter has faced critique from the media and civil rights movements. See 'EU Legislators Must Close Dangerous Loophole and Protect Human Rights in the AI Act', (7 September 2023) <https://edri.org/our-work/civil-society-statement-eu-close-loophole-article-6-ai-act-tech-lobby/> accessed 8 January 2025. Luca Bertuzzi, 'AI Act: EU Parliament's Legal Office Gives Damning Opinion on High Risk Classification "Filters"', *Euractiv* (19 October 2023) <www.euractiv.com/section/artificial-intelligence/news/ai-act-eu-parliaments-legal-office-gives-damning-opinion-on-high-risk-classification-filters/> accessed 8 January 2025.

32 Article 6(3) AIA.

33 EU Commission, Ethics Guidelines for Trustworthy AI, (2019) <https://digital-strategy.ec.europa.eu/en/library/ethics-guidelines-trustworthy-ai> accessed 8 January 2025.

34 Alessandro Mantelero, 'Fundamental Rights Impact Assessments in the DSA', *Verfassungsblog* (1 November 2022) <https://verfassungsblog.de/dsa-impact-assessment/> accessed 8 January 2025. See also Alessandro Mantelero, 'Human Rights Impact Assessment and AI', in *Beyond Data: Human*

practical experiences are taking place in the Netherlands,[35] and in Denmark.[36] As regards ERS, the requirement for a FRIA will particularly apply to ERS used by law enforcement and justice.

Sarah and Drew's scenarios (a), the personal mood tracker using face and voice recognition, will be considered an ERS and thus not only classified as a limited but also as a high-risk AI system under the AIA. This means that, in addition to the transparency requirements for limited risk AI systems, all the above-mentioned measures (except for the FRIA) must be taken and all requirements must be complied with.

Arguably, the AIA imposes significant compliance obligations on ERS, requiring substantial financial and time investments. Given the substantial risks posed by ERS to the fundamental rights and freedoms of individuals, these efforts, however, seem justified. Important voices have argued that the AIA should have gone so far as to entirely prohibit ERS. For example, the EDPB and EDPS strongly criticised the general practice of inferring emotions in their joint opinion on the Commission Proposal, advocating for a complete ban under the AIA, subject to specific exemptions:

> [T]he EDPB and the EDPS consider that the use of AI to *infer emotions of a natural person is highly undesirable and should be prohibited*, except for certain well-specified use-cases, namely for health or research purposes (e.g., patients where emotion recognition is important), always with appropriate safeguards in place and of course, subject to all other data protection conditions and limits including purpose limitation.[37]

3.1.3 *Unacceptable Risk*

The EDPB/EDPS's call for a general prohibition of ERS was not supported by EU legislators. On the contrary, the legislators chose to generally permit ERS, albeit with a stringent set of requirements following the regime for limited and high-risk systems, imposing a prohibition only in specific cases deemed to pose an unacceptable risk. This is remarkable, considering the legislators' own highly critical views on the scientific foundation of ERS, their reliability and potential impact on

Rights, Ethical and Social Impact Assessment in AI, Information Technology and Law Series, Vol. 36 (T. M. C. Asser Press, 2022), 45–91 <https://doi.org/10.1007/978-94-6265-531-7_2>. Alessandro Mantelero, 'The Fundamental Rights Impact Assessment (FRIA) in the AI Act: Roots, Legal Obligations and Key Elements for a Model Template' (2024) 54 *Computer Law & Security Review*, 106020 <https://doi.org/10.1016/j.clsr.2024.106020>.

35 'Dutch Ministry of the Interior and Kingdom Relations, Impact Assessment Fundamental Rights and Algorithms', (March 2022) <www.nldigitalgovernment.nl/wp-content/uploads/sites/11/2022/05/Impact-Assessment-fundamental-rights-and-algorithms.pdf> accessed 8 January 2025.

36 See <www.humanrights.dk/tools/human-rights-impact-assessment-guidance-toolbox/introduction-human-rights-impact-assessment> und <www.humanrights.dk/tools/human-rights-impact-assessment-guidance-toolbox> accessed 8 January 2025.

37 EDPB-EDPS, Joint Opinion 5/2021 on the Proposal for a Regulation of the European Parliament and of the Council Laying Done Harmonized Rules on Artificial Intelligence (Artificial Intelligence Act) (18 June 2021), 12.

fundamental rights and freedoms, such as non-discrimination, which they expressed in Recital 44 AIA:

> There are serious concerns about the scientific basis of AI systems aiming to identify or infer emotions, particularly as expression of emotions vary considerably across cultures and situations, and even within a single individual. Among the key shortcomings of such systems are the limited reliability, the lack of specificity and the limited generalisability. Therefore, AI systems identifying or inferring emotions or intentions of natural persons on the basis of their biometric data may lead to discriminatory outcomes and can be intrusive to the rights and freedoms of the concerned persons.[38]

Article 5 AIA lists the rare instances where AI systems to infer emotions are explicitly prohibited. Article 5 AIA has been among the most intensely discussed provisions during the legislative period.[39] This is not surprising, given that AI systems included in Article 5 AIA face a complete ban from the EU market, making the impact of this provision decisive. The inclusion of AI systems to infer emotions in Article 5 was first proposed by the Parliament Amendments. These suggested a total ban for AI systems to infer emotions in the workplace, in educational institutions, and in the areas of law enforcement and border management (Article 5(1)(dc) Parliament Amendments). During trilogue negotiations, the Parliament's stance was in principle supported by the Council, except for the prohibition in the area of law enforcement and border management. The finally adopted version of Article 5(1)(f) AIA therefore prohibits:

> (f) the placing on the market, the putting into service for this specific purpose, or the use of AI systems to infer emotions of a natural person in the areas of workplace and education institutions, except where the use of the AI system is intended to be put in place or into the market for medical or safety reasons;[40]

Article 5(1)(f) is banning the use of AI systems to infer emotions in the workplace context and in educational institutions under the AIA, except for medical or safety reasons.[41] Notably, the prohibition in Article 5(1)(f) AIA does not specifically mention the term 'ERS'. Article 5(1)(f) AIA could have simply stated that 'the placing on

38 Recital 44 AIA.

39 For discussions on the key points of critique surrounding Article 5 AIA, see, for instance: Michael Veale and Frederik Zuiderveen Borgesius, 'Demystifying the Draft EU Artificial Intelligence Act: Analysing the Good, the Bad, and the Unclear Elements of the Proposed Approach' (2021) 22(4) *Computer Law Review International*, 97–112 <https://doi.org/10.9785/cri-2021-220402>. Rostam J. Neuwirth, 'Prohibited Artificial Intelligence Practices in the Proposed EU Artificial Intelligence Act (AIA)', (2023) 48 *Computer Law & Security Review*, 105798 <https://doi.org/10.1016/j.clsr.2023.105798>; Mark Leiser, 'Psychological Patterns and Article 5 of the AI Act', (2024) Jahrgang 1, Ausgabe 1 *Journal of AI Law and Regulation*, 5–23 <https://doi.org/10.21552/aire/2024/1/4>.

40 Article 5(1)(f) AIA.

41 The impact of the prohibition in Article 5(1)(f) AIA on MDTs will be discussed more thoroughly in use case 4, Chapter 7, on 'Employment Monitoring'. Additionally, the possible effect of the prohibition in

the market, the putting into service for this specific purpose, or the use of *ERS* in the areas of workplace and education institutions' is prohibited.

Instead, the legislators used the wording, 'AI systems to infer emotions'; neither the identification of emotions is included in the provision, nor the concept of intentions. The choice of wording could potentially broaden the scope to include AI systems that do not rely on biometric data, in particular text-based applications. Conversely, Recital 44 AIA indicates that the prohibition in Article 5(1)(f) AIA is only referring to AI systems based on biometric data:

> Therefore, *AI systems identifying or inferring emotions or intentions* of natural persons *on the basis of their biometric data* may lead to discriminatory outcomes and can be intrusive to the rights and freedoms of the concerned persons. Considering the imbalance of power in the context of work or education, combined with the intrusive nature of these systems, such systems could lead to detrimental or unfavourable treatment of certain natural persons or whole groups thereof. Therefore, the placing on the market, the putting into service, or *the use of AI systems intended to be used to detect the emotional state of individuals in situations related to the workplace and education should be prohibited.* That prohibition should not cover AI systems placed on the market strictly for medical or safety reasons, such as systems intended for therapeutical use.[42]

When reading Article 5(1)(f) AIA in conjunction with Recital 44 AIA, the prohibition appears to factually apply only to AI systems based on biometric data, not including text-based MDTs. The Commission Guidelines on prohibited AI practices support this reading:

> (244) Article 3(39) AI Act defines 'emotion recognition systems' as AI systems 'for the purpose of identifying and inferring emotions or intentions of natural persons on the basis of their biometric data. The prohibition in Article 5(1)(f) AI Act does not refer to 'emotion recognition systems', but only to 'AI systems to infer emotions of a natural person'. Recital 44 further clarifies that that prohibition covers AI systems 'to identify or infer emotions'.
>
> (245) Inferring generally encompasses identifying as a prerequisite, so that the prohibition should be understood as including both AI systems identifying or inferring emotions or intentions. For consistency reasons, it is also important to construe the prohibition in Article 5(1)(f) AI Act as having a similar scope as the rules applicable to other emotion recognition systems (Annex III, point 1(c), and Article 50 AI Act) and to limit it to inferences based on a person's biometric data. The definition in Article 3(39) AI Act of emotion recognition systems should therefore be considered relevant in relation to Article 5(1)(f) AI Act.[43]

Article 5(1)(a) AIA on MDTs will be discussed in the AIA section concerning commercial and political advertising (end of use case 3, Chapter 6).

42 Recital 44 AIA (emphasis added).

43 EU Commission, Annex to the Communication to the Commission, Approval of the Content of the Draft Communication from the Commission – Commission Guidelines on Prohibited Artificial Intelligence Practices, section 244–245.

Considering the vast possibilities of inferring emotions through text-based MDTs – particularly in the contexts of work and education, where so many tasks and assignments nowadays are delivered in a written format – this reading is regrettable. At the same time, it is worth noting that only the Article itself is legally binding; neither the Recitals nor the Guidelines have binding force. In particular, the Guidelines could evolve and be amended over time. Any authoritative interpretation of the AIA can only be provided by the CJEU.

Sarah and Drew's scenario (b), the recruitment software employing gesture dynamics and (non-identifying) voice analytics (e.g. trembling and volume) to evaluate whether a candidate responds truthfully or not as described, falls in the category of an AI system to infer emotions of natural persons on the basis of their biometric data in the workplace.[44] Therefore, scenario (b) will be classified as unacceptable risk under the AIA. Its placing on the market, putting into service, or use will be prohibited in the EU.

The EU legislators' decision to prohibit ERS/AI systems to infer emotions only in the workplace and in educational institutions and not to impose a general prohibition on ERS has caused serious critique. Given the substantial reservations regarding the scientific foundation of ERS and the potential threats they pose to the fundamental rights and freedoms, as articulated both by the legislators as well as by the EDPB/EDPS, this critique is understandable.

However, this book argues against entirely dismissing the proposed regulatory approach to ERS under the AIA without fully considering the broader context. EU legislators, whether justly or not, are often criticised for over-regulation. In the case of ERS, they show a willingness to strike a balance between fostering innovation and implementing significant regulatory measures. First, all ERS are classified as limited-risk AI systems. Such systems must inform natural persons exposed thereto of the operation of the system, and process the personal data in accordance with the GDPR. This measure aims to prevent systems from identifying and inferring emotions or intentions of natural persons without their awareness. Second, ERS are classified as high-risk AI systems, the highest risk class under the AIA, subject to rigorous requirements and obligations. Third, AI systems to infer emotions are explicitly prohibited in two sectors: workplaces and educational institutions.

ERS are still evolving and their future capabilities remain uncertain. A uniform ban on ERS across all sectors would have stifled opportunities to discover new beneficial applications. Rather, this multilayered approach allows for the use of ERS across numerous sectors – whether for therapeutic purposes, enhancing well-being, leisure activities, gaming, or other domains where they can prove beneficial – provided adequate safeguards are in place and individuals are properly informed. This

[44] For a more granular analysis of the workplace-related prohibition in Article 5(1)(f) AIA, see use case 4 in Chapter 7 on Employment Monitoring.

approach enables innovation and use of ERS in sectors that may not be relevant today but could become important in the future.

Moreover, the AIA is inherently general legislation. Therefore, the approach towards ERS in the AIA must be understood as providing a basic level of protection, which should be complemented by more detailed measures in sector-specific laws. The fact that ERS are generally permitted under the AIA does not preclude their prohibition by leges speciales in specific sectors after careful legal analysis. The Platform Work Directive, which will be discussed in use case 4, Chapter 7, serves as an initial example. The book will also present additional instances where proactive prohibition by EU legislators should be considered. From this perspective, the AIA represents not the culmination of all regulatory efforts concerning ERS, but rather a foundational starting point.

In addition to sector-specific measures, a crucial element of such a multilayered approach could be the establishment of a sui generis special category for mind data within the GDPR, ensuring a consistently high level of data protection.

3.2 CLASSIFICATION AS PERSONAL DATA REMAINS CENTRAL

***Recalling scenario (e)**: a biometric system that infers customers' moods in a shopping mall using video cameras. Based on the emotions detected, the lights in the mall will be adjusted (e.g. dimmed/brightened) or a specific scent dispersed to enhance people's inclination to purchase products.*

ERS rely on the processing of biometric data. Although the AIA definition of biometric data is broader than the GDPR definition, it is still linked to its nature as personal data (argumentum: 'biometric data means personal data resulting from [...]', Article 3(33) AIA).[45] Unless the data processed by Sarah and Drew's system in scenario (e) is considered personal data, it does not qualify as biometric data under the AIA, meaning the system fails to meet the criteria for ERS and the provisions for ERS do not apply.

Initially, the AIA seems to present other options for regulating AI systems such as the one described in scenario (e): biometric categorisation systems or remote biometric identification systems. The AIA defines biometric categorisation systems as AI systems 'for the purpose of assigning natural persons to specific categories on the basis of their biometric data, unless it is ancillary to another commercial service and strictly necessary for objective technical reasons'.[46] However, the definition of biometric categorisation systems relies again on biometric data, which, as demonstrated before, only includes personal data. As long as the data in scenario (e) is not considered personal data, the provisions for biometric categorisation systems do not apply.

[45] Article 3(50) AIA defines 'personal data' referencing Article 4(1) GDPR.

[46] Article 3(40) AIA.

Remote biometric identification systems are defined as AI systems 'for the purpose of identifying natural persons, without their active involvement, typically at a distance through the comparison of a person's biometric data with the biometric data contained in a reference database'.[47] Once more, the AI systems are linked to the definition of biometric data, which requires the data to be personal data. Moreover, Sarah and Drew's scenario (e) does not identify natural persons through the comparison of their biometric data with the biometric data in a database. The requirements for remote biometric identification systems do not apply to scenario (e). In line with the existing legal framework, the most seamless approach to incorporate such AI systems would involve reassessing the classification of the data as (non-)personal data.

3.3 GENERAL-PURPOSE AI, GENERATIVE AI

Scenario (c_1): *Excited by media reports on the rise and potential of generative AI, Sarah and Drew start dreaming big and envision building a generative AI model to power their customer service chatbot, which infers emotions from clients' written complaints.*

Recent advancements in AI, particularly in general-purpose AI (GPAI) or generative AI, were not initially accounted for in the Commission's 2021 Proposal. However, integrating a regulatory regime for these forms of AI into the final Act became inevitable. Both the development of these AI techniques and their regulation remain in the early stages, and much of the current discourse is still speculative. Nonetheless, given the potential of MDTs when combined with these types of AI, this section will briefly outline the initial regulatory regime and offer preliminary observations.[48]

As the regulatory concept for GPAI was added ex post to the Commission Proposal – after the original design and structure of the draft AIA had already been completed – it serves as a supplementary element to the risk-based approach and the risk categories outlined above. Notably, legislators opted to address GPAI in a more nuanced manner compared to conventional forms of AI, introducing 'general-purpose AI models'.

The legal definition of GPAI models is provided in Article 3(63) AIA. According to this provision, a GPAI model is:

> an AI model, including where such an AI model is trained with a large amount of data using self-supervision at scale, that displays significant generality and is

[47] Article 3(41) AIA, Recital 17 AIA.

[48] For further analyses, see Claudio Novelli and others, 'Generative AI in EU Law: Liability, Privacy, Intellectual Property, and Cybersecurity', (2024) 55 *Computer Law & Security Review*, 106066 <https://doi.org/10.1016/j.clsr.2024.106066>. Sandra Wachter, 'Limitations and Loopholes in the EU AI Act and AI Liability Directives: What This Means for the European Union, the United States, and Beyond', (2024) 26(3) *Yale Journal of Law & Technology*, 671–718.

> capable of competently performing a wide range of distinct tasks regardless of the way the model is placed on the market and that can be integrated into a variety of downstream systems or applications, except AI models that are used for research, development or prototyping activities before they are placed on the market.[49]

GPAI models are therefore characterised by three key features:

- GPAI models have significant general usability,
- they can fulfil a wide range of different tasks competently,
- and they can be integrated into a variety of systems.

GPAI models do not constitute AI systems on their own; rather, they are integrated into and serve as essential components of AI systems.[50] For a GPAI model to form a complete AI system, additional elements – such as a user interface – are necessary.

Providers of GPAI models are required to meet documentation and information obligations, inter alia to enable downstream providers to comply with their own responsibilities. They must put in place a policy to comply with copyright laws, provide a sufficiently detailed summary of the training data, and cooperate with the Commission and competent national authorities when necessary (Article 53 AIA). If providers are established in a third country, they must appoint an authorised representative based in the Union (Article 54 AIA).

The term *generative AI* appears only in the recitals of the AIA and is absent from its legally binding provisions. Recital 99 AIA identifies large generative AI models as 'a typical example of a general-purpose AI model, given that they allow for flexible generation of content, such as text, audio, images, or video, which can readily accommodate a wide range of distinctive tasks'.[51] Essentially, generative AI can be understood as a subcategory of GPAI models. While GPAI models are designed for a wide range of applications, generative AI generates text, images, videos, music, and other content.

According to Recital 99 AIA, Sarah and Drew's generative AI model would be considered an example of a GPAI model. Since their GPAI model powers a chatbot, it is supplemented with additional components, particularly a user interface that directly interacts with users. Consequently, Sarah and Drew's GPAI model forms part of an AI system. The regulation of this AI system follows the regime outlined in

49 Recital 98 AIA adds that: 'models with at least a billion of parameters and trained with a large amount of data using self-supervision at scale should be considered to display significant generality and to competently perform a wide range of distinctive tasks'.

50 For the distinction between GPAI models and AI systems, see Recital 97 AIA:

> 'General-purpose AI models may be placed on the market in various ways, including through libraries, application programming interfaces (APIs), as direct download, or as physical copy. These models may be further modified or fine-tuned into new models. Although AI models are essential components of AI systems, they do not constitute AI systems on their own. AI models require the addition of further components, such as for example a user interface, to become AI systems. AI models are typically integrated into and form part of AI systems.' (Recital 97 AIA)

51 In addition, Recital 105 AIA mentions generative AI models in the context of copyright questions.

the previous section for scenario (c): Being a text-based application, the chatbot is not classified as an ERS and is therefore not subject to any of the requirements for ERS. However, it is considered an AI system intended to interact directly with natural persons. As such, it must comply with the transparency requirements for limited risk AI systems pursuant to Article 50(1) AIA. Additionally, Sarah and Drew must comply with the obligations for providers of GPAI models outlined in Article 53 AIA.

A stricter regulatory regime is envisaged for general-purpose AI models with systemic risks.[52] Article 51 AIA classifies GPAI models as GPAI models with systemic risks (a) if the model possesses high-impact capabilities, or (b) such a classification is determined by a decision of the Commission.[53] If the AI model described in Sarah and Drew's scenario (c_1) meets the established threshold for high-impact capabilities, they are required to take specific measures. These encompass conducting assessments of the model, including attack tests to identify systemic risks; implementing measures to mitigate systemic risks; documenting and reporting serious incidents and potential remedial measures, including notifying the AI Office; and ensuring an appropriate level of cybersecurity.[54]

Recital 110 AIA provides examples of systemic risks under the AIA, including major accidents, disruptions of critical sectors, and serious consequences for public health and safety. Other systemic risks listed in the Recital include actual or foreseeable negative effects on democratic processes, public and economic security, and the dissemination of illegal, false, or discriminatory content.

The notion of systemic risks is a relatively recent legal concept in the field of digital law, first introduced through the Digital Services Act (DSA).[55] The precise interplay between systemic risks addressed in the AIA and those under the DSA has yet to unfold fully. Recitals 120 and 136 AIA specify that obligations to identify and mitigate systemic risks arising from the dissemination of artificially generated or manipulated content – for instance, those affecting democratic processes, civic discourse, and electoral integrity – should be interpreted in relation to the obligations imposed on providers of very large online platforms and search engines under the DSA.[56]

52 Article 3(65) AIA defines a systemic risk as: 'a risk that is specific to the high-impact capabilities of general-purpose AI models, having a significant impact on the Union market due to their reach, or due to actual or reasonably foreseeable negative effects on public health, safety, public security, fundamental rights, or the society as a whole, that can be propagated at scale across the value chain'.

53 Article 51(2) specifies that a general-purpose AI model shall be presumed to have high impact capabilities when the cumulative amount of computation used for its training measured in floating point operations is greater than 10^{25}. According to Article 51(3), the thresholds can be amended in light of evolving technological developments (e.g. algorithmic improvements or increased hardware efficiency) to reflect the state of the art.

54 Article 55 AIA.

55 The Digital Services Act, including the concept and regulation of systemic risks therein, will be analysed in the context of use case 2 and 3, in Chapter 6.

56 This could become relevant for use case 3 in Chapter 6, provided a GPAI model with systemic risks is used.

However, while the DSA permits vetted researchers to access relevant platforms to investigate systemic risks and requires external auditors to evaluate these risks and assess the effectiveness of mitigation strategies under the DSA, the AIA does not incorporate similar external assessment mechanisms.[57] Instead, the AIA relies on the development of a GPAI code of practice to provide further guidance. This code aims to clarify the types and sources of systemic risks, methods for their assessment, and appropriate mitigation measures. The AI Office is tasked with facilitating the creation and adaptation of the GPAI code of practice under Article 56 AIA. The code shall also outline the obligations for providers of GPAI models, including those presenting systemic risks.[58]

Sarah and Drew could try to exempt themselves from the significantly stricter regulatory regime for GPAI models with systemic risks, provided they can present 'sufficiently substantiated arguments' to demonstrate that their AI model, due to its specific characteristics, does not pose systemic risks and should therefore not be classified as a GPAI model with systemic risks (Article 52(2) AIA). This self-assessment mechanism has attracted significant critique, as it may allow providers to bypass rigorous oversight by relying on their own judgement. The Commission retains the authority to reject these arguments should it deem them unconvincing (Article 52(3) AIA).

Overall, the legal landscape and regulatory requirements for GPAI, including generative AI, under the AIA are only beginning to take shape. Many aspects have yet to be specified in greater detail. Once these details are clarified, the regulatory concept and its requirements can be thoroughly explored and analysed.

Building on the foundational analysis of MDT regulation under the GDPR and the AIA, which apply across all sectors, the book will now turn to an in-depth examination of four specific use cases in Chapters 4–7. These use cases encompass areas such as mental health and well-being, commercial and political advertising, and workplace monitoring. By examining these use cases, the book seeks to deepen the understanding of the distinct regulatory challenges that MDTs pose in these key areas, while also offering suggestions into how existing legal frameworks could be adapted to address them effectively.

57 Wachter, 'Limitations and Loopholes'.

58 Recital 116 AIA.

4

Use Case 1: Mental Health and Well-Being

Is My Data Safe and Are the Devices Efficient?

Digital technologies hold immense potential in the domain of mental health and well-being, despite their inherent challenges.[1] They can support early detection and diagnosis, complement traditional therapy, deliver personalised interventions, enable innovative research and treatment options, and improve accessibility, availability, affordability, and scalability.[2] Propelled by the widespread acceptance of smartphones, increased internet connectivity, and rising investments, the e-mental health and well-being market has become an exponentially growing field.[3] Globally, the market for digital mental health is projected to grow from US$23.45 billion in 2023 to US$108.4 billion in 2032.[4]

Among the various domains where MDTs are deployed, this sector stands out as a focal point. In addition to their growing use in the distinct medical context, MDTs have increasingly expanded into the consumer mental health and well-being market. At the centre of this field of deployment lie two core challenges that drive intense discussions: (1) concerns about privacy/data protection and (2) doubts about efficacy. Both raise significant legal concerns regarding classification and compliance.

[1] Piers Gooding, 'Mapping the Rise of Digital Mental Health Technologies: Emerging Issues for Law and Society', (2019) 67 *International Journal of Law and Psychiatry*, 101498 <https://doi.org/10.1016/j.ijlp.2019.101498>. Jonah Bossewitch and others, *Digital Futures in Mind: Reflecting on Technological Experiments in Mental Health & Crisis Support* (University of Melbourne, 2021) <https://automatingmentalhealth.cc/> accessed 15 January 2025; World Health Organization (WHO), 'World Mental Health Report: Transforming Mental Health for All', (2022) <www.who.int/publications/i/item/9789240049338> accessed 30 January 2025.

[2] World Economic Forum and Deloitte, 'Global Governance Toolkit for Digital Mental Health: Building Trust in Disruptive Technology for Mental Health', White Paper (2021), 15 <www.weforum.org/publications/global-governance-toolkit-for-digital-mental-health/> accessed 8 January 2025.

[3] Recognising that the international expert community uses the terms 'digital mental health' and 'e-mental health' interchangeably, this book will use both terms consistently.

[4] Market Research Future, 'Global Digital Mental Health Market Overview' (2024) <www.marketresearchfuture.com/reports/digital-mental-health-market-11062> accessed 8 January 2025.

Sarah and Drew keep brainstorming about possible deployments of their future software. They consider the following scenarios:

Scenario (a): *an online program, including quizzes, voice analytics and a serious game, to diagnose and treat depression;*
Scenario (b): *an app drawing inferences about users' mood from geolocation and movement data together with social media entries to enhance self-awareness about mental health and well-being;*
Scenario (c): *a non-invasive BCI tracking users' mood based on brain activity to select music that helps them focus/relax, thereby enhancing their mental health and well-being.*

Sarah and Drew aim to seek certification as a medical device for scenario (a). In contrast, scenarios (b) and (c) would be freely available on the consumer market. Sarah and Drew discuss the legal nature of the processed data and the legal requirements they would have to comply with.

4.1 GDPR: ROBUST IN THEORY BUT LACKING IN PRACTICE

Once more, Sarah and Drew address the question concerning the legal nature and classification of the data processed by MDTs under the GDPR.[5] For Sarah and Drew, and many other manufacturers, this is not a matter of legal subtlety. If found in breach of GDPR requirements regarding sensitive data, they could face costly fines. In May 2023, a French website offering articles, tests, quizzes, and discussion forums related to health and well-being has been fined by the CNIL, the French DPA, with €380,000 for, inter alia, not providing any special warning or consenting mechanism on its online tests to ensure that the users were aware of the processing of their sensitive health data.[6]

Classifying the data processed by MDTs in the field of mental health and well-being as data concerning health, and thus as special category, has multiple facets. Contrary to the relatively young special category of biometric data, the protection of data concerning the health of natural persons has a long-standing tradition and predates today's data protection laws. The protection of health data is closely linked to safeguarding the fundamental rights of natural persons. In Europe, examples from the first half of the twentieth century (and beyond) illustrate vividly that unauthorised disclosure or access to health data can result in stigma, unjust discrimination, or even loss of life.

European data protection frameworks have incorporated health data in their list of special category data from the onset. Data concerning health was part of the

5 The classification as data concerning health may or may not be overlapping with the classification as special category biometric data.

6 CNIL, 'Health Data and Use of Cookies: DOCTISSIMO Fined €380,000', (17 May 2023) <www.cnil.fr/en/health-data-and-use-cookies-doctissimo-fined-eu380000> accessed 8 January 2025.

special categories in the Council of Europe's Convention 108.[7] Health data was included in the list of special categories in the DPD, and it continues to be listed in the GDPR as special category.[8] Health data, including mental health data, is therefore considered sensitive; it is guaranteed special safeguards and enjoys the highest level of protection under the GDPR.

Article 4(15) GDPR defines 'data concerning health' as data 'related to the physical or mental health of a natural person, including the provision of health care services, which reveal information about his or her health status'. The GDPR does not define the terms 'health', 'physical health', or 'mental health'.[9] However, Recital 35 GDPR gives several examples for data concerning health:

> Personal data concerning health should include all data pertaining to the health status of a data subject which reveal information relating to the past, current or future physical or mental health status of the data subject. This includes information about the natural person collected in the course of the registration for, or the provision of, health care services as referred to in Directive 2011/24/EU of the European Parliament and of the Council to that natural person; a number, symbol or particular assigned to a natural person to uniquely identify the natural person for health purposes; information derived from the testing or examination of a body part or bodily substance, including from genetic data and biological samples; and any information on, for example, a disease, disability, disease risk, medical history, clinical treatment or the physiological or biomedical state of the data subject independent of its source, for example from a physician or other health professional, a hospital, a medical device or an in vitro diagnostic test.[10]

European data protection legislation and jurisdiction apply a broad interpretation of the term 'data concerning health'. Already in *Lindqvist*, the CJEU confirmed that the term has to be 'given a wide interpretation so as to include information concerning all aspects, both physical and mental, of the health of an individual'.[11]

Regulatory guidance takes a broad approach as well. In an Annex to their letter to the EU Commission on the scope of health data in relation to lifestyle and well-being apps, the WP29 confirms that health data encompasses a much broader notion than simply medical data.[12] The list of examples for health data given in the Annex is indeed long, including information, such as;

7 See Article 6 of the Council of Europe's 'Convention for the Protection of Individuals with Regard to Automatic Processing of Personal Data' (1981).

8 See Article 8(1) DPD and Article 9(1) GDPR.

9 See also, Maria Tzanou, 'The GDPR and (Big) Health Data: Assessing the EU Legislator's Choices', in Maria Tzanou (ed.), *Health Data Privacy under the GDPR: Big Data Challenges and Regulatory Responses* (Routledge 2020), 6.

10 Recital 35 GDPR.

11 C-101/01 *Bodil Lindqvist* [2003] ECR I-12971, para 50.

12 Article 29 Data Protection Working Party, Annex – Health Data in Apps and Devices (2018) <https://ec.europa.eu/justice/article-29/documentation/other-document/files/2015/20150205_letter_art29wp_ec_health_data_after_plenary_annex_en.pdf> accessed 8 January 2025.

> that a woman has broken her leg (Lindqvist), that a person is wearing glasses or contact lenses, data about a person's intellectual and emotional capacity (such as IQ), information about smoking and drinking habits, data on allergies disclosed to private entities (such as airlines) or to public bodies (such as schools); data on health conditions to be used in an emergency (for example information that a child taking part in a summer camp or similar event suffers from asthma); membership of an individual in a patient support group (e.g. cancer support group), Weight Watchers, Alcoholics Anonymous or other self-help and support groups with a health-related objective; and the mere mentioning of the fact that somebody is ill in an employment context are all data concerning the health of individual data subjects.[13]

Similarly, scholarly literature and commentaries interpret the category of health data in the GDPR holistically, considering genetic/biometric data as well as data processed by patients through mobile health tools, wearables, apps and self-reported information as data concerning health.[14]

The increasing deployment of AI and data analytics, which both thrive on the merging of continual inputs of large amounts of different data to infer new information, has added more complexity to the distinction between health and non-health data.[15]

The WP29 lays out three scenarios indicating when data should be considered as data concerning health:

(i) when used in a professional medical context (as outlined in Recital 35),
(ii) when raw sensor data allows (independently or in combination with other data) conclusions about someone's health status or their health risks; and
(iii) when data allows for inferences to the health status or risk.

All three are relevant with regard to the deployment of MDTs in the field of mental health and well-being.

[13] Article 29 Data Protection Working Party, Annex – Health Data in Apps and Devices, 2.

[14] See Stefan Ernst, Article 4 Margin Number 106–110 in Boris Paal and Daniel Pauly (eds.), *Datenschutz-Grundverordnung Bundesdatenschutzgesetz: DS-GVO BDSG* (3rd edn, C. H. Beck 2021). For a more granular discussion, see also Anni-Mara Taka, 'A Deep Dive into Dynamic Data Flows, Wearable Devices, and the Concept of Health Data', (2023) 13(2) *International Data Privacy Law*, 124–140 <https://doi.org/10.1093/idpl/ipad007>.

[15] The ongoing challenge of distinguishing sensitive from non-sensitive data, with its doctrinal intricacies, will be addressed only as necessary for the use cases presented in this book, particularly with regard to use case 1 (data concerning health) in Chapter 4 and use case 3 (data revealing political opinions) in Chapter 6. For recent scholarly debates, see exemplarily, Gianclaudio Malgieri and Giovanni Comandé, 'Sensitive-by-Distance: Quasi-Health Data in the Algorithmic Era', (2017) 26(3) *Information & Communications Technology Law*, 229–249 <https://doi.org/10.1080/13600834.2017.1335468>; Quinn and Malgieri, 'The Difficulty of Defining Sensitive Data'; Daniel J. Solove, 'Data Is What Data Does: Regulating Risk, Based on Harm and Risk Instead of Sensitive Data', (2024) 118(4) *Northwestern University Law Review*, 1081–1138.

4.1.1 *Data Processed within the Distinct Medical Context*

The research and use of MDTs in the distinct medical field can take many forms. Examples based on emotion technology include glass devices for teenagers with autism disorder to help them read and understand other people's emotions and social behaviour,[16] algorithms used to predict aggressive outbursts in people with autism in advance by monitoring their physiological indicators of stress,[17] or certified mental health chatbots predicting mental health disorders and screening patients for e-triage.[18] In Australia, a large-scale study examines the onset of mental health issues in adolescence through the participation of more than 6,000 teenagers from 134 schools.[19] Over the course of five years, they engage with online questionnaires and apps analysing their data from memory games, logic games, voice recordings as well as typing tasks. Optionally, the participants also provide their location and movement data. Neurotechnologies have an even longer tradition in the medical sector. For instance, BCIs are deployed in the treatment of depression, dementia, locked-in syndrome, stroke, Parkinson's disease, epilepsy, as well as for the development of neuro-prosthetics or BCI-powered automatic wheelchairs.[20]

Provided these applications are deployed within the distinct medical field – such as by healthcare professionals, in a healthcare facility, or as certified medical devices – the data will undoubtedly be classified as health data and will require the full safeguards associated with special category data. Medical devices are mentioned explicitly by Recital 35 GDPR as a source for health information about a data subject. Regulatory guidance qualifies all data used in a professional medical context and processed in the distinct medical field as 'inherently/clearly medical data'.[21] In contrast to the category of biometric data, even data from a (text-based) certified medical chatbot would be considered sensitive, and so would biometric data processed for other purposes but identification if processed in the distinct medical field.

Sarah and Drew's scenario (a) is an online program to diagnose and treat symptoms of depression. Their plan is to seek official certification as a medical device for

16 Nick Haber and others, 'Upgraded Google Glass Helps Autistic Kids "See" Emotions', *IEEE Spectrum* (26 March 2023) <https://spectrum.ieee.org/upgraded-google-glass-helps-autistic-kids-see-emotions> accessed 8 January 2025.

17 Empatica, 'E4 Bytes: Predicting Aggressive Outbursts in People with Autism a Minute in Advance', (10 November 2020) <www.empatica.com/blog/e4-bytes-predicting-aggressive-outbursts-in-people-with-autism-a-minute-in-advance.html> accessed 8 January 2025.

18 Gordon Stribling, 'Mental Health Chatbot Gains Medical Device Status in World First', *Health Tech World* (17 January 2023) <www.htworld.co.uk/news/mental-health-chatbot-gains-medical-device-status-in-world-first/> accessed 8 January 2025.

19 Black Dog Institute, 'The Future Proofing Study' <www.blackdoginstitute.org.au/research-centres/future-proofing/> accessed 8 January 2025.

20 See, e.g., Future of Privacy Forum, 'Privacy and the Connected Mind'.

21 Article 29 Data Protection Working Party, Annex – Health Data in Apps and Devices, 5.

the program. The data processed in scenario (a), the certified online program, will be classified as data concerning health.

Sarah and Drew's scenarios (b) and (c) are both meant to be distributed on the consumer market and not within the distinct medical field. Their classification requires a different legal analysis.

4.1.2 *Data Processed beyond the Distinct Medical Context*

In addition to their deployment within the distinct medical market, MDTs have expanded widely into the consumer mental health and well-being market. Examples include mood trackers to facilitate self-awareness and self-care, conversational chatbots to cope with stress, anxiety, feelings of loneliness or sadness, BCIs to monitor one's concentration level or to help oneself relax and many more.

Many of these devices are not certified as a medical device. Nevertheless, multiple arguments point to classifying the data as data concerning health. In fact, the WP29 clarifies that the classification of data as health data is irrespective of the admission of a device as a medical device; it is not even necessary to establish 'ill-health' for qualifying the data as health data.[22]

4.1.2.1 Brain Data Invariably Constitutes Health Data

Recital 35 GDPR stipulates that personal data concerning health includes 'information derived from the testing or examination of a body part or bodily substance, including from genetic data and biological samples'. The brain constitutes a body part. BCIs collect data from that body part, deriving information from its testing or examination. In the context of the GDPR and its broad notion of data concerning health, the terms 'testing' or 'examination' should be interpreted broadly and not in a strictly medical sense, given its nature as general legislation.[23] Accordingly, the data constitutes information derived from the testing or examination of a body part and should be classified as data concerning health, regardless of whether the BCI is deployed in the distinct medical or the consumer market. Consequently, the data in Sarah and Drew's scenario (c), the non-invasive BCI selecting music based on brain activity to enhance mental health and well-being, should be qualified as data concerning health under the GDPR.

[22] Article 29 Data Protection Working Party, Annex – Health Data in Apps and Devices, 2. See also, Eike Michael Frenzel, Article 9 Margin Number 15 in Paal and Pauly (eds.), *Datenschutz-Grundverordnung Bundesdatenschutzgesetz*.

[23] In that, the GDPR differs fundamentally to the Medical Devices Regulation (MDR). The MDR is a sector-specific legislation that regulates devices with a medical purpose. Therefore, the rationale behind the Case C-219/11 *Brain Products GmbH* v *BioSemi VOF*, which will be discussed later in the context of non-medical BCIs under the MDR, does not apply here. (In *Brain Products GmbH* v *BioSemi VOF*, the CJEU insisted that BCIs cannot be considered a medical device merely by interpreting them as an investigation of the anatomy or of a physiological process.)

Moreover, and with specific regard to raw brain data, the WP29 considers data as health data when raw sensor data allows (independently or in combination with other data) conclusions about someone's health status or their health risks. Raw sensor data from the brain can be a treasure trove of health information. It has the potential to reveal neurophysiological and physiological insights, indicating predispositions to physical or mental conditions and enabling conclusions about a person's health status and health risks. While not all of this information may be currently decipherable or readily available in every sample – depending, among other factors, on its quality – the information is potentially present. With rapid technological advancement, what is unreadable in certain samples today could become comprehensible in the near future.

4.1.2.2 Health-Related Inferences

The classification of data as data concerning health, based on its capacity to allow for health-related inferences, warrants further examination. Sarah and Drew's scenario (b) potentially falls into this category, next to an ever-growing number of other well-being or lifestyle devices for the consumer health market. While the previously cited scenarios are relatively straightforward in their analysis, the category of health-related inferences has become progressively ambiguous. The main driver for this development is the growing ability to derive sensitive inferences from seemingly unrelated, often non-sensitive datapoints by combining them in unforeseen ways and discovering unexpected correlations through the power of AI and data analytics. As a result, the lines between health and non-health data have become blurrier than ever before. From a doctrinal perspective, the technological advancements put in question the entire binary concept of sensitive versus non-sensitive data in the GDPR.[24]

The app in Sarah and Drew's scenario (b) is drawing inferences from geolocation/movement data and random social media entries (not specifically health-related). By themselves, the single data points are not sensitive and do not allow for inferences about someone's health status or risk.[25] However, combined with one another and analysed for patterns over a longer period, they can allow for inferences about the health status or risk of a data subject.[26] For example, a decrease in mobility or physical activity can be among the possible signs of depression.

[24] Tal Z. Zarsky, 'Incompatible: The GDPR in the Age of Big Data', (2017) 47(4) *Seton Hall Law Review*, Article 2 Available at: <https://scholarship.shu.edu/shlr/vol47/iss4/2> accessed 30 January.

[25] Only in specific circumstances can geolocation data allow for health-related inferences, for instance when the data can be linked to the stay in a clinic or a health institution or the participation at patient or self-help groups, e.g. meetings of former alcoholics. See Stefan Ernst, Article 4 Margin Number 108 in Paal and Pauly (eds.), *Datenschutz-Grundverordnung Bundesdatenschutzgesetz*.

[26] See also EDPB, Guidelines 8/2020 on the Targeting of Social Media Uers, Version 2.0, Adopted on 13 April 2021, section 122.

Similarly, the language used on social media can indicate an increased risk of depression. Researchers found that depressed individuals are more likely to use words expressing negative emotions, particularly adjectives like 'lonely', 'sad' or 'miserable'.[27] Furthermore, depressed individuals tend to use first-person singular pronouns such as 'my', 'me', 'myself', or 'I' more frequently than third-person pronouns; and absolute words like 'always', 'never' or 'completely' appear more often in their texts. While the single data points in Sarah and Drew's scenario (b) – such as a single 'no', 'lonely', 'me' or a single piece of geolocation and movement data – do not allow for inferences about the health status or risk of a data subject, the combination of all these data points can. The data thus transforms into sensitive data.

The question of whether inferences derived from non-sensitive data can be considered special category data in their own right has been disputed among legal scholars.[28] However, regulatory guidance confirms this notion. The WP29 stipulates in their Guidelines on automated decision-making that normal personal data can transform into special category data and thus become new data.

> Profiling can create special category data by inference from data which is not special category data in its own right but becomes so when combined with other data. For example, it may be possible to infer someone's state of health from the records of their food shopping combined with data on the quality and energy content of foods.[29]

The EDPB confirmed this approach in their opinion 2/2022 when recalling that special categories of data could not only be directly collected from the data subject but also be inferred from and combined with other information.[30]

Additionally, the WP29 emphasised the importance of considering not only the data itself but also the intended purpose of the processing.[31] If the intended purpose is health-related, the data should be classified as data concerning health. In Sarah and Drew's scenario (b), the purpose of processing is to enhance self-awareness about mental health and well-being. The purpose of processing in scenario (b) is thus clearly health-related. As a result, also the data in Sarah and Drew's scenario (b) should be classified as data concerning health.

[27] Mohammed Al-Mosaiwi and T. Johnstone, 'In an Absolute State: Elevated Use of Absolutist Words Is a Marker Specific to Anxiety, Depression, and Suicidal Ideation', (2018) Jul 6(4) *Clinical Psychological Science*, 529–542 <https://doi.org/10.1177/2167702617747074>.

[28] Sandra Wachter and Brent Mittelstadt, 'A Right to Reasonable Inferences: Re-thinking Data Protection Law in the Age of Big Data and AI', (2019) 2019(2) *Columbia Business Law Review*, 494–620.

[29] Article 29 Data Protection Working Party, Guidelines on Automated Individual Decision-Making and Profiling for the Purposes of Regulation 2016/679 (WP251rev.01), Adopted on 3 October 2017, As Last Revised and Adopted on 6 February 2018, 15.

[30] EDPS, Opinion 2/2022 on the Proposal for Regulation on the Transparency and Targeting of Political Advertising (20 January 2022), section 29.

[31] Article 29 Data Protection Working Party, Annex – Health Data in Apps and Devices, 4.

4.1.3 *Weak Compliance with Data Protection Law*

Overall, data processed by MDTs in the context of mental health and well-being should be classified as data concerning health. In any event, Sarah and Drew's scenarios (a), (b), and (c) are to be considered health data. Accordingly, the data should be processed under the special regime for special category data and be protected by the highest standard available under the GDPR. Not only informed, but explicit consent, as the most obvious legal ground for processing, should be required;[32] adequate technical and organisational measures to safeguard the processing should be in place; a DPIA should be performed, and a DPO appointed for large-scale processing. As data protection law currently stands, the situation is essentially clear and the data should be safe.

Alas, regular reports in the media about unethical or unauthorised data sharing and security breaches in the e-mental health and well-being sector bear witness to a different reality. Privacy International conducted an analysis in 2019 of over 136 popular web pages focusing on depression in Germany, France, and the UK. It was found that 97.78 per cent of these web pages had third-party components to track users for advertising and marketing objectives.[33] Mozilla ran a study on the privacy and security practices of some of the most popular mental health apps in 2022. The results were again concerning: Out of the thirty-two analysed apps, twenty-eight were found having worrisome user data management practices, and twenty-five failed to meet even the basic security standards. Despite handling data that related to highly sensitive topics, such as depression, anxiety, suicidal thoughts, domestic violence, eating disorders, or PTSD, these apps routinely shared data with third parties, allowed weak passwords, targeted vulnerable users with personalised ads and featured privacy policies that were poorly written and lacked clarity.[34]

In 2022, the British mental health helpline 'Shout' was found to share full conversation data about suicidal thoughts, self-harm, abuse, and bullying with Imperial College London.[35] A similar case was reported in the US, where the suicide hotline

[32] The coerced employment of MDT-based applications against a patient's will is conceivable, especially in institutionalised settings. However, such a scenario raises very different legal questions that are not being discussed here.

[33] Privacy International, Report: 'Your Mental Health for Sale', (2019) <https://privacyinternational.org/node/3193> 8 January 2025.

[34] Mozilla, 'Top Mental Health and Prayer Apps Fail Spectacularly at Privacy, Security', (2022) <https://foundation.mozilla.org/en/blog/top-mental-health-and-prayer-apps-fail-spectacularly-at-privacy-security/> accessed 8 January 2025. For a recent empirical investigation, see also, Leonardo Horn Iwaya and others, 'On the Privacy of Mental Health Apps', (2023) 28(2) *Empirical Software Engineering* <https://doi.org/10.1007/s10664-022-10236-0>.

[35] Shanti Das, 'Mental Health Helpline Funded by Royals Shared Users' Conversations', *The Guardian* (19 February 2022) <www.theguardian.com/society/2022/feb/19/mental-health-helpline-funded-by-royals-shared-users-conversations> accessed 8 January 2025.

'Crisis Text Line' shared data with its for-profit spinoff 'Loris.ai'.[36] Both incidents made headlines in the quality press and caused an enormous public outcry. Both hotlines claimed to have the users' consent to the data sharing and to fully anonymise and aggregate the data. Nonetheless, both had to end their data sharing relationship due to the public pushback.

The practice of health data sharing is generally disputed. In the case of the British helpline, data was shared with a trusted academic partner for research purposes to benefit the service and a broader public. The EU Commission strongly supports the idea of sharing health data for treatment, innovation, and research. The Commission has made the common European Health Data Space a declared policy project,[37] proposing the European Health Data Space Regulation (COM/2022/197 final) to further encourage and facilitate the sharing of data for primary and secondary use. On the EHDS see further section 4.5.

Conversely, patients and consumers have a differentiated, rather restrictive attitude towards health data sharing. Considering the fierce public outcry against the data sharing practices by the two e-mental health hotlines mentioned above, the willingness to share data concerning mental health seems to be even more limited. The stigma surrounding mental health is still an important factor. One of the service users noted: 'My understanding was that the conversation would stay between me and the person I was messaging and wouldn't go any further [...] If I had known that it would, then I can't say for certain that I still would have used the service.'[38]

The greatest concerns users have about health data sharing relates to the possibility of data theft (44%), unauthorised access (40%), or use (39%) of their health data, according to a study by the European Consumer Organisation BEUC.[39] The risks involved appear to be of even greater impact when it comes to mental health data. In Vastaamo (Finland), a mental health start-up fell victim to a cyber attack in 2020.[40] Patients' notes on adultery, suicide attempts, paedophilic thoughts, and abuse landed in the dark net. Many patients, among them politicians and public figures, were confronted with attempted blackmail.

In summarising the core problems for MDTs in these incidental yet exemplary cases, the foremost data protection challenges in the field of e-mental health and well-being revolve around poor data protection practices. In theory, the existing

36 Alexandra S. Levine, 'Suicide Hotline Shares Data with For-Profit Spinoff, Raising Ethical Questions', *Politico* (28 January 2022) <www.politico.com/news/2022/01/28/suicide-hotline-silicon-valley-privacy-debates-00002617> accessed 8 January 2025.

37 EU Commission, European Health Data Space <https://health.ec.europa.eu/ehealth-digital-health-and-care/european-health-data-space_en> 8 January 2025.

38 Das, 'Mental Health Helpline Funded by Royals Shared Users' Conversations'.

39 Bureau Européen des Unions de Consommateurs (BEUC) (European Bureau of Consumers' Unions). BEUC, 'Consumer Attitudes to Health Data Sharing', (2023), 5 <www.beuc.eu/sites/default/files/publications/BEUC-X-2023-051_consumer_attitudes_to_health_data.pdf> accessed 8 January 2025.

40 William Ralston, 'They Told Their Therapists Everything: Hackers Leaked It All', *Wired* (4 May 2021) <www.wired.com/story/vastaamo-psychotherapy-patients-hack-data-breach/> accessed 8 January 2025.

legal framework provides adequate protection for the data processed by MDTs in the context of mental health and well-being. In practice, this sector suffers from remarkable compliance weaknesses with prevailing data protection law. This includes the common occurrence of unwanted data sharing, coupled with the risk of unauthorised access to the data. Compliance is considered particularly poor among devices which are not certified as medical devices but distributed on the consumer market.[41] Therefore, improving data protection compliance among consumer health devices is especially critical.

4.1.4 *How to Enhance Poor Data Protection Practices*

One way of addressing compliance weaknesses is by enhancing enforcement ex post. In the Finnish case regarding the psychotherapy centre, the national Data Protection Ombudsman was notified and started an investigation. The authority found that the start-up had neglected their duties related to the safe processing of personal data and to reporting the data breach without delay. The data had not been appropriately protected; the company had not implemented basic measures to ensure the safe processing; and documentation of the appropriate safety requirements was insufficient. As a result, the Data Protection Ombudsman imposed an administrative financial sanction of €608,000 on the company.[42] The company went bankrupt. Alas, the damage had already been done, the data had already reached the dark net. Reportedly, at least one suicide can be linked to the case.[43]

Alternatively, the EU data protection framework offers complementing governance instruments that could be tailored ex ante for the mental health and well-being sector. Specifically, the GDPR provides two co-regulatory instruments, a data protection code of conduct and a data protection certificate according to Article 40 and 42 GDPR.[44]

[41] It should be noted, however, that poor data protection and data security practices are not strictly limited to non-medical devices. In Germany, cyber activists attacked an e-mental health app in 2023 to make the company and the market aware of the serious security concerns in the field – this app had been officially recognised as a DiGA (an app on prescription, certified as a medical device and refunded by the German health care service). See Eva Wolfangel, 'Wenn Hacker mit Gesundheits-Apps besonders leichtes Spiel haben', *Die Zeit* (9 May 2023) <www.zeit.de/digital/datenschutz/2023-05/gesundheitsapp-datenschutz-depression-edupression-sicherheitsluecke> accessed 8 January 2025. Meanwhile, the German Federal Institute for Drugs and Medical Devices is planning to introduce a new certification scheme to enhance data protection and security for DiGAs: DiGA und DiPA Datenschutzkriterien <www.bfarm.de/DE/Medizinprodukte/Aufgaben/DiGA-und-DiPA/Datenschutzkriterien/_node.html> accessed 8 January 2025.

[42] Office of the Data Protection Ombudsman, 'Administrative Fine Imposed on Psychotherapy Centre Vastaamo for Data Protection Violations', (2021) <https://tietosuoja.fi/en/-/administrative-fine-imposed-on-psychotherapy-centre-vastaamo-for-data-protection-violations> accessed 8 January 2025.

[43] Joey Tidy, 'Hacker Jailed for Blackmailing Therapy Patients', (BBC 1 May 2024) <www.bbc.com/news/articles/c97zndooq7mo> accessed 8 January 2025.

[44] For a detailed comparative discussion on data protection certificates and data protection codes of conduct in the context of digital mental health devices, see Elisabeth Steindl, 'Safeguarding Privacy and

A data protection certificate, seal, or mark appears to be the preferable option for consumer devices, as it not only enhances user safety but also provides clearer guidance for consumers and mental health professionals navigating a diverse and fragmented market.[45] Such a certification would also contribute to improving the overall quality of the sector by raising the data protection standards through the establishment of best practices and an accountability framework. A sector-specific GDPR certification could thus serve multiple purposes, benefiting users, individual companies, and, if widely adopted, the entire market.

A sector-specific GDPR certificate could enhance data protection practices for mental health and well-being devices.

Once such a certificate is available on the market, Sarah and Drew could demonstrate the data protection compliance of their devices by getting them GDPR certified.

4.2 MDR: CLASSIFICATION RULES RESULT IN AVOIDANCE OF CERTIFICATION

Beyond severe concerns about data protection and privacy in the field of e-mental health and well-being, MDTs for mental health are facing recurring doubts regarding their promised effectiveness. Efficacy is essentially a matter addressed by product safety law.[46] The General Product Safety Directive (2001/95/EC),[47] known as the GPSD, has ensured product safety for nearly two decades. Opting for comprehensive adaptation, EU legislators have recently replaced the GPSD with the General Product Safety Regulation (EU) 2023/988 (hereinafter referred to as 'GPSR'),[48] aiming to better address the needs of product safety in an increasingly digitised environment.[49] The GPSR has come into effect in December 2024.

Efficacy in E-mental Health: Policy Options in the EU and Australia', (2023) 13(3) *International Data Privacy Law*, 207–224 <https://doi.org/10.1093/idpl/ipad009>.

45 Recital 100 GDPR.

46 For a brief history of product safety in the EU, see Ruohonen, 'A Review of Product Safety Regulations in the European Union'.

47 Directive 2001/95/EC of the European Parliament and of the Council of 3 December 2001 on General Product Safety, OJ 2001 L 11. The General Product Safety Regulation (EU) 2023/988 (GPSR), published in the *Official Journal* on 23 May 2023 (OJ L 135), will replace Directive 2001/95/EC and will apply from 13 December 2024.

48 Regulation (EU) 2023/988 of the European Parliament and of the Council of 10 May 2023 on General Product Safety, Amending Regulation (EU) No 1025/2012 of the European Parliament and of the Council and Directive (EU) 2020/1828 of the European Parliament and the Council, and repealing Directive 2001/95/EC of the European Parliament and of the Council and Council Directive 87/357/EEC. OJ L 135.

49 For a brief overview over the provisions enhancing product safety for digital products in this context, see Steindl, 'Consumer Neuro Devices?', section 'The GPSR Enhances the Horizontal Regulation'.

Similar to the GDPR, which is the lex generalis for the protection of personal data and applies to all processing of personal data, the GPSR functions as the lex generalis for product safety and applies to all consumer products. A range of sector-specific product safety laws, which take precedence as lex specialis whenever a product falls within their scope, complements the GPSR. Being designed as a general legislation, the GPSR does not include any sector-specific requirements for medical devices, such as the need for clinical evidence. Instead, clinical evaluation as a requirement is addressed by the Medical Devices Regulation (EU) 2017/745 (hereinafter referred to as 'MDR'),[50] which is the sector-specific product safety law in the health sector. The MDR applies to all devices with an intended medical purpose, as well as to certain BCIs without an intended medical purpose.

The MDR foresees a rigorous regime, creating a cautiously regulated environment for medical devices and ensuring the safety of patients. The MDR requires extensive documentation and monitoring by the manufacturer. Moreover, the MDR mandates that clinical evidence is provided for every medical device: According to Article 61 MDR, all medical devices must undergo clinical evaluation as a component of the overall requirements for safety and performance documentation. Whether an MDT-based device is governed by the MDR or not is therefore pivotal for its demonstrated efficacy.

Recalling Sarah and Drew's ideas discussed above:
Scenario (a)*: an online program, including quizzes, voice analytics and a serious game, to diagnose and treat depression;*
Scenario (b)*: an app drawing inferences about users' mood from geolocation and movement data together with social media entries to enhance self-awareness about mental health and well-being;*
Scenario (c)*: a non-invasive BCI tracking users' mood based on brain activity to select music that helps them focus/relax, thereby enhancing their mental health and well-being.*

4.2.1 *Certified Medical Devices*

Article 1(1) MDR specifies that the Regulation applies to the placing on the market, making available on the market, or putting into service of medical devices. Pursuant to Article 2(1) MDR, a medical device is defined as:

> any instrument, apparatus, appliance, software, implant, reagent, material or other article intended by the manufacturer to be used, alone or in combination, for human beings for one or more of the following specific medical purposes:

[50] Regulation (EU) 2017/745 of the European Parliament and of the Council of 5 April 2017 on Medical Devices, Amending Directive 2001/83/EC, Regulation (EC) No 178/2002 and Regulation (EC) No 1223/2009 and repealing Council Directives 90/385/EEC and 93/42/EEC (hereinafter referred to as MDR), OJ 2017 L117/1.

> – diagnosis, prevention, monitoring, prediction, prognosis, treatment or alleviation of disease
> – diagnosis, monitoring, treatment, alleviation of, or compensation for, an injury or disability,
> – investigation, replacement or modification of the anatomy or of a physiological or pathological process or state,
> – providing information by means of in vitro examination of specimens derived from the human body, including organ, blood and tissue donations, […].

Sarah and Drew's scenario (a) is an online program intended to be used for the diagnosis and treatment of a mental disease (depression). Thus, it is a software intended to be used for a medical purpose and falls within the material scope of the MDR.

The requirements that Sarah and Drew have to meet for scenario (a) depend on the assigned risk class of the device. The higher the risk class, the more rigorous the requirements. Compared to the previous Medical Devices Directive (MDD),[51] the MDR has specified new rules to classify software. Software is now classified according to Rule 11 Annex VIII MDR. Rule 11 Annex VIII MDR defines that: '[s]oftware intended to provide information which is used to take decisions with diagnosis or therapeutic purposes is classified as class IIa'. If the impact may cause death or an irreversible deterioration of a person's state of health, it is classified as risk class III. If it may cause a serious deterioration of a person's state of health or a surgical intervention, it is classified as risk class IIb. Software that is intended to simply monitor physiological processes is classified as class IIa, whereas all other software is classified as class I.

For many digital mental health devices, the implementation of specified risk classes for software under the MDR meant a shift from classification as risk class I to risk class IIa. This change brought about a substantial increase in the time, financial resources, and effort required by manufacturers to comply with the regulations. The demands placed on risk class IIa medical devices are substantial. They encompass comprehensive technical documentation, a certified quality management system that includes post-market surveillance, and engagement with notified bodies. Reports indicate that market entry for a risk class IIa medical device is delayed considerably compared to a risk class I medical device, and audits result in costs reaching a mid five-figure amount.[52]

Nonetheless, the purpose of Sarah and Drew's online program in scenario (a) is to diagnose and treat depression, the software is intended to provide information, which is used to take decisions with diagnostic and therapeutic purposes. Accordingly, their online program will be classified as risk class IIa.

[51] Council Directive 93/42/EEC of 14 June 1993 Concerning Medical Devices, OJ 1993 L 169.

[52] See here, <https://openregulatory.com/question/how-long-does-medical-device-compliance-take/> and here <https://openregulatory.com/question/how-much-does-medical-device-compliance-cost/> accessed 8 January 2025.

4.2.2 *Lifestyle and Well-Being Devices*

Scenario (b) and scenario (c) offer a broader scope for interpretation, allowing for different legal rationales and analyses. Scenario (b) is an app to enhance mental health and well-being self-awareness by drawing inferences from geolocation and movement data together with social media entries, and scenario (c) is a non-invasive BCI that selects music based on users' brain activity to help them focus/relax, thereby enhancing their mental health and well-being.

Scenarios (b) and (c) intend to both support and/or improve 'mental health and well-being'. Mental health and well-being are often mentioned in one breath. This aligns with the definition of mental health by international organisations, such as the WHO. The concepts in mental health are defined by the WHO as follows:

> Mental health is a state of mental well-being that enables people to cope with the stresses of life, realize their abilities, learn well and work well, and contribute to their community. It is an integral component of health and well-being that underpins our individual and collective abilities to make decisions, build relationships and shape the world we live in. Mental health is a basic human right. And it is crucial to personal, community and socio-economic development.
>
> Mental health is more than the absence of mental disorders. It exists on a complex continuum, which is experienced differently from one person to the next, with varying degrees of difficulty and distress and potentially very different social and clinical outcomes.
>
> Mental health conditions include mental disorders and psychosocial disabilities as well as other mental states associated with significant distress, impairment in functioning, or risk of self-harm. People with mental health conditions are more likely to experience lower levels of mental well-being, but this is not always or necessarily the case.[53]

This notion of mental health is remarkably comprehensive, reflecting how multifaceted the matters of our mental well-being are and how many areas of our lives both affect and are affected by them. This complexity, coupled with the ability of digital technologies to detect subtle changes in mental states and study patterns granularly over extended periods, explains why digital technologies hold such significant potential for enhancing the diagnosis and treatment of mental health. However, the comprehensive notion of mental health poses practical challenges for legal analysis under the MDR in determining whether a device falls within its scope or not.

Software with an intended medical purpose is clearly within the scope of the MDR, whereas simple well-being and lifestyle devices are beyond. Recital 19 MDR stipulates that: 'software for general purposes, even when used in a healthcare setting, or software intended for lifestyle and well-being purposes is not a medical device'.

53 WHO, 'Mental Health: Concepts in Mental Health', (17 June 2022) <www.who.int/news-room/fact-sheets/detail/mental-health-strengthening-our-response> accessed 8 January 2025.

The MDR does not provide a legal definition of well-being or lifestyle purposes, nor does it give any guidance on where to draw defining lines between medical and well-being purposes. Decisive for determining whether a device has an intended medical purpose or not is the intended purpose of the manufacturer. Article 2(12) MDR defines the 'intended purpose' as: 'the use for which a device is intended according to the data supplied by the manufacturer on the label, in the instructions for use, or in promotional or sales materials or statements, and as specified by the manufacturer in the clinical evaluation'. It is therefore the instructions, statements, and the documentation provided by the manufacturer that decide whether a device has an intended medical purpose or a lifestyle or well-being purpose. This stance has been confirmed by the Medical Device Coordination Group (MDCG) in their Guidance notes for manufacturers of class I medical devices.[54]

As long as Sarah and Drew describe the intended purpose of scenario (b) as merely for well-being, ensuring that the documentation and instructions support their statement and avoiding any details suggesting otherwise, their device will not be subject to the MDR. Briefly, Sarah and Drew consider enhancing their device's functionality by adding extra features (e.g. offering users personalised recommendations based on the inferred data on how to improve their current mental state) and certifying it as a medical device. However, they cannot find clear guidance and illustrative examples ensuring them that their device would not be classified higher than risk class I. Deterred by the sums that classification of their device as risk class IIa medical device would cost, Sarah and Drew decide to keep all their documentation within the scope of 'well-being' software, avoiding the MDR and adhering solely to the product safety requirements outlined in the general framework of the GPSR. Accordingly, scenario (b) will not be required to provide any proof of clinical evidence or efficacy, nor will it be subject to any other requirements under the MDR.

Scenario (c), Sarah and Drew's non-invasive BCI for mental health and well-being, deserves an individual legal assessment under the MDR.

4.2.3 *BCIs without an Intended Medical Purpose*

BCIs have also found their way into the consumer mental health and well-being market. In the consumer market they are, for instance, used to facilitate a deeper state of relaxation or meditation, or to monitor and enhance attention and concentration. Earlier scholarly discussions to consider all BCIs, regardless of their intended purpose, as medical devices have been put to an end by the CJEU.[55] In *Brain Products*

[54] MDCG, 2019-15 rev.1 Guidance Notes for Manufacturers of Class I Medical Devices, (December 2019, July 2020 rev.1) <https://health.ec.europa.eu/document/download/349a2d4c-ea2a-4279-861c-7c063bc077e4_en?filename=md_guidance-manufacturers_en.pdf> accessed 8 January 2025.

[55] See, e.g., Hannah Maslen and others, 'The Regulation of Cognitive Enhancement Devices: Extending the Medical Model', (2014) 1(1) *Journal of Law and the Biosciences*, 68–93 <https://doi.org/10.1093/jlb/

GmbH v *BioSemi VOF* (CJEU C-219/11),[56] the court held that BCIs cannot be considered medical devices merely by interpreting them an 'investigation, replacement or modification of the anatomy or of a physiological process'.[57] On the contrary, an intended medical purpose can only be assumed if declared by the manufacturer.[58] Scenario (c) is therefore not automatically considered a medical device.

Under the previous MDD, this would have given Sarah and Drew a free card to market scenario (c) as well-being product. They could have added a disclaimer to their website, stating that their BCI was not intended for a medical purpose but was instead a consumer health, lifestyle, or well-being device. All accompanying documentation would have been tailored accordingly – similar to their plans for scenario (b). By doing so, they could have deliberately circumvented the requirements of medical devices legislation without giving it a second thought.[59]

However, with the adoption of the MDR, particularly the introduction of Annex XVI, significant changes have occurred. Simply marketing a BCI off-label as consumer BCI to escape the strict regime of medical devices legislation is no longer an option. Annex XVI incorporates a group of products within the scope of medical devices legislation that do not have an intended medical purpose – among them, specific BCIs.[60] Sarah and Drew, being increasingly cautious, want to ensure that their BCI in scenario (c) does not fall within the scope of Annex XVI MDR.

Section 6 Annex XVI MDR specifies that '[e]quipment intended for brain stimulation that apply electrical currents or magnetic or electromagnetic fields that penetrate the cranium to modify neuronal activity in the brain' lies within the scope of the MDR and has to comply with its requirements. Article 61(9) MDR provides that the requirement for Annex XVI-BCIs to demonstrate a clinical benefit

> shall be understood as a requirement to demonstrate the performance of the device. Clinical evaluations of those products shall be based on relevant data concerning safety, including data from post-market surveillance, PMCF, and, where applicable, specific clinical investigation. Clinical investigations shall be performed for those products unless reliance on existing clinical data from an analogous medical device is duly justified.

Therefore, Annex XVI-BCIs do have to provide a performance evaluation.

The revolutionary aspect of Annex XVI MDR lies in the fact that, unlike the rest of the MDR, it takes a purely technological approach. The focus of Annex XVI is not on the intended purpose of the device but on functional and technological

lst003>; Commission Staff Working Document Impact Assessment on the Revision of the Regulatory Framework for Medical Devices, SWD/2012/0273 final.

56 Case C-219/11 *Brain Products GmbH* v *BioSemi VOF* [2012].

57 Third indent of Article 1(2)(a) MDD, now similar under third indent of Article 2(1) MDR.

58 Case C-219/11 *Brain Products GmbH* v *BioSemi VOF*, section 18.

59 See also Maslen and others, 'The Regulation of Cognitive Enhancement Devices', 82.

60 For a more detailed analysis of consumer BCIs under the MDR, see Steindl, 'Consumer Neuro Devices?'

characteristics only: The BCI must apply electrical currents or magnetic or electromagnetic fields that penetrate the cranium to modify neuronal activity in the brain. The intended purpose is irrelevant – it does not matter whether the BCI is used for well-being, enhancement, security, leisure, or any other purpose (as long as the purpose is not medical; BCIs with an intended medical purpose naturally fall within the scope of Article 1(1) MDR). The only issue that matters is whether the BCI cumulatively meets the required technological criteria. If it does, the BCI falls automatically within the scope of Annex XVI and has to comply with the strict regime of the MDR, irrespective of the purpose stated by the manufacturer.

The approach taken by EU legislators regarding non-medical BCIs in product safety law is sophisticated, even from a dogmatic point of view. While the inclusion of non-medical products in medical devices legislation may initially seem incompatible with the systematic nature of such a sector-specific legislation, a closer look reveals that Annex XVI exclusively integrates non-medical BCIs that pose very specific health-related risks and potentially cause a variety of serious health-related effects.[61] Possible side effects considered by the legislators include 'atypical brain development, abnormal patterns of brain activity, increase metabolic consumption, fatigue, anxiety, irritability, headaches, muscle twitches, tics, seizures, vertigo and skin irritation at the electrode site'.[62] EU legislators had no intention of leaving the regulation of these health-related risks and side effects to general product safety laws, given that these are not well equipped to handle this type of risks. Instead, they address these concerns in the legislation best suited for them: health-specific product safety law. Moreover, in response to the seriousness of the mentioned side effects, legislators have elevated Annex XVI-BCIs to risk class III, the highest possible risk class under the MDR.[63]

Overall, the approach taken by EU legislators to include specific non-medical BCIs in medical devices legislation is remarkably innovative. By shifting from the generally purpose-based approach of the MDR to a purely technology-based perspective in Annex XVI, the EU has created a novel pathway to govern specific aspects of consumer neurotechnology within health-specific product safety law. This approach holds the potential to serve as an international regulatory blueprint.

At the same time, EU legislators abstain from over-regulating BCIs that do not pose known health-related risks within medical devices legislation. Key element in the definition of Annex XVI-BCIs is their ability to modulate neuronal activity. Arguably, this excludes the majority of consumer BCIs currently available on the

[61] For the specific risks that may be caused by Annex XVI-BCIs, see Annex VII, section 3 of the Commission Implementing Regulation (EU) 2022/2346 OJ L 311/60 <https://eur-lex.europa.eu/legal-content/EN/TXT/?uri=CELEX%3A32022R2346> accessed 8 January 2025.

[62] Recital 7 of the Commission Implementing Regulation (EU) 2022/2347 OJ L 311/94 <https://eur-lex.europa.eu/legal-content/EN/TXT/?uri=celex:32022R2347> accessed 8 January 2025.

[63] Article 1(c) of the Commission Implementing Regulation (EU) 2022/2347.

market from the scope and regime of medical devices legislation. Consumer BCIs on today's market are typically not designed to modulate users' brain activity, but rather to monitor or record it. Sarah and Drew's BCI in scenario (c), for instance, applies electrical currents that penetrate the cranium, as specified in the definition in Annex XVI; however, it is not designed to modify neuronal activity. Simply playing a certain type of music based on tracked brain waves to help a person relax or focus is not considered modulating neuronal activity in neuroscientific terminology. Consequently, scenario (c) falls outside the scope of Annex XVI and, therefore, the MDR. Sarah and Drew can distribute the device on the consumer market without facing any further costs or assessments; no additional requirements regarding efficacy apply to scenario (c).

4.2.4 *Policy Options to Improve Efficacy Standards*

The current lack of evidence supporting the effectiveness of large parts of digital mental health and well-being devices impedes the broader acceptance and implementation of digital technologies, including MDTs. Moreover, their failure to deliver on their promised outcomes due to inadequate clinical evaluation may cause delays in getting effective care and thus have indeed harmful effects on vulnerable users.

The shift in classification for seemingly most digital mental health devices from risk class I to risk class IIa in the MDR has inadvertently produced a consequence that contradicts the initial intentions of the legislator.[64] Instead of achieving improved governance and establishing strong regulatory frameworks for software as a medical device, the new classification rules have resulted in a greater number of mental health devices choosing to bypass certification entirely due to the additional costs and requirements. The effect of the existing legislation is therefore a prevalence of devices in the consumer mental health market lacking substantiated clinical evidence, while also posing a risk of impeding innovation and restricting patient access to novel therapeutic and diagnostic technologies.

Encouraging more manufacturers to pursue certification for their devices and adhere to the stricter MDR regulations could significantly improve the effectiveness and reliability of digital mental health devices, including those based on MDTs. This approach would not only ensure a higher standard of safety and efficacy but also bolster greater confidence among users regarding digital technologies for mental health and well-being. Moreover, expanding the number of devices governed by the MDR would contribute to the overall improvement of quality and reliability of MDT-based mental health and well-being devices available on the European market. Ultimately, this would foster the development of a

[64] See also EU Parliament Resolution of 23 October 2024 on the urgent need to revise the Medical Devices Regulation (2024/2849(RSP)), section P.

more resilient and trustworthy ecosystem in this domain, benefiting both manufacturers and users.

An effective strategy to encourage more manufacturers to seek certification for their devices under the MDR and comply with its regime could involve reopening risk class I for certain mental health devices through targeted revisions to Rule 11 Annex VIII MDR. Such a change would require only minor adjustments while maintaining the overall conceptual framework and systematic integrity of the MDR. De lege lata, Rule 11 Annex VIII MDR reads:

> Software intended to provide information which is used to take decisions with diagnosis or therapeutic purposes is classified as class IIa, except if such decisions have an impact that may cause:
>
> – death or an irreversible deterioration of a person's state of health, in which case it is in class III; or
>
> – a serious deterioration of a person's state of health or a surgical intervention, in which case it is classified as class IIb.
>
> Software intended to monitor physiological processes is classified as class IIa, except if it is intended for monitoring of vital physiological parameters, where the nature of variations of those parameters is such that it could result in immediate danger to the patient, in which case it is classified as class IIb.
>
> All other software is classified as class I.

An additional paragraph could be added de lege ferenda:

> **Rule 11 Annex VIII MDR new:** [...] Software intended to inform about, diagnose, monitor or treat a mental health condition that is not a serious disease or serious condition, ailment or defect, is classified as class I.

Such an amendment may prompt more manufacturers genuinely committed to quality and user safety to voluntarily consider certification. Currently deterred by the complexity, costs, and duration of meeting risk class IIa requirements, manufacturers may find it more appealing to (self-)certify their devices under risk class I.

Alternatively, the MDCG could provide additional guidance, expanding the eligibility of software for risk class I. This guidance could specifically embrace more software applications for the mental health sector, including relevant examples and further clarifying the criteria for manufacturers.[65]

[65] For current guidance, see Guidance – MDCG Endorsed Documents and Other Guidance <https://health.ec.europa.eu/medical-devices-sector/new-regulations/guidance-mdcg-endorsed-documents-and-other-guidance_en> accessed 8 January 2025. In particular, MDCG, 2019-15 rev.1 Guidance Notes for Manufacturers of Class I Medical Devices, December 2019, July 2020 rev.1. MDCG, Manual on Borderline and Classification for Medical Devices under Regulation (EU) 2017/745 on Medical Devices and Regulation (EU) 2017/746 on in Vitro Diagnostic Medical Devices, Version 3 – September 2023.

Enhanced MDCG guidance on the eligibility of software as risk class I, incorporating specifically examples for the sector of mental health and well-being, may encourage more manufacturers to seek certification.

Another option would be to address digital mental health devices separately within the MDR. Regulating digital mental health tools distinctly within the sector-specific product safety law for medical devices is not unprecedented. For example, Australia has reformed its health legislation and singled out digital mental health devices therein.[66] Provided they follow established clinical practice guidelines that are referenced and can clearly be seen by the user, they are exempt from all other requirements normally imposed under the Australian medical devices legislation. Thus, the Australian legislator requires the efficacy of digital mental health devices to be assured, while lifting the rest of the requirements.[67]

If EU lawmakers were to follow the Australian model, they might consider introducing a similar conditioned exemption in the MDR. The notion of exempting certain devices from the requirements of the MDR, while imposing only the indispensable ones, has its own charm. The clinical practice guidelines proposed by the Australian model could be replaced by a certificate or label that guarantees appropriate quality and efficacy assessment. However, if the principal idea of introducing a conditioned exemption was to limit the requirements to the essential ones only, EU lawmakers may want to complement the quality and efficacy assessment with a mandatory demonstration of compliance with data protection, like the one proposed in the previous section.

The implementation of sector-specific co-regulatory mechanisms would contribute to the smooth transfer of high-quality applications throughout Europe and thus foster the growth and functioning of a sustainable European e-mental health industry, which is in alignment with Recital 2 MDR.[68] Such an approach in the EU could therefore be as follows:

A conditioned exemption for e-mental health devices under the MDR could include:
- a Quality and Efficacy Assessment Label together with
- a GDPR Certificate.

Another possibility for EU lawmakers would be to amend Annex XVI MDR. The list in Annex XVI is exhaustive, but it can be amended according to Article 1(5)

66 For a detailed analysis, see Steindl, 'Safeguarding Privacy and Efficacy in E-mental Health'.

67 In addition, Australia has introduced soft law instruments for digital mental health devices, i.e. Standards and an Accreditation Scheme. See Sandra Rigby and others, 'Implementation of the Australian National Safety and Quality Digital Mental Health Standards', (2024) 32(4) *Australasian Psychiatry*, 314–318 <https://doi.org/10.1177/10398562241246488>.

68 'This Regulation aims to ensure the smooth functioning of the internal market as regards medical devices, taking as a base a high level of protection of health for patients and users, and taking into account the small- and medium-sized enterprises that are active in this sector…' (Recital 2 MDR).

MDR. However, the notion of amending Annex XVI MDR by adding another section for mental health and well-being devices, raises conceptual concerns. In fact, this approach might inadvertently increase the confusion surrounding the ambiguous boundary between medical and well-being devices, rather than resolving it. The MDR is the applicable product safety law for medical devices. If a device has an intended medical purpose, it is within the scope of the MDR and has to comply with all of its requirements. In that case, there is no need to include it in Annex XVI MDR. For mental health devices with an intended medical purpose this means, they must adhere to the existing classification rules. As previously discussed, the probable outcome is that the device will need to undergo certification as risk class IIa. If a device is instead intended for lifestyle or well-being purposes, it is beyond the scope of the MDR. Lawmakers have clearly stated their intention to exclude simple lifestyle and well-being products from the scope of the medical device legislation, as expressed in Recital 19 MDR. Adding all well-being devices to Annex XVI MDR would contradict both the intention and Recital 19 MDR. Moreover, the notion of forcing all well-being products under the MDR would have unpredictable legal ramifications across various related regulations and would be practically unfeasible.

Considering the options discussed, reopening risk class I for a larger number of mental health devices or introducing a conditioned exemption similar to the Australian model – tailored to the EU legal framework and including instruments to demonstrate data protection compliance – are in better alignment with the systematics of the MDR. They appear to be sounder policy choices compared to amending Annex XVI MDR.

Finally, it should be stressed that none of the presented options will be able to compel manufacturers into certifying their device. Any approach taken may therefore require additional incentives for manufacturers. For example, certification could grant access to certain public funding or facilitate the integration of the device into the statutory health care system.

4.3 AIA: HIGH STANDARDS FOR MEDIUM- TO HIGH-RISK MEDICAL DEVICES

The AIA is a horizontal law, modelled after product safety regulations. While not specifically tailored for the medical sector, it does include provisions relevant to medical devices. Notably, the AIA does not replace the GPSR/MDR but is designed to complement existing product safety legislation, establishing a framework that addresses the specific requirements of AI.

Article 6(1) AIA lays down two conditions for classifying medical devices as high risk AI systems. Both conditions have to be met cumulatively:

a) the AI system is either a safety component of a product, or it is itself a product, which is covered by Union harmonisation legislation (Annex I);
b) the product is required to undergo a third-party conformity assessment.

As regards lit (a, medical products are covered by Union harmonisation legislation and the MDR is listed in Annex I section A para 11. Concerning lit (b, all medical devices in risk class IIa or above have to undergo third-party conformity assessment. Medical devices classified as risk class IIa or higher are therefore considered a high risk AI system, provided they use an AI system that meets the definition under the AIA.

The requirements for medical devices risk class IIa and above are already significant under the MDR. AI adds another layer of complexity to these requirements.[69] To ensure consistency, minimise additional burden, and avoid duplication of procedures and bureaucracy, the AIA requirements can be integrated into those under Union harmonisation legislation.[70] The application of requirements under the AIA and the MDR should be simultaneous and complimentary; whenever requirements under the AIA are deemed equivalent to those under the MDR, they shall be considered as covered to the extent that they are covered under the MDR. For instance, the quality management system (QMS) required by the AIA, documenting the strategies, policies and procedures to cover regulatory compliance, risk management, post-market monitoring, document retention, quality control, and compliance with technical specifications, should be incorporated into the QMS required under the MDR.[71] The conformity assessment required by the AIA should be integrated into the conformity assessment required under the MDR.[72] As a result, there should be one single conformity assessment and one single, integrated, technical documentation for medical devices to demonstrate compliance with both, the AIA and the MDR.

In addition to the requirements under the MDR, significant responsibilities will be applicable concerning data quality and data governance. The AIA puts a particular focus on the quality of training, validation and testing data sets.[73] Moreover, the AIA adds requirements regarding transparency,[74] and human oversight.[75] For practical guidance, the EU Commission is obliged to issue detailed guidance on the interplay between the AIA and the MDR.[76]

Following the current classification rules and practices according to Rule 11 Annex VIII MDR, a majority of digital mental health devices will be classified as high risk AI system. This intensifies the dilemma for manufacturers: whether to certify their device as a medical device or bypass certification altogether. As a result, a

69 See also, Elisabetta Biasin and others, 'New Cybersecurity Requirements for Medical Devices in the EU: The Forthcoming European Health Data Space, Data Act, and Artificial Intelligence Act', (2023) 5(2) *Law, Technology and Humans*, 43–58 <https://doi.org/10.5204/lthj.3068>; Daria Onitiu and others, 'How AI Challenges the Medical Device Regulation: Patient Safety, Benefits, and Intended Uses', (2024) lsae007 *Journal of Law and the Biosciences* <https://doi.org/10.1093/jlb/lsae007>.

70 Article 8(2) AIA.

71 Article 17(3) AIA.

72 Article 43(3) AIA.

73 Article 10(3) AIA.

74 Article 13 AIA.

75 Article 14 AIA.

76 Article 96(1)(e) AIA.

large number of mental health and well-being applications may not be affected by Article 6(1) AIA due to the fact that manufacturers tend to circumvent MDR certification. Notably, reopening risk class I for a larger number of devices would have no effect on their classification under the AIA, as risk class I does not require a third-party conformity test and thus does not meet the requirements for Article 6(1) AIA. Whether a conditioned exemption from the MDR, involving a quality and efficacy assessment along with a data protection assessment, would bring changes needs to be analysed carefully. It depends on how this conditioned exemption is crafted, what kind of devices it should apply to, whether legislators intend for these devices to be considered high risk and what kind of assessment or certification schemes they require. For example, data protection certification schemes according to Article 42 GDPR necessitate third-party conformity assessment, whereas data protection codes of conduct according to Article 40 GDPR do not.

In Sarah and Drew's scenarios, only scenario (a), the certified online program to diagnose and treat depression, will be subject to the regime for risk class IIa MDR and consequently to the regime for high risk AI systems. Scenarios (b) – the app to enhance mental health and well-being self-awareness by drawing inferences from geolocation and movement data together with social media entries – and scenario (c) – the non-invasive BCI that selects music based on users' brain activity to help them focus/relax, thereby enhancing their mental health and well-being – will not fall within the scope of Article 6(1) AIA for medical devices.

Article 6(2) in conjunction with Annex III section 1(c) AIA for ERS could serve as an alternative way to classify scenarios (b) and (c) as high-risk AI systems. However, scenario (b) does not qualify as an ERS, as it does not involve the use of biometric data. Depending on its functioning, scenario (b) may be subject to limited risk requirements, provided it interacts directly with a natural person (e.g. by exchanging tailored information, and giving personalised responses to the user, based on the inferred data), pursuant to Article 50(1) AIA. Otherwise, scenario (b) will not be subject to additional requirements under the AIA. In contrast, scenario (c), the non-invasive BCI tracking users' mood based on brain activity to select music that helps them focus/relax, thereby enhancing their mental health and well-being, can be classified as an ERS. As such, it falls within the scope of Annex III section 1(c) AIA, initiating the regime for high risk AI systems, as well as the regime for limited risk AI systems according to Article 50(3) AIA.

4.4 EHDS: CONTROVERSIAL INTEGRATION OF WELLNESS APPS

With the Regulation (EU) 2025/327 on the European Health Data Space[77] (EHDS), EU legislators have agreed on another piece of health-related legislation that will

[77] Regulation (EU) 2025/327 of the European Parliament and of the Council of 11 February 2025 on the European Health Data Space and amending Directive 2011/24/EU and Regulation (EU) 2024/284. OJ L.

become relevant for MDT-based mental health and well-being devices. The EHDS is designed to establish a health-specific data sharing framework in the EU, expanding the right to data portability already enshrined in the GDPR.[78] The regulation aims to foster increased digital access to and control of electronic personal health data for patients (primary use), and to provide a trustworthy and efficient environment for the use of health data for research, innovation, policy-making, and regulatory activities (secondary use).[79] Moreover, the EHDS wishes to establish a single market for electronic health record (EHR) systems.

Trilogue negotiations for the EHDS have been challenging. The potential benefit of enhanced data access for research and development clashed with concerns about data privacy. Most controversially discussed were opt-out options for primary and/or secondary use.[80] In a compromise solution, Article 10 EHDS provides Member States with the possibility to introduce a right for natural persons to opt out from primary use, except where necessary for protecting the vital interests of the data subject or another person. Moreover, Article 71 EHDS introduces a reversible right for natural persons to opt out of the processing of personal electronic health data for secondary use. In addition, Member States have the possibility to strengthen the safeguards for specific categories in secondary use.[81]

Notably, the EHDS does not only apply to certified medical devices, but it also incorporates well-being devices. The integration of wellness applications in secondary use has been subject of intense debate during the legislative process. Therefore, the following outlook will focus on this aspect. Provisions of particular interest in that respect are in Chapter 3 (setting the framework for electronic health record systems and wellness applications) and Chapter 4 (regulating the secondary use of electronic health data) EHDS.

In contrast to the MDR, the EHDS provides a legal definition for wellness applications. According to Article 2(2)(ab) EHDS, wellness application means 'any software, or any combination of hardware and software, intended by the manufacturer to be used by a natural person, for the processing of electronic health data, specifically for providing information on the health of natural persons, or the delivery of care for purposes other than the provision of healthcare'. MDT-based well-being devices meeting

[78] Wenkai Li and Paul Quinn, 'The European Health Data Space: An Expanded Right to Data Portability?', (2024) 52 *Computer Law & Security Review*, 105913 <https://doi.org/10.1016/j.clsr.2023.105913>.

[79] European Commission, European Health Data Space <https://health.ec.europa.eu/ehealth-digital-health-and-care/european-health-data-space_en> accessed 8 January 2025; European Commission, Questions and Answers – EU Health: European Health Data Space (EHDS) (3 May 2022) <https://ec.europa.eu/commission/presscorner/detail/en/qanda_22_2712> accessed 8 January 2025.

[80] Mari Eccles and Giedre Peseckyte, 'Why Is It So Hard to Deliver a European Health Data Deal?', *Politico* (8 March 2024) <www.politico.eu/article/why-is-it-so-hard-to-deliver-a-european-health-data-deal/> accessed 8 January 2025.

[81] According to Article 51(4) EHDS, this applies to human genetic, epigenomic and genomic data; other human molecular data such as proteomic, transcriptomic, metabolomic, lipidomic, and other omic data; data from wellness applications; and health data from biobanks and associated databases.

this definition can therefore participate in the European Health Data Space, provided they claim interoperability with an EHR system and are labelled accordingly.

Electronic health data includes personal as well as non-personal electronic health data (Article 2(2)(c) EHDS), with personal electronic health data being defined as 'data concerning health and genetic data, processed in an electronic form' (Article 2(2)(a) EHDS). Recital 6 EHDS introduces a remarkably broad concept of personal electronic health data, including even determinants of health like behaviour, environmental and physical influences, medical care, and social or educational factors:

> Such personal electronic health data could include personal data related to the physical or mental health of a natural person, including related to the provision of healthcare services, and which reveal information about their health status, personal data relating to the inherited or acquired genetic characteristics of a natural person which give unique information about the physiology or the health of that natural person and which result, in particular, from an analysis of a biological sample from the natural person in question, as well as data determinants of health, such as behaviour, environmental and physical influences, medical care, and social or educational factors. Electronic health data also include data that have been initially collected for research, statistical, health threat assessment, policy making or regulatory purposes and it should be possible to make them available in accordance with the rules laid down in this Regulation. Electronic health data consist of all categories of those data, irrespective of whether such data are provided by the data subject or other natural or legal persons, such as health professionals, or are processed in relation to a natural person's health or well-being and should also include inferred and derived data, such as diagnostics, tests and medical examinations, as well as data observed and recorded by automated means.[82]

The data in scenarios (b) and (c) has been classified as data concerning mental health (see Section 4.1.2), meeting the definition of personal electronic health data under the EHDS. If Sarah and Drew wish to include scenarios (b) and (c) in the EHDS for secondary use, they can claim interoperability of their apps with an EHR system and label them.

The inclusion of wellness applications for secondary use has caused significant critique before and during the trilogue negotiations. In their joint opinion, the EDPB/EDPS recommended excluding data from wellness applications and other digital applications from secondary use in the EHDS.[83] The reasons given by EDPB/EDPS relate to the intrusiveness of these devices, the high privacy risks involved, and their inferior data quality compared to certified medical devices. With reference to wellness applications and other digital health applications, the EDPB/EDPS noted that: 'these applications generate an enormous amount of data and can be highly invasive

[82] Recital 6 EHDS.

[83] EDPB-EDPS, Joint Opinion 03/2022 on the Proposal for a Regulation on the European Health Data Space (2022), 22.

since it relates to every step individuals takes [*sic*] in their everyday lives. Even if health data could be indeed separated from other kinds of data, inferences such as food practices and other habits could be easily made, revealing particularly sensitive information such as religious orientation.'[84] Moreover, the EDPB/EDPS warned that: '[m]ore than tracking humans' actions and decisions, it is now possible to track humans' bodies, minds and emotions at a level that even humans themselves might not be able to do. These data can then be used to predict people's actions and manipulate their behaviour, even at a group level.'[85] These concerns are even more present in the context of MDT-based applications.

BEUC supported the EDPB/EDPS' recommendation to exclude wellness applications, expressing further apprehensions regarding the inclusion of genetic, genomic, and proteomic data.[86] According to BEUC, these types of data have not only imminent but also long-term predictive qualities.[87] They are practically impossible to anonymise, bear an inherent risk of re-identification, and encompass characteristics relating to a natural person that can never be changed. BEUC advocated therefore for the exclusion of genetic, genomic and proteomic data from secondary use.

In the EHDS, legislators did not follow the recommendation to completely exclude the previously mentioned categories from secondary use. Instead, Article 51 EHDS mandates data holders to make certain categories of electronic data available for secondary use, including:

- data on factors impacting on health, including socio-economic, environmental and behavioural determinants of health (para 1 lit b),
- human genetic, epigenomic and genomic data (para 1 lit f)
- other human molecular data such as proteomic, transcriptomic, metabolomic, lipidomic and other omic data (para 1 lit g)
- data from wellness applications (para 1 lit i)
- health data from biobanks and associated databases (para 1 lit q).[88]

In response to the discussed critique, however, legislators introduced the option for Member States to implement stricter measures and additional safeguards at the national level for some of these categories, aiming to protect their sensitivity and value. These categories include the categories listed in Article 51 (1) points (f), (g), (i), and (q). Member States can implement a more rigorous regime for secondary use inter alia for human genetic, epigenomic, and genomic data and for data from

84 EDPB-EDPS, Joint Opinion 03/2022 on the Proposal for a Regulation on the European Health Data Space (2022), 4.
85 EDPB-EDPS, Joint Opinion 03/2022 on the Proposal for a Regulation on the European Health Data Space (2022), 11.
86 BEUC, 'Consumers Need Strong Safeguards to Protect Their Health Data: BEUC Position Paper on the Proposed European Health Data Space', (2022), 15.
87 BEUC, 'Consumers Need Strong Safeguards to Protect Their Health Data' (2022), 13.
88 Article 51 EHDS.

wellness applications.[89] Depending on Member State law, Sarah and Drew's scenario (b) and (c) could therefore be subject to stricter requirements.

The purposes for secondary use are listed in Article 53 EHDS. They include, public interest in the areas of public or occupational health, public health surveillance or activities ensuring high levels of quality and safety of healthcare and of medicinal products or medical devices (para 1 lit a); policymaking and regulatory activities (para 1 lit b); and scientific research related to health or care sectors that contributes to public health or health technology assessments, or ensures high levels of quality and safety of healthcare, of medicinal products or of medical devices (para 1 lit e). The comprehensiveness of the purposes for secondary use is remarkable, reflecting the diverse needs and potential applications of the data. Simultaneously, it carries significant implications for data privacy.

Article 67(1) EDHS provides that any 'natural or legal person may submit a health data access application for the purposes referred to in Article 53(1) to a health data access body'. Hence, also private businesses and non-profit organisations, such as political parties, can submit a data access application and utilise the data categories mentioned in Article 51 EHDS for the purposes described. The data format they get access to would preferably be anonymised – however, '[w]here the health data user has sufficiently demonstrated that the purpose of processing cannot be achieved with anonymised data in accordance with Article 68(1), point (c), health data access bodies shall provide access to electronic health data in pseudonymised format'.[90] This means they will not only have access to anonymised data but also to (pseudonymised) personal data, depending on the stated purpose.

Article 54 EHDS lists prohibited secondary use, including those pertaining to job offers, offering less favourable terms in the provision of goods or services, or excluding people from insurance or credit benefits (lit b). Additionally, the purpose of advertising or marketing purposes is forbidden (lit c).

If Sarah and Drew seek integration of scenarios (b) and (c) into the EHDS for secondary use, they have to label their apps, complying with the requirements in Annex II EHDS and the common specifications in Article 36 EHDS.[91] The format and content of the label shall be determined by the Commission through implementing acts.[92] The validity of the label is restricted to three years.[93] Market surveillance authorities shall check the device's compliance with the requirements in Annex II.[94] Before placing on the market or putting into service, they have to register the required data into an EU database.[95]

89 Article 51(4) EHDS.
90 Article 66 (2) and (3) EHDS.
91 Article 47 EHDS.
92 Article 47(3) EHDS.
93 Article 47(5) EHDS.
94 Article 47(7) EHDS.
95 Article 49(2) EHDS.

Article 48 EHDS imposes an obligation on manufacturers to duly inform the users about the interoperability of the device with an EHR system and its effects. However, the mere interoperability itself shall not imply automatic sharing of all or part of the health data from the wellness application with or automatic transmission to the EHR system. On the contrary, the sharing or transmission of such data is subject to the consent of the natural person, in accordance with Article 5 EHDS.[96]

Furthermore, the EHDS requires that users of wellness applications shall be able to choose the categories of health data they want to insert in the EHR system and also the circumstance for sharing or transmission.[97] This concession to the Parliament's negotiation position aligns well with studies about consumers' willingness to share their health information. According to a study about consumers' attitude to health data sharing by the European Consumer Organisation BEUC, consumers' willingness to share their health data varies significantly depending on what types of data are shared, with whom, and for what purpose. Generally, a majority of consumers are unwilling to share data about their health habits (67–70%, depending on the purpose), with an even larger majority unwilling to share wellness and health applications data (79–84%) or genetic data (77–80%).[98] While 88% are comfortable sharing their health data with their general practitioner for care purposes, only 17% are willing to share it with the pharmaceutical industry and only 5% would share their health data with digital technology companies for scientific research.[99] An overwhelming majority (81%) want control over who they share their data with and for what purpose; more than half of the survey participants believe that access to their health information should be subject to their explicit consent (51–57%, depending on the purpose), and a significant majority (69%) insist that highly sensitive data, such as genetic information that cannot be anonymised, should not be used for research purposes without explicit consent.[100]

Brain data was not specifically addressed in any of the opinions on the draft EHDS, nor is it mentioned anywhere in the final act. Considering the arguments made on behalf of genetic, genomic, and proteomic data and their similarities to brain data, there is reason to argue that brain data should have been listed along with these categories. Few types of data contain as much intimate information or render people as vulnerable to sensitive inferences about their present and future state as brain data does. The prospect of having brain data included in the EHDS without further safeguards amplifies the apprehensions surrounding advancements

[96] Article 48(2) EHDS.
[97] Article 48(2) EHDS.
[98] BEUC, 'Consumer Attitudes to Health Data Sharing', (2023), 8 <www.beuc.eu/sites/default/files/publications/BEUC-X-2023-051_consumer_attitudes_to_health_data.pdf> accessed 8 January 2025.
[99] BEUC, 'Consumer Attitudes to Health Data Sharing', 9.
[100] BEUC, 'Consumer Attitudes to Health Data Sharing', 11.

in neurotechnology and heightens user concerns related to data privacy. As the EHDS currently stands, Member States have the option to introduce stricter measures and safeguards for brain data processed by wellness applications in their national regulations. However, unlike with genetic, genomic, and proteomic data, they do not have that same regulatory flexibility regarding brain data processed by medical devices.

5

Use Case 2: Commercial Advertising

May Commercial Companies Use Mind Data for Targeted Advertising?

Advertisers have long recognised the crucial role emotions play in human decision-making and have capitalised on this insight for decades. Today, MDT-based targeted advertising is capturing their attention.[1] Targeted advertising is a field most controversially discussed by privacy scholars, consumer organisations, digital rights organisations, advertisers, and industry.[2] Targeted advertising is the practice of customising and delivering ads that are specifically relevant to consumers, with the goal of increasing engagement and driving product purchases. Targeted online advertising manifests in a variety of forms and designs.[3] Display advertising utilises pop-up windows, info-bars, banners, or videos to deliver personalised ads on websites or on

[1] In this context, the terms 'targeted' and 'personalised' advertising will be used interchangeably. For a study on the broader impact of targeted advertising and its regulatory context, see Niklas Fourberg and others, 'Online Advertising: The Impact of Targeted Advertising on Advertisers, Market Access and Consumer Choice', Study Requested by the European Parliament's Committee on the Internal Market and Consumer Protection (IMCO) (2021) <www.europarl.europa.eu/RegData/etudes/STUD/2021/662913/IPOL_STU(2021)662913_EN.pdf> accessed 8 January 2025.

[2] For comprehensive scholarly studies, see Giovanni Sartor and others, 'Regulating Targeted and Behavioural Advertising in Digital Services: How to Ensure Users' Informed Consent', Study Requested by the European Parliament's Committee on Legal Affairs (JURI committee) (2021) <www.europarl.europa.eu/thinktank/en/document/IPOL_STU(2021)694680> accessed 8 January 2025; Natali Helberger and others, 'EU Consumer Protection 2.0: Structural Asymmetries in Digital Consumer Markets: A Joint Report from Research Conducted under the EUCP2.0 Project', BEUC (2021) <www.beuc.eu/sites/default/files/publications/beuc-x-2021-018_eu_consumer_protection_2.0.pdf> accessed 8 January 2025; Natali Helberger and others, 'EU Consumer Protection 2.0: The Regulatory Gap: Consumer Protection in the Digital Economy. Addendum to the Report "Structural Asymmetries in Digital Consumer Markets"', BEUC (2021) <www.beuc.eu/sites/default/files/publications/beuc-x-2021-116_the_regulatory_gap-consumer_protection_in_the_digital_economy.pdf> accessed 8 January 2025; Natali Helberger and others, 'Digital Fairness for Consumers', BEUC (2024) <www.beuc.eu/sites/default/files/publications/BEUC-X-2024-032_Digital_fairness_for_consumers_Report.pdf> accessed 8 January 2025.

[3] See Sartor, 'Regulating Targeted and Behavioural Advertising', 31 subsequential.

social media platforms. These ads may appear in a user's feed, timeline, or story, alongside user-generated content. They are tailored based on a mix of provided information, browsing history, and behavioural data collected on the platforms, including groups, followers, likes, shares, clicked videos, and preferences. Keyword advertising matches keywords entered into search engine boxes with those chosen by advertisers to describe their products or service. Conversational advertising uses chatbots to send real-time messages seamlessly integrated into user conversations. Virtual assistants play audio ads and promotional offers in response to specific user requests.

Targeted advertising can differ significantly in the degree of intrusiveness, depending on what kind of data is used and whether or not consumers are tracked. The prevalent types of targeted advertising encompass contextual advertising, segmented advertising, and behavioural advertising. Contextual advertising builds upon the real-time content a data subject is viewing (e.g. the content of a web page a data subject is visiting, their search keywords, previous search queries, or even the user's IP address if it is indicating the likely geographical location).[4] Segmented advertising is based on known characteristics (e.g. sex, age, or location), which have been provided by users themselves in the sign-up or registration stage. Both contextual and segmented targeted advertising operate without observing or tracking the behaviour of users.[5] They are perceived as significantly less intrusive when contrasted with the third type, behavioural advertising.[6]

Behavioural advertising involves the tracking of consumers' online behaviour over time and virtual space and the building of individual consumer profiles. Based on these profiles, inferences are drawn and ads are targeted, matching the inferred interests of the consumers.[7] Behavioural advertising observes the behaviour of individuals by studying their online actions. These actions include which websites they visit, when, how often, if they visit a site repeatedly, how long they look at certain items, which ads they click on and in which order, the keywords they use, the online content they produce, and many more. The tracking can happen via cookies, tracking walls, web beacons, or device fingerprinting. Behavioural targeting companies often use a combination of tracking techniques, cookie-based technologies, and data mining software. Moreover, they deduct data from the IP address or the

4 Article 29 Data Protection Working Party, Opinion 2/2010 on Online Behavioural Advertising (WP 171), Adopted on 22 June 2010, 5.

5 Sartor, 'Regulating Targeted and Behavioural Advertising', 24.

6 The effects of online behavioural advertising on privacy, non-discrimination, and group-privacy have been discussed, for example, in Sandra Wachter, 'Affinity Profiling and Discrimination by Association in Online Behavioural Advertising', (2020) 35(2) *Berkeley Technology Law Journal* <https://doi.org/10.15779/Z38JS9H82M>; Johann Laux and others, 'Neutralizing Online Behavioural Advertising: Algorithmic Targeting with Market Power As an Unfair Commercial Practice', (2021) 58(3) *Common Market Law Review*, 719–750 <https://doi.org/10.54648/cola2021048>.

7 WP 171, 4.

Wifi access point to complete the profile. They create a predictive profile, which is combined with the explicit profile of users, that is to say, information provided by the users themselves (e.g. when registering for the service).[8]

Overall, behavioural advertising collects a comprehensive data portfolio about consumers and paints a very detailed picture of a consumer's online life and behaviour. The data necessary for building a complete consumer profile includes various types of data. Typically, the data set includes volunteered data, that is to say, data that has been provided by the users themselves, so they are aware of the existence of that data but may not know it is used for this particular processing (e.g. data provided when registering for an online profile, used for a payment by credit card or for publishing on social media). It encompasses observed data, that is to say, data that is captured about activities of the user (e.g. from online cookies, loyalty cards, and enabled location sensors on their devices). Finally, it includes inferred data based on probability analytics.[9]

In practice, MDTs are best suited to enhance online behavioural advertising, complementing the predictive behavioural profile of consumers. However, it is also conceivable that mind data builds the sole basis for emotional targeting or emotion-based advertising.

5.1 GDPR: WHEN ALL ELSE FAILS, CONSENT PREVAILS

In their opinion on online behavioural advertising, the WP29 stated that targeted advertising most likely involves the processing of personal data as it entails the collection of IP addresses and the processing of unique identifiers via cookies; thus, data subjects are singled out (irrespective of whether their real names are known or not).[10] Moreover, the collected information relates to a person's characteristics or behaviour and is used to influence them. Accordingly, the processing of data, including mind data, for targeted advertising is within the scope of the GDPR and has to comply with all principles outlined in Article 5.

The very first principle stipulates that all processing of personal data has to be lawful, fair, and transparent.[11] For the processing to be lawful, it must have a valid legal basis. Article 6 GDPR specifies that processing of personal data shall be lawful only if one of the criteria listed in Article 6(1) GDPR is met. In other words, without having one of the legal bases given in Article 6(1) GDPR, all processing of personal

8 WP 171, 7.

9 Sometimes, the classification is further narrowed down and there is an additional category of derived data. 'Derived data' means data derived from other data, i.e. by deterministic computations, related either to an individual or to a group of people who share certain attributes, such as age, gender, or purchased items (see Sartor, 'Regulating Targeted and Behavioural Advertising', 38 subsequential).

10 WP 171, 9.

11 Article 5(1)(a) GDPR.

data is unlawful.[12] For the processing of special category data, one of the exemptions from the general prohibition in Article 9(2) GDPR has (additionally) to apply. The parameters for lawful processing of sensitive data are considerably more restricted than for normal personal data.

Discussing alternative forms for the deployment of MDTs, Sarah and Drew turn their attention to the commercial advertising sector. They are intrigued by the idea of using MDTs for targeted advertising. They consider the following options for their potential software:

Scenario (a): *a text-based chatbot for a medium-sized ticketing platform. The chatbot handles ticket sales, facilitates access to content, provides notifications of events as well as updates on postponements and cancellations, and infers people's emotional state and their emotional reaction from the written interaction to target ads;*

Scenario (b): *a software for a very large social media platform which combines mind data inferred from written posts and likes/dislikes/emojis, with other information from across websites (if and how long users watch certain videos/ ads, what they click, what they search for, etc.) for personalising the content of the users' social media feed and displaying targeted ads in the timeline. Additionally, the algorithm gives preference to sad/controversial posts to increase people's social media engagement and the time they stay on the platform;*

Scenario (c): *EEG-based earbuds as a special promotional tie-in for subscriptions to a music streaming platform. The earbuds personalise the music playlist and target ads based on users' inferred emotions.*

After discussing the complexities surrounding the legal nature of the processed data in the previous section, Sarah and Drew take data protection to the next level and contemplate the appropriate legal basis for these innovative endeavours. Moreover, they explore the implications under consumer protection law and new pieces of digital law.

Online advertising practises and their legal basis have spurred discussions by regulators and legal scholars very early on. Article 6(1) GDPR names six possible legal grounds for processing normal personal data. Among these six, none has normative priority over the other and there is no ranking between lit (a) to lit (f).[13] Three out of the six legal bases in Article 6(1) GDPR are potentially appropriate for targeted advertising: consent (lit a), performance of a contract (lit b), and legitimate interest (lit f).

[12] The following analysis will focus on possible legal bases according to the GDPR only and not include the e-Privacy Directive. For the interplay between Article 5(3) e-Privacy Directive and GDPR-related legal bases in general, see, e.g., Frederik J. Zuiderveen Borgesius, 'Personal Data Processing for Behavioural Targeting: Which Legal Basis?', (2015) 5(3) *International Data Privacy Law*, 163–176 <https://doi.org/10.1093/idpl/ipv011>.

[13] Article 29 Data Protection Working Party, Opinion 06/2014 on the Notion of Legitimate Interests of the Data Controller under Article 7 of Directive 95/46/EC (WP 217), 10.

Being aware of the intricacies of consent and that GDPR-compliant consent has to be informed, freely given, specific, unambiguous, and easy to withdraw,[14] companies started diverting from consent and giving preference to performance of a contract and legitimate interest as legal bases for processing of data for targeted advertising. Therefore, the analysis will delve into these.

Article 6(1)(b) stipulates that processing is lawful if the 'processing is necessary for the performance of a contract to which the data subject is party or in order to take steps at the request of the data subject prior to entering into a contract'.[15] The provision goes back to Article 7 DPD and was transferred to the GDPR. This provision includes all stages necessary for the fulfilment of a contract (e.g. administration, billing, and processing for defect liability), including pre-contractual situations (processing for pre-contractual relationships is, however, limited to what a data subject would reasonably expect and what is 'typically adequate' for this kind of request).[16] The necessity for the performance of the contract has to be established ex ante, including an assessment of whether there are less intrusive means.

Notably, lit b (performance of a contract) and lit a (consent) are mutually exclusive.[17] A controller can therefore only choose one of the two. If the targeting of ads was indeed a necessity for the contract, consent would be the wrong legal basis and vice versa. Moreover, the ways to remove the legal basis and thus end the processing differ in both cases: While consent gives data subjects the right to withdraw their consent (as easily as it was given), the data subject cannot simply 'withdraw' the contractual necessity to remove the legal basis for processing – only terminating the contract will remove lit b.

The crux of the matter is to determine what is truly necessary for the performance of a contract and what is not. The WP29 has outlined a strict interpretation of what is to be considered necessary.[18] Notably, the WP29 has stated that performance of a contract is not a legal ground for direct marketing at the sole initiative of the retailer/controller.[19] The EDPB confirms the WP29's strict interpretation of performance of a contract as in 'impossible to perform without', clarifying that vague or general purposes, for example improving users' experience, marketing purposes, IT-security purposes, or future research, will not suffice, unless specified by more details.[20] Moreover, the EDPB reiterates that lit b is not

14 Article 4(11) and Article 7 GDPR.

15 See also, Recital 44 GDPR: 'Processing should be lawful where it is necessary in the context of a contract or the intention to enter into a contract'.

16 Waltraut Kotschy, Article 6 in Kuner and others, *The EU General Data Protection Regulation (GDPR)*.

17 Article 29 Data Protection Working Party, Guidelines on Consent under Regulation 2016/679 (WP259 rev.01), Adopted on 28 November 2017, as last Revised and Adopted on 10 April 2018, 8.

18 WP 217, 16.

19 WP 217, 18.

20 EDPB, Guidelines 2/2019 on the Processing of Personal Data under Article 6(1)(b) GDPR in the Context of the Provision of Online Services to Data Subjects, Version 2.0 (8 October 2019), 7.

a legal ground for unsolicited marketing solely upon the initiative of the controller or at the request of a third party; neither is it a valid legal basis for online behavioural advertising.[21]

The EDPB stresses that in order for something to be necessary for the performance of a contract, it has to be objectively necessary. Purposes that are merely useful but not objectively necessary – even though they might be necessary for other business purposes of the controller – are excluded from the scope of lit b.[22] As guiding questions to establish whether a processing is objectively needed for the performance of a contract or not, the EDPB suggest the following questions:

- What is the nature of the service being provided to the data subject?
- What are its distinguishing characteristics?
- What is the exact rationale of the contract (i.e. its substance and fundamental object)?
- What are the essential elements of the contract?
- What are the mutual perspectives and expectations of the parties to the contract?[23]

In scenario (a), the chatbot for the ticketing platform, the nature of the service is an exchange of information related to the purchase/selling of tickets. Facilitating access to content, handling of ticket sales, and providing notifications (cancellations, postponements, updates) can all be considered (pre-)contractual necessities to the purchase contract. All these different functions meet the expectations of both parties, the buyer and the seller. Performance of a contract is therefore the correct legal basis for the processing of all data that is required for these features. Arguably, the inference and processing of mind data is not required for these kinds of services. Neither the operating of ticket sales, nor information about cancellations or postponements require the inference and further processing of data on the emotional state of the consumer. The inference and processing of mind data for these services cannot therefore be based on performance of a contract.

Rationale of the contract in scenario (a) is the provision of information related to the purchase of tickets and the facilitation of purchasing activity. Targeting users and displaying ads are not objectively necessary for the contract, it is not part of the exact rationale of the contract, and it is not an essential element thereof. Additionally, the inference and processing of mind data for targeted ads does not comply with the expectations of the users. An average user does not expect for their mind data to be inferred when they are buying a ticket for a concert or a theatre play then to be targeted with ads. Moreover, and as per regulatory guidance above, unsolicited direct marketing at the sole initiative of the controller cannot be based

[21] EDPB, Guidelines 2/2019, 13–14.
[22] EDPB, Guidelines 2/2019, 8.
[23] EDPB, Guidelines 2/2019, 10.

on performance of a contract as legal basis. As a result, the inference and processing of mind data for targeted advertising cannot be based on performance of a contract in scenario (a).

Scenario (b) is more complex in its legal analysis than scenario (a). Scenario (b) is the software for a very large social media platform, drawing mind data from written posts and combining them with other information from across websites to personalise the content of the users' social media feed, including targeted ads. In addition, the algorithm highlights and increases the quantity of sad or controversial posts in the timeline to intensify users' social media engagement and the time spent on the platform.

In scenario (b), the behavioural tracking and targeting of ads forms part of the personalisation of content. Social media platforms could argue (and they have been arguing similarly in the past) that the behavioural tracking and targeting of ads, including the inference and processing of mind data and targeting of ads based on mind data, contribute to improving the service and making the content people see more relevant and engaging. Accordingly, the inference and processing of people's mind data would merely serve to fulfil the actual contract and be objectively necessary for the performance of the contract in that it helps to personalise the content and provide users with a timeline, which is personally relevant.

The EDPB takes a differentiated stance regarding the personalisation of content in their Guidelines on the processing of data under the legal basis of contractual necessity, not rejecting the concept in its entirety:

> The EDPB acknowledges that personalisation of content may (but does not always) constitute an intrinsic and expected element of certain online services, and therefore may be regarded as necessary for the performance of the contract with the service user in some cases. Whether such processing can be regarded as an intrinsic aspect of an online service, will depend on the nature of the service provided, the expectations of the average data subject in light not only of the terms of service but also the way the service is promoted to users, and whether the service can be provided without personalisation. Where personalisation of content is not objectively necessary for the purpose of the underlying contract, for example where personalised content delivery is intended to increase user engagement with a service but is not an integral part of using the service, data controllers should consider an alternative lawful basis where applicable.[24]

If the social media platform in scenario (b) relied on performance of a contract as legal basis for the inference and processing of mind data, the inference and processing of mind data would have to be intrinsic to the service, be part of the core elements and of the rationale of the contract between user and social media platform. The EDPB points to three elements that must be taken into account when

[24] EDPB, Guidelines 2/2019, 15–16, emphasis in original.

considering the personalisation of content intrinsic to the service and thus necessary to the underlying contract:

- the nature of the service
- the expectations of the average user
- if the service can be provided without personalisation.[25]

Social media users have many reasons for being on a social media platform. Being on a platform is a way to stay in touch with friends, to connect with business partners, to learn about personal or professional news, to learn about world or national news, and to be seen and heard by personal peer groups or professional communities. In essence, though, one could argue that the users personalise the service and their timeline themselves, simply by defining who they choose to follow or to connect with and what group they decide to join. This self-determined form of personalisation is the pure nature of the service and the kind of service the users agree to. All the purposes described meet the expectations of the users. All of them can be achieved without online behavioural tracking, without remote-controlled personalisation of content, and without being sent targeted ads. Particularly, they can be achieved without inferring and processing mind data.

In 2022, the EDPB issued two binding decisions (3/2022 and 4/2022) concerning targeted advertising on social media platforms. Following the platforms' own statements, the EDPB considers sharing content and communicating with others as the main purpose for using a service like Facebook or Instagram – not receiving personalised advertisements:

> Meta IE presents its Facebook service in its landing website as a platform enabling users to 'connect with friends and the world around you on Facebook' and at the beginning of its Facebook Terms of Service as being its mission 'to give people the power to build community and bring the world closer together. To help advance this mission, we provide the Products and services described below to you: (…)' which include in consecutive headings 'Connect you with people and organizations you care about: (…)'; 'Empower you to express yourself and communicate about what matters to you: (…)" and 'Help you discover content, products and services that may interest you: (…).'[26]

According to the EDPB, this purpose can be achieved without the personalisation of commercial content. No contractual obligations in the Terms of Service oblige Facebook to offer personalised ads, there are no penalties in case it would fail to do so.[27] Further, the EDPB points to realistic, less intrusive alternatives for achieving the same goal, for example by offering contextual advertising based on geography,

[25] EDPB, Guidelines 2/2019, 15–16.

[26] EDPB, Binding Decision 3/2022 on the Dispute Submitted by the Irish SA on Meta Platforms Ireland Limited and Its Facebook Service (Article 65 GDPR), Adopted on 5 December 2022, 32.

[27] EDPB, Binding Decision 3/2022, 32.

language, and content, or providing the option to choose between a chronological and a personalised newsfeed.[28]

As regards the expectations of the average user towards MDT-enhanced behavioural advertising, it is very unlikely that the social media platform in scenario (b) promotes in full transparency that the mind data of users will be inferred and processed for personalising their timeline, including targeted advertising. However, if the intended inference and processing of mind data has not been fully disclosed, the average user cannot expect this to be part of the service. The EDPB also stresses the great technical complexity of the techniques involved. The EDPB finds it 'extremely difficult to argue that an average user can fully grasp it, be aware of its consequences and impact on their rights to privacy and data protection, and reasonably expect it solely based on the Facebook Terms of Service'.[29] Considering the particular complexities of inferring mind data and their potential impact, this argument is even more true. The EDPB concludes that behavioural advertising is not an essential or core element of the service and contractual necessity, therefore, is not a suitable legal basis for the processing activities.

Scenario (b)'s extra feature of preferencing negative posts over positive posts in the timeline of users merits separate attention. In the realm of (social) media, bad news is good news; negative news raises attention and lures people into staying longer on the site or platform.[30] Controversial posts trigger active engagement. Anger and hate keep people on the platform.[31] The longer people stay on the platform, the more ads can be displayed to them. The practise described in scenario (b) recalls a true story happening several years ago: Facebook conducted a mass-scale emotional contagion experiment by manipulating the feeds of nearly 700,000 users.[32] They filtered the flow of comments, videos, pictures, and web links posted by other people, deliberately favouring sad over happy content. The study concluded that emotions expressed by our connections influence our moods. In defending the study, a spokesperson of Facebook explained the study was carried out 'to improve our services and to make the content people see on Facebook as relevant and engaging as possible'.[33]

28 EDPB, Binding Decision 3/2022, 33.

29 EDPB, Binding Decision 3/2022, 34.

30 For a recent study, see Claire E. Robertson and others, 'Negativity Drives Online News Consumption', (2023) 7 *Nature Human Behaviour*, 812–822 <https://doi.org/10.1038/s41562-023-01538-4>.

31 Jeremy B. Merrill and Will Oremus, 'Five Points for Anger, One for a "Like": How Facebook's Formula Fostered Rage and Misinformation', *Washington Post* (26 October 2021) <www.washingtonpost.com/technology/2021/10/26/facebook-angry-emoji-algorithm/> accessed 8 January 2025.

32 Adam D. I. Kramer and others, 'Experimental Evidence of Massive-Scale Emotional Contagion through Social Networks', (2014) *Proceedings of the National Academy of Sciences (PNAS)* <https://doi.org/10.1073/pnas.1320040111>.

33 Robert Booth, 'Facebook Reveals News Feed Experiment to Control Emotions', *The Guardian* (30 June 2014) <www.theguardian.com/technology/2014/jun/29/facebook-users-emotions-news-feeds> accessed 8 January 2025.

The EDPB's Guidelines on processing personal data under contractual necessity states that measures for personalising content to increase user engagement which are not an integral part of using the service cannot rely on contractual necessity; they are not objectively necessary.[34] Inferring and processing mind data to prioritise sad or controversial content in order to prolong people's time on a platform is not an integral part of using the service. The processing cannot therefore be based on performance of a contract, either.

Overall, the inference and processing of mind data for behavioural advertising in scenario (b) is neither objectively necessary nor within the expectations of the average consumer. Therefore, performance of a contract is not an appropriate legal basis for processing with regard to behavioural tracking and targeting ads based on mind data in scenario (b).

In scenario (c), the EEG-based earbuds interpret users' brain activity to tailor music lists and target audio ads. Contrary to scenario (b), the personalisation of content in scenario (c), that is to say, the personalisation of the music list, is intrinsic to the product and part of the service. Companies selling EEG-based earbuds with this unique innovation would highlight it in their promotion; users would choose these very earbuds specifically for this functionality; and would anticipate this specific feature as an integral part of the earbuds. Performance of a contract is therefore a reasonable choice for the legal basis. However, as illustrated earlier, the processing of brain data constitutes processing of special category data. Consequently, the processing in scenario (c) necessitates an exemption from the general prohibition of processing under Article 9(2) GDPR, in addition to the legal basis according to Article 6(1) GDPR. In scenario (c), the processing of brain data for personalising music could be based on explicit consent according to Article 9(2)(a) GDPR, coupled with performance of a contract according to Article 6(1)(b) GDPR.[35] Importantly, this grants users the right to opt out or withdraw their consent to the processing of their brain data. In such cases, the earbuds would limit their service to a standard earbud service, devoid of the special feature of personalising music lists based on mind data.

As regards the targeting of ads based on brain activity, similar arguments apply as in the aforementioned examples. Targeting of ads is not an integral part of the service, and users do not anticipate it unless explicitly informed otherwise. Contractual necessity is therefore not applicable for the targeting of ads in scenario (c). Moreover,

[34] EDPB, Guidelines 2/2019, 15–16.

[35] As noted by Sartor, explicit consent under Article 9(2)(b) GDPR does not necessarily need to be linked to the legal basis of consent under Article 6(1) GDPR: 'In the case of using the legal base set out in Article 6 para 1 lit. b (when processing is necessary for the performance of a contract), processing of special categories of data will in many cases be based on explicit consent.' See Giovanni Sartor, Article 9 Margin Number 45, in Indra Spiecker gen. Döhmann and others (eds.), *General Data Protection Regulation. Article-by-Article Commentary*, (2023) <https://doi.org/10.5771/9783845276984>.

the processing would require a derogation from the general ban of processing special category data.

With contractual necessities not being an appropriate legal basis for the targeting of ads, advertisers turned to another option: legitimate interest. Article 6(1)(f) GDPR provides that processing is legitimate, where it 'is necessary for the purposes of the legitimate interests pursued by the controller or by a third party, except where such interests are overridden by the interests or fundamental rights and freedoms of the data subject which require protection of personal data, in particular where the data subject is a child'. The provision applies only to the interests of private sector controllers; processing carried out by public authorities in the performance of their tasks is explicitly excluded.[36] Targeted commercial advertising is typically undertaken by private controllers, and legitimate interest is therefore worth considering. The legal basis of legitimate interests can be removed by objecting to the processing according to Article 21 GDPR. Related to Article 21 GDPR, the data subject has the right to erasure ('right to be forgotten') according to Article 17(1)(c) GDPR.

Legitimate interests encompass three components, which need to apply cumulatively: (i) the pursuit of a legitimate interest by the controller or a third party; (ii) the need to process the data for these purposes; and (iii) that the interests are not overridden by fundamental rights and freedoms of the data subject.[37] Establishing an exact scope of 'legitimate interests' is a complex matter. Recital 47 GDPR gives some details and mentions fraud prevention and direct marketing as possible legitimate interests. Recital 48 GDPR extends legitimate interests to transmitting personal data within a group of undertakings for internal administrative purposes, Recital 49 stipulates that network and information security constitute a legitimate interest of a controller.

According to the WP29, the concept of 'interest' is broader than the concept of 'purpose'.[38] It includes, inter alia, the exercise of the right to freedom of expression or information, enforcement of legal claims, fraud prevention, the monitoring of employees for safety or management, whistle-blowing, physical as well as IT and network security, and processing for historical, scientific, or statistical purposes. Conventional direct marketing and other forms of marketing or advertisement are mentioned, alongside unsolicited non-commercial messages, including for political campaigns or charitable fundraising. Moreover, the WP29 explicitly includes processing for marketing research.[39] Areas like commercial marketing, commercial advertising, and political advertising, which are all relevant for the deployment of MDTs, are therefore included in this non-exhaustive list.

36 Article 6(1) GDPR and Recital 47 GDPR.
37 See EDPB, Guidelines 8/2020, 15.
38 WP 217, 24 subsequential.
39 WP 217, 25.

For an interest to be 'legitimate', it must be in accordance with applicable EU and national law, it has to be 'sufficiently clearly articulated', that is to say, sufficiently specific (otherwise no serious fundamental rights balancing test can be done), and represent 'a real and present' interest (an interest that is only speculative would not suffice).[40] Advertising per se is lawful, it is not forbidden by the law, neither is the targeting of ads. The interest of advertising is real and present; although the expectations about the success for an ad may be speculative, the interests in promoting a product or service are not. The interest of advertising is also sufficiently specific. Further narrowing the analysis down to the inference/processing of mind data for advertising, the arguments would largely remain the same: Inferring and processing mind data for advertising is lawful; to date, there is no law forbidding it. The interest in doing so is present and real, although the success of it may be speculative. The interest of inferring and processing mind data for advertising is also sufficiently specific.

Legitimate interests require a balancing test against the fundamental rights of the data subject. More precisely, Article 6(1)(f) GDPR reads that legitimate interests of a controller or a third party may be overridden by the 'interests or fundamental rights and freedoms' of a data subject. The balancing test is therefore not restricted to the fundamental rights but also takes into consideration the interests of the data subject.[41] According to the WP29, such a balancing test involves assessing the controller's legitimate interest, the impact on the data subjects, provisional balance, and additional safeguards implemented by the controller.[42]

If the inference and processing of mind data for the purpose of targeted advertising is based on legitimate interests, it will have to pass this balancing test. For the legitimate interests to prevail, the inference and processing has to be necessary and proportionate. Advertising, including targeted advertising, can be achieved without inferring and processing mind data. This raises doubts about the necessity of such inference and processing. Moreover, inferring people's mind data and using these inferences for targeted advertising is not in their interests as it renders them vulnerable and at high risk of manipulation. Additionally, the inference and processing of mind data infringes on a number of their fundamental rights. At a minimum, the non-transparent inference and further processing of mind data violates their right to privacy and data protection. The potential impact of the processing on the interests and fundamental rights of the data subjects is significant. As they lack proportionality, such impact cannot be justified by the interests of the advertiser.

With regard to the building of a consumer profile, the WP29 notes that the interest in getting to know the preferences of customers to then be able to personalise offers and offer products or services that better match the needs and desires of the

[40] WP 217, 24.

[41] See WP 217, 29.

[42] WP 217, 33.

customers is legitimate for certain types of marketing. In the same breath, the WP29 continues that this does not imply controllers can rely on legitimate interest to

> monitor the on-line or off-line activities of their customers, combine vast amounts of data about them from different sources that were initially collected in other contexts and for different purposes, and create […] complex profiles of the customers' personalities and preferences without their knowledge, a workable mechanism to object, let alone informed consent. Such a profiling activity is likely to present a significant intrusion into the privacy of the customer, and when this is so, the controller's interest would be overridden by the interests and rights of the data subject.[43]

In other words, the WP29 recognises the building of a profile as a legitimate interest of the controller, immediately adding that the interests and rights of the data subject override this legitimate interest due to the intrusiveness of this kind of profiling activity. Incorporating mind data into the consumer profile data set does not make the profile and the associated techniques less intrusive; on the contrary, it increases their intrusiveness.

The EDPB continues this way of reasoning in their Guidelines 8/2020 on the targeting of social media users, outlining in some detail the impact on the fundamental rights of data subjects. The EDPB underscores that the combination and analysis of data stemming from different sources, together with the opaqueness of the underlying processing of potentially sensitive data, cause risks for the fundamental rights and freedoms of natural persons. According to the EDPB, targeting that relies on personal data, or even potentially sensitive data, can involve uses of data that are against the reasonable expectations of social media users and deprive data subjects from their control over their data. Thus, it is a risk to their informational self-determination.[44] Similarly, the EDPS states that when data is used outside its original context, this repurposing of data can affect an individual's informational self-determination and reduce the control over their data.[45] As a second risk, the EDPB stresses that targeting can exacerbate existing biases and lead to discriminatory effects for data subjects in the context of advertising, for instance related to job offers, housing, or credits.

Moreover, the EDPB highlights the risk of manipulation, given that the targeting mechanisms, by definition, aim to influence the behaviour or choices of the users, 'whether it be in terms of their purchasing decisions as consumers or in terms of their political decisions as citizens'.[46] Directly following these considerations, the EDPB shares their concerns specifically regarding the inference of emotions by analysing social media content (e.g. by looking for certain key words). They stress that information about individual emotions can be used to 'target the individual with

[43] WP 217, 26.
[44] EDPB, Guidelines 8/2020, 5.
[45] EDPS, Opinion 3/2018 on online manipulation and personal data (9 March 2018), 15.
[46] EDPB, Guidelines 8/2020, 5.

specific messages and at specific moments to which he or she is expected to be more receptive, thereby surreptitiously influencing his or her thought process, emotions and behaviour'.[47] According to the EDPB, the practice of delivering individualised messages, designed to exploit vulnerabilities, values, or concerns, can aggravate these vulnerabilities, thereby undermining individual autonomy and freedom.

Recital 47 GDPR stresses that the reasonable expectations of data subjects based on their relationship with the controller must be taken into account, if considering legitimate interest as a legal basis. The Recital continues in more detail that existence of a legitimate interest requires a thorough assessment, 'including whether a data subject can reasonably expect at the time and in the context of the collection of the personal data that processing for that purpose may take place'.[48] An average user does not expect their mind data to be inferred and processed by a controller for their targeting practices.

Overall, the analysis illustrates that the inference and processing of mind data for targeted advertising generally fails to pass the balancing test. The intrusive and non-transparent inference and processing of mind data, violating consumers' privacy and their right to data protection, as well as the exploitation of consumers' vulnerability to the unilateral advantage of the advertisers do not pass the provisional balancing test. No additional safeguards outweigh the non-transparency and intrusiveness. Accordingly, legitimate interest is not an appropriate legal basis for the inference and processing of mind data for targeted ads.

Based on the legal analysis, both performance of a contract and legitimate interest must be excluded as a legal basis for inferring and processing mind data for targeted advertising and personalising content. Therefore, the only remaining legal basis is consent/explicit consent. Importantly, this does not imply that consent/explicit consent is the optimal or even a favourable solution.[49] However, it is the only GDPR-compliant option currently available.

Consent as the only available legal basis has also been confirmed by a CJEU decision. In a landmark decision in July 2023, the CJEU clarified comprehensively the interpretation of Article 6(1) GDPR concerning the appropriate legal basis for personalising ads and content. In *Meta Platforms Inc and Others* v *Bundeskartellamt*

[47] EDPB, Guidelines 8/2020, 6.

[48] Recital 47 GDPR.

[49] For a discussion about the deficiencies of consent, see, for instance, Daniel J. Solove, 'Murky Consent: An Approach to the Fictions of Consent in Privacy Law', (2024) 104 *Boston Law Review*, 593 <www.bu.edu/bulawreview/files/2024/04/SOLOVE.pdf> accessed 8 January 2025; Sourya Joyee De and Abdessamad Imine, 'Consent for Targeted Advertising: The Case of Facebook', (2020) 35 *AI & Society*, 1055; Alessandro Mantelero, 'The Future of Consumer Data Protection in the E.U. Re-thinking the "Notice and Consent" Paradigm in the New Era of Predictive Analytics', (2014) 30(6) *Computer Law & Security Review*, 643–660; Gabriela Zanfir, 'Forgetting about Consent: Why the Focus Should Be on "Suitable Safeguards" in Data Protection Law', in Serge Gutwirth and others (eds.), *Reloading Data Protection: Multidisciplinary Insights and Contemporary Challenges* (Springer Netherlands 2014) <https://doi.org/10.1007/978-94-007-7540-4_12>.

(C-252/21), the CJEU held that for Article 6(1)(b) GDPR, performance of a contract, to be applicable, the processing needs to be 'objectively indispensable for a purpose that is integral to the contractual obligation', it must be 'essential for the proper performance of the contract', with 'no workable, less intrusive alternatives' available.[50] The court acknowledges that the personalisation of content may be useful to the user, however,

> personalised content does not appear to be necessary in order to offer that user the services of the online social network. Those services may, where appropriate, be provided to the user in the form of an equivalent alternative which does not involve such a personalisation, such that the latter is not objectively indispensable for a purpose that is integral to those services.[51]

The court hereby confirms the binding decisions by the EDPB from 2022, which exclude performance of a contract as an appropriate legal basis for personalised behavioural advertising.

With regard to Article 6(1)(f), legitimate interest, the court recalls that the need for processing ought to be examined in conjunction with the principle of minimisation (personal data shall be 'adequate, relevant and limited to what is necessary in relation to the purposes for which they are processed', Article 5(1)(c) GDPR). Concerning the reasonable expectations of the data subject, the court concludes that the user of a social media network like Facebook 'cannot reasonably expect that the operator of the social network will process that user's personal data, without his or her consent, for the purposes of personalised advertising' and that 'the interests and fundamental rights of such a user override the interest of that operator in such personalised advertising by which it finances its activity, with the result that the processing by that operator for such purposes cannot fall within the scope of point (f) of the first subparagraph of Article 6(1) of the GDPR'.[52] The CJEU thus leaves no doubt that legitimate interest cannot serve as legal basis, either, as the rights and interests of the data subjects, in particular their right to private life and data protection, override the legitimate marketing interests of the controller.

As a possible way forward, the court recommends exploring alternative ways that satisfy just as effectively the legitimate interest in marketing of the controller but that are less restrictive of the fundamental rights of the data subjects. Such less intrusive alternatives would, for instance, be segmented or contextual advertising, which both do not rely on tracking users' behaviour and preferences.

The CJEU confirms that the dominant position and the existing power asymmetry of social network operators do not preclude users from being able to validly consent. Consent remains therefore an available legal basis. In the same context,

[50] Case C-252/21 *Meta Platforms Inc and Others* v *Bundeskartellamt* [2023], section 98–99.
[51] Case C-252/21 *Meta Platforms Inc and Others* v *Bundeskartellamt*, section 102.
[52] Case C-252/21 *Meta Platforms Inc and Others* v *Bundeskartellamt*, section 117.

the court anticipates the option of offering the service for payment. According to the CJEU, users must be free to refuse to give their consent to specific data processing operations, without being obliged to completely refrain from using the service, 'which means that those users are to be offered, if necessary for an appropriate fee, an equivalent alternative not accompanied by such data processing operations'.[53]

Following the decision by the CJEU, the Norwegian DPA has temporarily banned targeted behavioural advertising by Meta based on Article 6(1)(b) or (f) GDPR in July 2023 by issuing an emergency sanction pursuant to Article 58(2)(f) and 66(1) GDPR,[54] referring the case to the EDPB. In October 2023, the EDPB extended the Norwegian ban on behavioural targeted advertising without consent to the whole of the EU/EEA and made it permanent. Meta introduced a mechanism to make EU users choose between a free service including personalised advertising or a service upon payment.[55] First experiences suggested that a vast majority of users (over 99%) is rather willing to consent than to pay for a service without personalised ads.[56] Following that, the EDPB has adopted an Opinion on valid consent in the context of 'consent or pay models', addressing specifically large online platforms in April 2024.[57] Therein, the EDPB emphasises the requirements for valid consent under the GDPR, most importantly that it has to be truly freely given. Considering the position of large online platforms in the market, the existence of lock-in or network effects, and the extent of dependence on the service, the EDPB outlines that these platforms will not be able to rely on consent in the majority of cases, if confronting their users with just a binary choice between either consenting to processing of personal data for behavioural advertising purposes or paying a fee. Rather, the EDPB recommends for large online platforms to offer a further alternative without behavioural advertising, free of charge, deploying advertisement that involves the processing of less (or no) personal data. As regards the 'appropriate fee' for an equivalent service, the EDPB is not condemning this option in its entirety. However, it recalls that its appropriateness should be assessed case by case and that the fundamental right to data protection cannot be transformed into a feature people have to pay to enjoy.

In October 2024, in *Maximilian Schrems* v *Meta Platforms Ireland Ltd* (C–446/21), the CJEU reaffirmed the principle of data minimisation and ruled

53 Case C-252/21 *Meta Platforms Inc and Others* v *Bundeskartellamt*, section 150.

54 Norwegian Data Protection Authority, Urgent and Provisional Measures – Meta (14 July 2023) <www.datatilsynet.no/contentassets/36ad4a92100943439df9a8a3a7015c19/urgent-and-provisional-measures--meta_redacted.pdf> accessed 8 January 2025. Segmented and generalised advertising are not within the scope of the banning order (see 3).

55 Alessia Sophia D'Amico and others, 'Meta's Pay-or-Okay Model: An Analysis under EU Data Protection, Consumer and Competition Law', (2024) *Technology and Regulation*, 254–272 <https://doi.org/10.26116/techreg.2024.019>.

56 Noyb, 'Noyb Files GDPR complaint against Meta over "Pay or Okay"', (28 November 2023) <https://noyb.eu/en/noyb-files-gdpr-complaint-against-meta-over-pay-or-okay> accessed 8 January 2025.

57 EDPB, Opinion 08/2024 on Valid Consent in the Context of Consent or Pay Models Implemented by Large Online Platforms, Adopted on 17 April 2024.

that storing personal data indefinitely for targeted advertising constitutes a disproportionate interference with the rights protected under the GDPR (section 58).[58] The Court held that Article 5(1)(c) must be interpreted to mean that the principle of data minimisation prohibits that all of the personal data obtained by a controller can be aggregated, analysed, and processed for the purposes of targeted advertising without time limits or distinctions based on the type of data (section 65).

In addition to considerations about the lawfulness of processing pursuant to Article 6, the regime for automated processing under the GDPR should be taken into account. Article 4(4) GDPR defines profiling as 'any form of automated processing of personal data consisting of the use of personal data to evaluate certain personal aspects relating to a natural person, in particular to analyse or predict aspects concerning that natural person's performance at work, economic situation, health, personal preferences, interests, reliability, behaviour, location or movements'. MDTs rely on automated processing, they analyse personal aspects, preferences, and interests, they evaluate these aspects, and, in the context of targeted advertising, predict which ads are most likely to successfully influence the data subject's consumer behaviour. MDTs categorise individuals into groups according to their attitudes, preferences, psychological states, intentions, emotions, or thoughts to predict their future behaviour, deploying analytics, and computing technologies. The inference and processing of mind data thus meets the definition of profiling.

Profiling under the GDPR initiates a number of provisions, with Article 22 GDPR being the most prominent. Article 22 GDPR concerns the right of the data subject to not be object to decision-making solely based on automated processing, including profiling, that has legal effects or similarly concerns them, unless for contractual necessities, authorisation by Union or Member State law or explicit consent. Processing operations that are within the scope of Article 22 GDPR have to meet specific transparency and fairness requirements and comply with greater accountability obligations. According to Recital 70 GDPR, data subjects have the right to oppose profiling for direct marketing. Being within the scope of Article 22 GDPR therefore initiates significant obligations and restrictions for the controller.

In general, Article 22 GDPR is not considered applicable for advertising practices, as receiving an ad is not understood as an action that has a legal effect or similarly affects the data subject under Article 22 GDPR.[59] However, with regard to the specificities of MDTs, it is worth remembering that the WP29 points to a more differentiated approach. In their Guidelines on Automated individual decision-making and

[58] Case C-446/21 *Maximilian Schrems* v *Meta Platforms Ireland Ltd, formerly Facebook Ireland Ltd* [2024].

[59] Sartor and others discuss that targeted advertising may fall within the scope of Article 22 GDPR, when it involves unfair discrimination that result in non-trivial economic consequences, e.g. when personalised pricing mechanisms lead to significantly higher prices (Sartor and others, 'Regulating Targeted and Behavioural Advertising', 72).

profiling, the WP29 reflects on the possibility that targeted advertising could indeed have a significant effect. The criteria outlined for such a significant effect include: (i) the intrusiveness of the profiling process, (ii) the expectations and wishes of the individuals concerned, (iii) the way the advert is delivered and (iv) knowledge of the vulnerabilities of the data subject being used.[60] Undoubtedly, the inferring and processing of people's mind data by MDTs is intrusive. Data subjects are mostly unaware of the profiling process by MDTs and do not expect this type of processing. The knowledge about the inferred information is used purposefully to influence data subjects into buying a certain product, hence the knowledge of the vulnerability is used. It could therefore be argued that Article 22 GDPR may be applicable for the use of MDTs in advertising.

Applying the regime of Article 22 GDPR would further confirm that consent is the only legal basis for inferring and processing mind data for targeted advertising, narrowing it down to explicit consent as per Article 22(2)(c) GDPR.

5.2 UCPD: GREAT POTENTIAL, AMENDMENTS NEEDED

Limiting the legal basis to consent/explicit consent is unlikely to end the practice of inferring and processing mind data for targeted advertising. Therefore, the analysis of the legal framework should be expanded beyond mere data protection. One legal field with an established tradition in restricting certain forms of advertising is consumer protection law.[61]

In principle, all advertising aims to persuade people to purchase items they may not necessarily need, leading them to spend money that could be used differently, and potentially causing them economic harm. As such, this is neither unethical nor unfair. Considering the inherently intrusive nature of MDTs, largely operating without the knowledge of the consumers, the question arises though as to whether Sarah and Drew's scenarios – or possibly all advertising based on MDTs – qualify as unfair commercial practices.

The primary legal source for delineating fair from unfair commercial practices is the Unfair Commercial Practices Directive 2005/29/EC (UCPD), amended in 2019 by the Modernisation Directive 2019/2161/EU to address new market developments, especially in online marketing.[62] The UCPD's main objective is to regulate

60 WP251, 22.

61 For a discussion of the many challenges for consumer protection in the digital age, see, for instance, Helberger and others, 'EU Consumer Protection 2.0: Structural Asymmetries'; Natali Helberger and others, 'EU Consumer Protection 2.0: The Regulatory Gap: Consumer Protection in the Digital Economy: Addendum to the Report "Structural Asymmetries in Digital Consumer Markets"'; Lex Zard and Alan M. Sears, 'Targeted Advertising and Consumer Protection Law in the European Union', (2023) 56(3) *Vanderbilt Journal of Transnational Law*, 799–852; Natali Helberger and others, 'Digital Fairness for Consumers'.

62 Hereinafter, references will be to the consolidated version (28 May 2022) of the UCPD.

commercial practices, thereby enhancing consumer protection and promoting cross-border trade, particularly for small and medium-sized enterprises. The UCPD establishes restrictions for a wide range of unfair business practices, including to provide consumers with false information or to employ aggressive marketing techniques in an attempt to influence their choices. The Directive prohibits techniques intended to limit consumers' freedom of choice or conduct with regard to a product, thereby distorting their economic behaviour.

The scope of the UCPD is broad. It applies to the totality of business-to-consumer transactions, covering online intermediaries, including social media, online market places and app stores, search engines, comparison tools, and other traders operating in the digital sector, before, during, and after a commercial transaction in relation to a product.[63] Article 2(d) UCPD defines business-to-consumer commercial practices as 'any act, omission, course of conduct or representation, commercial communication including advertising and marketing, by a trader, directly connected with the promotion, sale or supply of a product to consumers'.

In 2021, the EU Commission adopted a Commission Notice on the interpretation and application of the UCPD ('UCPD Guidance'), exploring in more detail unfair advertising practices online.[64] The UCPD Guidance is not legally binding; however, it provides additional information on how to interpret the UCPD. In Section 4.2.7 of the UCPD Guidance, the Commission outlines that the UCPD applies to data driven business-to-consumer commercial practices, including tracking, targeting, algorithmic personalisation, and dynamic optimisation, complementing other instruments in the EU legal framework, such as the GDPR. Targeted advertising practices based on MDTs are therefore within the scope of the UCPD and have to be compliant with the Directive's regime. The UCPD applies to all of Sarah and Drew's scenarios (a), (b), and (c).

In scenario (b), the algorithm is not only used to target ads based on MDTs but also to personalise the content of people's social media feed and to keep people longer on the platform by giving preference to up-setting or controversial posts. Ethically, these practices may be questionable or perceived as unfair. However, they do not qualify as business-to-consumer commercial practices in a narrow sense. These practices are not 'directly connected with the promotion, sale or supply of a product', as required by Article 2(d) UCPD. They are not within the scope of the UCPD.

A possible approach for how to include these kinds of practices within the scope of the UCPD has been suggested by BEUC. BEUC recommends expanding the

[63] Pursuant to Article 2(c) UCPD, 'product' includes digital services and digital content.

[64] EU Commission, Guidance on the Interpretation and Application of Directive 2005/29/EC of the European Parliament and of the Council Concerning Unfair Business-to-Consumer Commercial Practices in the Internal Market (2021/C 526/01) <https://eur-lex.europa.eu/legal-content/EN/TXT/?uri=oj:JOC_2021_526_R_0001> accessed 30 January 2025.

definition of 'transactional decision' in the UCPD.[65] Following BEUC's recommendation, the concept of transactional decision should

> reflect all cases where the behaviour of the consumer is connected to the revenue-earning model of the trader. In other words, if the business model is that of providing unpaid access to a social media platform, where various types of interaction of the consumer with the platform (e.g., clicking on ads and other content, scrolling the newsfeed, sharing, liking) are monetised, engaging in such types of interaction should be treated as transactional decisions on the part of the consumer.[66]

If the notion of transactional decisions in the UCPD were adapted accordingly, the use of MDTs for the personalisation of content and for giving preference to certain posts to keep people longer on the platform in scenario (b) would be within the scope of the UCPD. However, without a similar adaptation, it is not.

In scenario (c), the personalisation of music lists based on mind data is not an act or a communication 'directly connected with the promotion, sale or supply of a product'; instead, this feature is a key element of the product itself. It is not within the scope of the UCPD, either.

The UCPD combines a mix of general and specific prohibitions of unfair commercial practices. Broadly, advertising practices are considered unfair if they are employed to manipulate consumers into actions contrary to their better judgement, their will, or their interests, or without their awareness, leading to an economic disadvantage. Article 5(2) UCPD is a safety net that prohibits any unfair practice, which is not caught by other provisions of the UCPD, that is to say, practices that are neither misleading, nor aggressive, nor listed in Annex I UCPD.[67] The provision addresses commercial practices, which are contrary to the requirements of professional diligence,[68] and likely to materially distort the purchasing behaviour of the average consumer.[69] Article 5(3) UCPD sets the general level of protection higher if the commercial practice is targeting vulnerable groups of consumers. Article 5(4) UCPD prohibits misleading and aggressive practices pursuant to Articles (6) to (9)

[65] The definition in Article 2(k) UCPD reads that transactional decision means: 'any decision taken by a consumer concerning whether, how and on what terms to purchase, make payment in whole or in part for, retain or dispose of a product or to exercise a contractual right in relation to the product, whether the consumer decides to act or to refrain from acting'.

[66] BEUC, 'EU Consumer Protection 2.0. Protecting Fairness and Consumer Choice in a Digital Economy', (2022), 10 <www.beuc.eu/sites/default/files/publications/beuc-x-2022-015_protecting_fairness_and_consumer_choice_in_a_digital_economy.pdf> accessed 8 January 2025.

[67] EU Commission, Guidance on the Interpretation and Application of Directive 2005/29/EC, 37.

[68] Article 2(h) UCPD defines 'professional diligence' as: 'the standard of special skill and care which a trader may reasonably be expected to exercise towards consumers, commensurate with honest market practice and/or the general principle of good faith in the trader's field of activity'.

[69] Article 2(e) UCPD defines the meaning of 'to materially distort the economic behaviour of consumers' as: 'using a commercial practice to appreciably impair the consumer's ability to make an informed decision, thereby causing the consumer to take a transactional decision that he would not have taken otherwise'.

UCPD. Article 5(5) UCPD points to Annex I UCPD with its blacklist of explicitly prohibited practices.

The most straightforward way to identify Sarah and Drew's scenarios as unfair commercial practices would be to find them, expressis verbis, on the UCPD blacklist. Annex I UCPD contains an exhaustive list of practices, which are considered unfair under all circumstances without a case-by-case assessment.[70] Alas, MDTs or the inferring and processing of mind data are not mentioned in Annex I UCPD, none of the items on the blacklist of Annex I UCPD is exactly suitable for the practices in Sarah and Drew's scenarios. Article 5(5) UCPD is therefore not applicable.

Article 5(3) UCPD addresses groups of consumers 'who are particularly vulnerable [...] because of their mental or physical infirmity, age or credulity in a way which the trader could reasonably be expected to foresee'. Arguably, none of the criteria for vulnerability mentioned in Article 5(3) UCPD is appropriate for Sarah and Drew's scenarios or for the employment of MDTs in general. The list in Article 5(3) UCPD is however indicative and non-exhaustive.[71] The UCPD Guidance introduces novel dimensions within the concept of vulnerability, particularly in the context of online practices, which are of possible interest for the employment of MDTs as they, inter alia, refer to the collection of data on moods[72]: 'Multi-dimensional forms of vulnerability are particularly acute in the digital environment, which is increasingly characterised by data collection on socio-demographic characteristics but also personal or psychological characteristics, such as interests, preferences, psychological profile and mood.'[73]

The UCPD Guidance acknowledges that in the digital age, vulnerability is no longer a static phenomenon but rather fluid, dynamic, situational:

> The concept of vulnerability in the UCPD is dynamic and situational, meaning, for instance, that a consumer can be vulnerable in one situation but not in others. For example, certain consumers may be particularly susceptible to personalised persuasion practices in the digital environment, while less so in brick-and-mortar shops and other offline environments. The use of information about

[70] Recital 17 UCPD.

[71] Recital 19 UCPD.

[72] For the concept of vulnerability in the digital age in consumer and data protection law, see, for instance, Nadine Bol and others, 'Vulnerability in a Tracked Society: Combining Tracking and Survey Data to Understand Who Gets Targeted with What Content', (2020) 22(11) *New Media & Society*, 1996–2017 <https://doi.org/10.1177/1461444820924631>; Gianclaudio Malgieri and Jędrzej Niklas, 'Vulnerable Data Subjects', (2020) 37 *Computer Law & Security Review*, 105415 <https://doi.org/10.1016/j.clsr.2020.105415>; Natali Helberger and others, 'Choice Architectures in the Digital Economy: Towards a New Understanding of Digital Vulnerability', (2022) 45 *Journal of Consumer Policy*, 175–200 <https://doi.org/10.1007/s10603-021-09500-5>; Christine Riefa, 'Protecting Vulnerable Consumers in the Digital Single Market', (2022) 33 *European Business Law Review*, 607–634 <https://doi.org/10.54648/eulr2022028>; Gianclaudio Malgieri, *Vulnerability and Data Protection Law* (Oxford 2023; online edn, Oxford Academic) <https://doi.org/10.1177/1461444820924631>.

[73] EU Commission, Guidance on the Interpretation and Application of Directive 2005/29/EC, 35.

> the vulnerabilities of specific consumers or a group of consumers for commercial purposes is likely to have an effect on the consumers' transactional decision. Depending on the circumstances of the case, such practices could amount to a form of manipulation in which the trader exercises 'undue influence' over the consumer, resulting in an aggressive commercial practice prohibited under Articles 8 and 9 of the UCPD. When assessing the presence of undue influence, according to Article 9(c) one should take into account the exploitation of any specific misfortune or circumstance of such gravity as to impair the consumer's judgement, of which the trader is aware.[74]

Knowledge about consumers' emotions, intentions, and thoughts allows traders to target them at the very time or situation when they are most susceptible, exploiting their specific moments of weakness, impairing their judgement, and luring them into purchase decisions they would not otherwise take. Inferring consumers' mind data and targeting them with corresponding personalised ads makes them vulnerable in exactly this dynamic and situational way. An OECD report on consumer vulnerability in the digital age gives the very targeting of mental states as an example for the increasing vulnerability of consumers with regard to advertising.[75]

However, for being granted the higher level of protection of Article 5(3) UCPD, the vulnerable group must be 'clearly identifiable'. This criterion will be hard to fulfil, as there is no common denominator for that group other than that their mind data is inferred – all the rest is dynamic and situational. Moreover, the assessment for Article 5(3) UCPD should be based on the perspective of the average member of that clearly identifiable group, not just the average consumer. It is hard to define what the average member of that group would be like and to what extent they would be different to the normal average consumer. In theory, the considerations about this new notion of digital vulnerability can only be supported; in practise, its impact on the application of Article 5(3) UCPD appears still limited.[76]

Applying Article 5(4) UCPD could prove to be more promising for the use of MDTs for advertising. Article 5(4) UCPD prohibits misleading and aggressive commercial practices. Contrary to the blacklist in Annex I UCPD, all other unfair practices must undergo a case-by-case assessment and be evaluated in the context of an average consumer, including misleading and aggressive practices. The benchmark for the average consumer is that they are 'reasonably well-informed and reasonably observant and circumspect, taking into account social, cultural and linguistic factors'.[77]

74 EU Commission, Guidance on the Interpretation and Application of Directive 2005/29/EC, 100.

75 OECD, Consumer Vulnerability in the Digital Age, *OECD Digital Economy Papers*, No. 355, 25, OECD Publishing, (2023) <https://doi.org/10.1787/4d013cc5-en>.

76 On the practical limits of the current concept of vulnerability in the UCPD and the nature of digital vulnerability as a universal condition that can potentially affect anyone at any time, see particularly, Helberger and others, 'Choice Architectures in the Digital Economy'.

77 Recital 18 UCPD.

Article 6 and 7 UCPD specify misleading actions and omissions, among them hidden commercial practices. In Sarah and Drew's scenario (a), the targeted ads appear in the middle of a written chatbot conversation. Inserting targeted ads in the middle of a conversation with a chatbot could arguably blur the line between advertisement and the service of the chatbot. However, for ads to be compliant with Article 6 e-Commerce Directive 2000/31/EC, they have to be clearly recognisable. Additionally, Article 7(2) UCPD considers practises misleading where the trader 'fails to identify the commercial intent of the commercial practice if not already apparent from the context, and where, in either case, this causes or is likely to cause the average consumer to take a transactional decision that he would not have taken otherwise'. Provided therefore, the case-by-case assessment finds that the ads are clearly identifiable as commercial content, as required by the law, inserting ads in the middle of a conversation does not qualify per se as a misleading hidden practice pursuant to Article 7(2) UCPD. The same applies for the ads in the middle of a newsfeed in scenario (b) and the EEG-based ads played in the middle of a music playlist in scenario (c).

Articles 8 and 9 UCPD specify aggressive commercial practices. Article 8 UCPD stipulates that a commercial practice is aggressive

> if, in its factual context, taking account of all its features and circumstances, by harassment, coercion, including the use of physical force, or undue influence, it significantly impairs or is likely to significantly impair the average consumer's freedom of choice or conduct with regard to the product and thereby causes him or is likely to cause him to take a transactional decision that he would not have taken otherwise.

Applied to the employment of MDTs in our examples, the practices in scenarios (a), (b) and (c) would be aggressive if, (i) by undue influence; (ii) they impaired or were likely to impair an average consumer's freedom of choice or conduct; and (iii) thus caused them to take a transactional decision, for example a purchase decision.

First, the practice needs to (i) exert undue influence. Article 2(j) UCPD defines the term undue influence as 'exploiting a position of power in relation to the consumer so as to apply pressure, even without using or threatening to use physical force, in a way which significantly limits the consumer's ability to make an informed decision'. In all of Sarah and Drew's scenarios, traders exploit their position of power to infer and process mind data for targeted advertising. Consumers have not been informed in any of the examples about the inference and processing of their mind data. The practices are employed without their knowledge; hence, they cannot object or end them. According to the UCPD Guidance, the exploitation of power imbalance is one of the exacerbating elements of unfair commercial practices in the digital world.[78] Article 9(a) UCPD stipulates that also the nature of the

[78] EU Commission, Guidance on the Interpretation and Application of Directive 2005/29/EC, 100.

practise must be taken into account when determining whether a practice applies undue influence. The nature of the practice of inferring and processing mind data to target ads is very opaque. Moreover, the UCPD Guidance explicitly mentions that knowledge about the vulnerabilities of specific consumers is likely to have an effect on their transactional decision and that these practices can amount to a form of manipulation where traders exert undue influence.[79] MDTs allow traders to target consumers exactly at a point in time when they are most susceptible and to tailor the most suitable ad accordingly; thus, using MDTs for advertisement allows traders to benefit from the weakest points of consumers. Hence, the employment of MDTs can be considered as exercising a form of undue influence.

Second, these practices have to (ii) significantly impair or be likely to significantly impair an average consumer's freedom of choice or conduct. By inferring mind data and using the inferences to target ads, MDTs reveal the perfect individual pressure point of consumers to traders. Traders thus apply psychological or emotional pressure, limiting people's ability to make an informed decision. BEUC even strengthens this argument in their opinion on consumer protection 2.0, saying that knowledge about the individual pressure points and the fluctuation of emotional states in real time allows the trader to manipulate consumers into purchasing decisions as easy as to deny them access to products or services when they do not match the desired race or gender.[80] Hence, the employment of MDTs is also likely to significantly impair an average consumer's freedom of choice or conduct.

The impaired freedom of choice or conduct shall (iii) lead to a transactional decision. The MDTs used in Sarah and Drew's examples are all intended to make consumers buy a product or a service they would not have bought otherwise. Considering the impact of emotions on decision-making, it can be argued that MDTs are likely to cause consumers to make a purchase decision. The Commission itself points out in their UCPD Guidelines that the use of information about consumers' vulnerabilities is likely to have an effect on their transactional decisions they would not have otherwise taken.[81]

In summary, the practices in scenarios (a), (b), and (c) exert undue influence, significantly impairing the average user's freedom of choice or behaviour and influencing consumers' purchasing decisions. These practices exploit a position of power, employing psychological and emotional pressure, and abusing the situational vulnerability of the consumer. They limit the consumer's ability to make an informed decision. The opacity adds to the unfairness of these practices.

Sarah and Drew's scenarios are illustrative examples of how MDT's can typically be utilised in advertising. Consequently, the arguments go well beyond the

79 EU Commission, Guidance on the Interpretation and Application of Directive 2005/29/EC, 100.

80 BEUC, 'EU Consumer Protection 2.0. Protecting Fairness and Consumer Choice in a Digital Economy', 3.

81 EU Commission, Guidance on the Interpretation and Application of Directive 2005/29/EC, 100.

individual examples discussed, encompassing the broader landscape of MDT usage in advertising in its entirety. The analysis provides grounds to argue that the utilisation of MDTs for advertising should be categorised as an aggressive commercial practice as such, due to the intrusiveness, the technical opaqueness, and the fact that they are typically employed without the consumers' knowledge. The power imbalance and knowledge asymmetry undoubtedly play crucial roles in the assessment, too. It is questionable whether merely disclosing the use of MDTs for advertising would rectify this form of commercial practice.[82] There is reason to believe that even with comprehensive disclosure, the situation would not be substantially alleviated, given the complexity of the underlying system and procedures.[83] Simply asking for consent/explicit consent, pursuant to the GDPR, will unlikely solve the problem. In fact, the analysis above supports advocating a general prohibition of inferring and processing mind data for business-to-consumer transactions and including them in the existing blacklist of Annex I UCPD, as per Article 5(5) UCPD. Such a provision could be formulated as follows:

> **Annex I UCPD, Aggressive commercial practices:**
> **32. (new):** Inferring and processing mind data.

The layout of scenario (b) adds more complexity to the analysis. In scenario (b), mind data is merged with a seemingly unlimited amount of other data sets, contributing to the development of a psychographic consumer profile,[84] which encompasses consumers' interests, preferences, moods, and vulnerabilities. This psychographic profile is then leveraged to employ manipulative personalised persuasion practices, as referred to by the Commission in their UCPD Guidance.[85] The Commission delineates the boundaries between normal persuasive advertising or sales techniques and unfair practices as follows:

> Persuading consumers to engage with the trader's content is an essential part of commercial practices and of advertising in particular, both in the online and offline world. However, the digital environment enables traders to employ their practices more effectively on the basis of consumer data, with high scalability and even dynamically in real time. Traders can develop personalised persuasion practices

[82] See also Karina Grisse, 'Recommender Systems, Manipulation and Private Autonomy: How European Civil Law Regulates and Should Regulate Recommender Systems for the Benefit of Private Autonomy', in S. Genovesi and others (eds.), *Recommender Systems: Legal and Ethical Issues*, International Library of Ethics, Law and Technology, Vol. 40 (Springer 2023) <https://doi.org/10.1007/978-3-031-34804-4_6>.

[83] BEUC, 'EU Consumer Protection 2.0. Protecting Fairness and Consumer Choice in a Digital Economy', 4.

[84] A 'psychographic profile' is a detailed profile, mapping a person's personality, biases, and vulnerabilities. See BEUC, 'EU Consumer Protection 2.0. Protecting Fairness and Consumer Coice in a Digital Economy', 11.

[85] EU Commission, Guidance on the Interpretation and Application of Directive 2005/29/EC, 99.

> because they benefit from superior knowledge based on aggregated data about consumer behaviour and preferences, for example by linking data from different sources. Traders can also have the possibility to make adjustments to improve the effectiveness of their practices, as they continuously test the effects of their practices on consumers and thereby learn more about their behaviour (e.g. through A/B testing). Furthermore, such practices could often be employed without the full knowledge of the consumer. It is the presence of these factors and their opaqueness that distinguishes, on the one hand, highly persuasive advertising or sales techniques from, on the other hand, commercial practices that may be manipulative and, hence, unfair under consumer law. In addition, they may be in breach of transparency obligations under GDPR or the ePrivacy Directive.[86]

A possible approach to stop targeted advertising practices based on psychographic profiles, including, inter alia, the inference and processing of mind data, could entail an immediate ban of these practices under the UCPD, similar to the ban suggested above for the inference and processing of mind data. BEUC, for instance, proposes to extend the blacklist in Annex I by adding 'the use of psychographic profiles or similar to exercise emotional or psychological pressure' to the list of explicitly prohibited practices.[87]

Such a ban would also be in alignment with the expectations and wishes of consumers. Consumers perceive tracking and commercial surveillance as unjust. According to a study by BEUC, less than one-fifth of consumers (19%) believe it is fair for individuals to be subjected to targeted ads and content based on details about their lives, weaknesses, and vulnerabilities.[88] A significant portion, half of the consumers (50%), deems this practice unfair.

The prohibition of psychographic profiles would affect the deployment of MDTs in all cases where the inferred mind data is combined with other data sets to build such a psychographic profile. This would be the case in scenario (b). However, the sole prohibition of targeted advertising based on psychographic profiling would fail cases that do not build an entire psychographic profile but only rely on the inferences by MDTs, as is the case in scenario (a) and (c). Putting pervasive tracking on the blacklist should be considered along with the previously mentioned ban for the inference and processing of mind data as such, as they essentially address different (albeit sometimes overlapping) objectives.

Completing the analysis, dark patterns in online advertising practices should also be addressed briefly. Dark patterns represent a specific type of unfair commercial

86 EU Commission, Guidance on the Interpretation and Application of Directive 2005/29/EC, 100.

87 BEUC, 'EU Consumer Protection 2.0. Protecting Fairness and Consumer Choice in a Digital Economy', 12. A similar call to ban psychographic profiles was also suggested in Helberger and others, 'EU Consumer Protection 2.0: Structural Asymmetries', 79.

88 BEUC, 'Connected, but Unfairly Treated: Consumer Survey Results on the Fairness of the Online Environment', (2023), 10 <www.beuc.eu/sites/default/files/publications/BEUC-X-2023-113_Fairness_of_the_digital_environment_survey_results.pdf> accessed 8 January 2025.

practice. Dark patterns encompass tactics or tricks deliberately designed to push or mislead consumers into actions that do not align with their true desires or could be even detrimental to them – all to the advantage of the advertiser. A primary characteristic for dark patterns is their hidden, subtle, and manipulative nature. They invade consumers' privacy, causing economic harm or a cognitive burden (e.g. frustration induced by the time, energy, and attention spent unnecessarily).[89] While nudging techniques help users make decisions that align with their presumed medium- or long-term preferences or promote overall societal goals, dark patterns influence decisions solely in favour of the advertiser's agenda. Therefore, dark patterns are also referred to as dark nudging.[90]

In the context of emotions and psychological states, relevant forms of dark patterns include emotional stirring/steering, toying with emotions, and confirmshaming. Emotional steering involves manipulating or exploiting a person's emotions. It is employed to persuade or pressure individuals into taking actions they might not otherwise choose if they were making a rational, unemotional decision. The forms vary and include using emotionally charged language, imagery, or design elements to create a sense of urgency, fear, excitement, or desire. The EDPB describes emotional steering as:

> [u]sing wording or visual elements (such as style, colours, pictures or others) in a way that confers the information to users in either a highly positive outlook, making users feel good, safe or rewarded, or in a highly negative one, making users feel scared, guilty or punished. Influencing the emotional state of users in such a way is likely to lead them to make an action that works against their data protection interests.[91]

For instance, a website might use aggressive pop-up messages with alarming language to get users to subscribe to a service or make a purchase. By evoking emotions like fear of missing out, emotional steering aims to influence the user's decision. Confirmshaming refers to the manipulative practice of applying emotional pressure – often through guilt, fear, or insecurity – to discourage users from opting out of an offer or subscription. It typically appears when users are asked to confirm their choice to decline, often through language that subtly or overtly shames them for doing so.

Dark patterns are not mentioned expressis verbis in the main text of the UCPD or in Annex I UCPD. Dark patterns are, however, referred to in the UCPD Guidance. Therein, they are described as 'a type of malicious nudging, generally incorporated

89 Francisco Lupiáñez-Villanueva and others, 'Behavioural Study on Unfair Commercial Practices in the Digital Environment: Dark Patterns and Manipulative Personalisation', Final Report (European Commission), (2022), 90.

90 Mario Martini and others, 'Dark Patterns', (2021) 01 *Zeitschrift für Digitalisierung und Recht*, 52.

91 EDPB, Guidelines 03/2022 on Deceptive Design Patterns in Social Media Platform Interfaces: How to Recognise and Avoid Them, Version 2.0, Adopted on 14 February 2023, 67.

into digital design interfaces'.[92] In the same vein, the EDPB describes dark patterns in their Guidelines on Dark patterns in social media platform interfaces as 'interfaces and user experiences implemented on social media platforms that lead users into making unintended, unwilling and potentially harmful decisions regarding the processing of their personal data'.[93] Traditional dark patterns are therefore inherently associated with design interfaces leading users to make harmful decision regarding the processing of their personal data.

Over time, the term 'dark patterns' began evolving. Version 2 of the EDPB Guidelines formerly on 'dark patterns' transforms the term in its title into 'deceptive design patterns', defining these as:

> interfaces and user journeys implemented on social media platforms that attempt to influence users into making unintended, unwilling and potentially harmful decisions, often toward a decision that is against the users' best interests and in favour of the social media platforms interests, regarding the processing of their personal data. Deceptive design patterns aim to influence users' behaviour and can hinder their ability to effectively protect their personal data and make conscious choices.[94]

An even broader notion of deceptive and manipulative practices has been developed in the DSA and the AIA.[95]

5.3 AVMSD: ADS USING SUBLIMINAL TECHNIQUES ARE PROHIBITED

Complementing the general framework of the UCPD, the Audiovisual Media Services Directive (AVMSD) (Directive (EU) 2010/13, amended by Directive (EU) 2018/1808), applies in contexts or scenarios where audiovisual commercial communication is shared.[96] The Directive is specifically aimed at regulating television broadcasts, on-demand audiovisual media services, and audiovisual commercial communication.[97] Following a revision of the original Directive in 2018, the

92 EU Commission, Guidance on the Interpretation and Application of Directive 2005/29/EC, 101.

93 EDPB, Guidelines 3/2022 on Dark Patterns in Social Media Platform Interfaces: How to Recognise and Avoid Them, Version 1.0, Adopted on 14 March 2022, 2.

94 EDPB, Guidelines 03/2022 on Deceptive Design Patterns in Social Media Platform Interfaces: How to Recognise and Avoid Them, Version 2.0, Adopted on 14 February 2023, 3.

95 New regulatory approaches to such practices will be discussed in the concluding sections on the DSA and the AIA towards the end of use case 3 in Chapter 6.

96 Directive 2010/13/EU on the Coordination of Certain Provisions Laid Down by Law, Regulation or Administrative Action in Member States Concerning the Provision of Audiovisual Media Services (Audiovisual Media Services Directive), OJ L 95/1; Directive (EU) 2018/1808 of the European Parliament and of the Council of 14 November 2018 amending Directive 2010/13/EU on the Coordination of Certain Provisions Laid Down by Law, Regulation or Administrative Action in Member States Concerning the Provision of Audiovisual Media Services (Audiovisual Media Services Directive) in View of Changing Market Realities, OJ L 303/69. Hereinafter, references will refer to the consolidated version (18/12/2018).

97 Article 2(1) in conjunction with Article 1(1) AVMSD.

AVMSD also applies to video-sharing platform services, including certain social media services.[98]

In the context of MDT-based advertising, the provisions on audiovisual commercial communication may become relevant. The Directive intends to ensure that audiovisual commercial communication is clearly identifiable.[99] Further, the AVMSD prohibits certain types of content (e.g. tobacco advertising), protects minors from content that may harm their physical, mental, or moral development, and limits the quantity of advertising per hour and the interruption of programming by ads.

Article 9(1)(b) AVMSD provides that audiovisual communications shall not use subliminal techniques. Subliminal techniques in the context of the AVMSD are understood as commercial manipulation techniques that are designed to circumvent the users' awareness.[100] Subliminal techniques try to influence users subconsciously by operating below the threshold of normal perception, making them covert and not apparent to the viewer. Given the opaque functioning and intrusive effects of MDTs, this provision may be relevant.

Article 1(1)(h) AVMSD defines audiovisual commercial communication as 'images with or without sound which are designed to promote, directly or indirectly, the goods, services or image of a natural or legal person pursuing an economic activity', citing television advertising, sponsorship, teleshopping, and product placement as prominent examples. Essentially, audiovisual commercial communication under the AVMSD refers to various forms of advertising and promotional activities that are integrated into audiovisual content. Importantly, the definition of audiovisual commercial communication under the AVMSD primarily refers to audiovisual content – to the ads themselves, their content, and their compliance with content-related rules – rather than to the mechanisms used to target those ads to specific audiences. While regulating the content and presentation of audiovisual commercial communication, the AVMSD does not specifically cover targeting practices.

Applying the AVMSD to Sarah and Drew's scenarios requires a differentiated analysis. Scenario (c) is an audio streaming platform, tailoring music and targeting

98 Article 1(1)(aa) AVMSD determines the criteria for video sharing platforms: either the provision of audiovisual content is the principal purpose of the service or it is an essential functionality of the service. Recital 5 AVMSD refers to the inclusion of social media services, explaining that regulating social media services as such is not the Directive's objective. However, social media services will be covered 'if the provision of programmes and user-generated videos constitutes an essential functionality of that service'. In further explanation to the essential functionality criterion, the Commission published: Guidelines on the Practical Application of the Essential Functionality Criterion of the Definition of a 'Video-Sharing Platform Service' under the Audiovisual Media Services Directive (2020/C 223/02).

99 Article 9(1)(a) AVSMD.

100 Maja Cappello (ed.), *New Actors and Risks in Online Advertising*, IRIS Special, European Audiovisual Observatory, Strasbourg, 2022, 33. Report on the Novelties of the Audiovisual Media Services Directive (AVMSD) and Its Relevance for National Legislative Transposition, (2023), 88 <www.osce.org/files/f/documents/a/1/539114.pdf> accessed 17 May 2024.

ads based on users' mind data. Being an audio medium, scenario (c) does not contain visual content as in 'images with or without sound' (Article 1(1)(h) AVMSD). Hence, it cannot display audiovisual commercial communication. Scenario (a) is a ticketing chatbot, engaging in written conversation and targeting ads based on mind data. Scenario (b) is a social media platform, enhancing the personalisation of content and the targeting of ads with mind data. Both scenarios could potentially display audiovisual commercial communication. However, even if they did, it is worth noting that the MDTs in scenarios (a) and (b) are not used as an integral part of the image or the audiovisual content itself. They do not form part of the television advertising, sponsorship, teleshopping, or product placement itself. The MDTs serve rather to decide which audiovisual content to display, to whom, and when.

In both scenarios (a) and (b), the MDTs may be considered as part of subliminal targeting practices. However, the 'images with or without sound which are designed to promote, directly or indirectly, the goods, services or image of a natural or legal person pursuing an economic activity' (i.e. the audiovisual commercial content) are not using MDTs as a subliminal technique to circumvent the users' awareness. Therefore, even if Sarah and Drew's scenarios (a) and (b) involved audiovisual commercial communication, the prohibition in Article 9(1)(b) AVMSD would not apply to their targeting practices.

In cases where MDTs are indeed used as an integral part of audiovisual commercial communication, the AVMSD and the prohibition of subliminal techniques for audiovisual commercial communication may apply.

In addition to established legislation, new horizontal laws, particularly the Digital Services Act and the Artificial Intelligence Act, are expected to impact targeted advertising in the coming years. Given the evident similarities between commercial and political advertising, along with the definition of advertisement in the Digital Services Act, which encompasses both types of practices, a collective analysis will be provided after preliminary reflections on MDTs used in the context of political advertising.

6

Use Case 3: Political Advertising

Is There a Higher Bar for Political Advertisers?

Beyond their use in commercial settings, MDTs harbour remarkable potential within the intricate landscape of political practices. As with commercial companies, political players are keen on establishing a recognisable brand, with a focus on expanding their base of party supporters and voters, especially as elections approach.

Throughout history, political parties and candidates have employed various methods to communicate and build relationships with different segments of potential voters. Traditional political communication addresses a mass audience through media channels such as TV or radio, which tend to be expensive and demanding in terms of production.[1] In contrast, tailored online communication targets individuals through online channels and requires considerably fewer financial investments. Strategically, social media-based online political campaigns confer distinct advantages over traditional counterparts, especially beneficial for smaller political parties. Their cost-effectiveness, coupled with precision-targeting strategies, makes them highly attractive to political actors.

In many European countries, political parties utilise online political advertising for electoral purposes. In the twenty weeks leading up to the 2019 European Parliament elections, €43 million were dedicated to advertising on platforms such as Facebook, Instagram, Google, and YouTube.[2] Investments for political advertising spent on Google in Europe between March 2019 and January 2022 were highest in Germany (€5.35 million), followed by Hungary (€2.96 million) and the Netherlands (€2.43 million).[3] Global spending on online political advertising reached US$522.5 billion in 2021, with projections anticipating an increase to US$836 billion by 2026.[4]

1 F. J. Zuiderveen Borgesius and others, 'Online Political Microtargeting: Promises and Threats for Democracy', (2018) 14(1) *Utrecht Law Review*, 82–96 <https://doi.org/10.18352/ulr.420>.

2 European Council, 'Transparency and Targeting of Political Advertising' (2023) <www.consilium.europa.eu/en/infographics/political-advertising/> accessed 8 January 2025.

3 European Council, 'Transparency'.

4 European Council, 'Transparency'.

Online targeting mechanisms promise to exert a strong influence on people during political discourse or democratic electoral processes.[5] The advent of big data analytics and modelling has expanded access to political inferences well beyond the capabilities of traditional databases, involving methods that neither the entity collecting the data nor the data subject could have imagined in the past. Even if users provide only a limited set of distinct data points, there is a likelihood that these data points are combined, resulting in the creation of second and even third generations of data about them.[6] By collecting a tangled net of data points, such as website visits, time spent on these sites, and user likes, a detailed psychographic voter profile is gradually formed, including inferences about political leanings.

The outcomes can be surprisingly detailed. In a study examining the Facebook likes of nearly 60,000 participants, researchers managed to determine political party affiliations with an 85 per cent accuracy rate.[7] A separate UK-based study utilised an algorithm that correctly identified political leanings in 86 per cent of cases based on Twitter activity. An analysis of individuals' Twitter engagement, including retweets and hashtag use, achieved a 91 per cent accuracy rate in pinpointing political affiliations. Another study demonstrated the ability to predict political ideology with high accuracy based solely on a user's activity in non-political discussion forums. For instance, the frequent use of the word 'feel' was found to correlate with economically left-wing views.

In the context of democratic decision-making and electoral processes, political psychographic profiling is often referred to as 'online political microtargeting'. In essence, online political microtargeting describes the practice of online behavioural advertising within a political context.[8] Political parties apply microtargeting to choose and promote policy views matching the preferences or interests of the voters; they employ it to mobilise voters in times of an election, referendum, or protest; and they use it at moments when people are most susceptible to influence their political opinion. The potential impact of online political microtargeting has become evident in recent election cycles. The Facebook Cambridge Analytica data scandal stands as an early example, vividly displaying the magnitude and repercussions that can arise from the improper use of online political microtargeting. Reportedly, Cambridge Analytica used psychological profiles of 87 million Facebook users in support of the

5 At the same time, it should be noted that scholars are starting to question whether the effect of targeted political advertising is indeed living up to its promises. Some countries appear to show a countermovement, shifting away from targeting ultra-niche audiences. See Kobi Hackenburg and Helen Margetts, 'Evaluating the Persuasive Influence of Political Microtargeting with Large Language Models', PNAS, (2024) 121(24) *Political Sciences*, e2403116121 <https://doi.org/10.1073/pnas.2403116121>; Jim Waterson, '"Show This to Everyone": UK Political Ads Move Away from Microtargeting', *The Guardian* (31 May 2024) <www.theguardian.com/politics/article/2024/may/31/show-this-to-everyone-uk-political-ads-move-away-from-microtargeting> accessed 8 January 2025.

6 EDPS, Opinion 3/2018 on Online Manipulation and Personal Data, 15.

7 For the following examples in this paragraph, see Solove, 'Data Is What Data Does', 1106–1107.

8 Zuiderveen Borgesius and others, 'Online Political Microtargeting'.

presidential campaigns of Ted Cruz and Donald Trump in an attempt to gain an advantage over political rivals.[9]

Utilised responsibly, online political microtargeting has the capacity to promote democratic values and instigate positive changes within society. At their core, they serve as a dynamic conduit for establishing connections, imparting information, and mobilising individuals who may otherwise be indifferent to political affairs. Reportedly, Facebook's get-out-the-vote button, first used in the USA in 2008, has proven effective in marginally boosting voter turnout.[10] Facebook provided a link to find local polling places, featured a clickable 'I Voted' button, and included a counter indicating how many other Facebook users reported voting. Enhanced with a 'social message', such as profile pictures or messages of close friends, the techniques work even better.

Conversely, the power of online political microtargeting can also be misused, jeopardising democratic values and principles. These practices often fuel disinformation campaigns that exacerbate societal division. They selectively amplify certain messages, while marginalising others, potentially chilling freedom of expression and fostering self-censorship. Additionally, they pose risks of limiting access to diverse information sources for specific groups or individuals, which harm the pluralism of perspectives in public debate and impede overall access to information.[11] The primary risks of online microtargeting in political practices include potential discrimination and exclusion of individuals or groups of people, as well as possible manipulation of their behaviour or political decisions as citizens.[12] The impact of such practices is thus far more profound compared to mere commercial practices, as they can undermine the democratic electoral process and public political opinion.[13]

Political microtargeting claims to help push voters toward desired political attitudes and voting choices, profiting not only from their ignorance and biases but also from their emotional weak spots. The EDPB notes accordingly:

> Certain targeting approaches may however go so far as to undermine individual autonomy and freedom, e.g. by delivering individualized messages designed to exploit or even accentuate certain vulnerabilities, personal values or concerns. For example, an analysis of content shared through social media can reveal information about the emotional state (e.g. through an analysis of the use of certain key words). Such information could be used to target the individual with specific messages and

9 Sam Meredith, 'Facebook-Cambridge Analytica: A Timeline of the Data Hijacking Scandal', CNBC (10 April 2018) <www.cnbc.com/2018/04/10/facebook-cambridge-analytica-a-timeline-of-the-data-hijacking-scandal.html> accessed 8 January 2025.

10 Vian Bakir, 'Psychological Operations in Digital Political Campaigns: Assessing Cambridge Analytica's Psychographic Profiling and Targeting', (2020) 5(67) *Frontiers in Communication*, 3 <https://doi.org/10.3389/fcomm.2020.00067>.

11 EDPB, Guidelines 8/2020 on the Targeting of Social Media Users, 6.

12 EDPB, Guidelines 8/2020, 5.

13 See Sartor and others, 'Regulating Targeted and Behavioural Advertising', 26.

> at specific moments to which he or she is expected to be more receptive, thereby surreptitiously influencing his or her thought process, emotions and behaviour.[14]

Enhanced with MDTs, targeting mechanisms can be tailored to pinpoint moments when people are most susceptible, leveraging insights into their inner state of mind to craft more resonant and impactful campaigns and mobilise supporters. The ability to discern psychological states at specific moments or in specific contexts – be it related to a candidate, party, or a particular political agenda – emerges as a formidable asset in the political arena. The use of MDTs thus represents a powerful tool with substantial potential for refining political advertising.

6.1 GDPR: CONSENT REMAINS PREVALENT

In the EU, 'data revealing political opinions' qualifies as special category data pursuant to Article 9(1) GDPR. In addition to the legal basis, it therefore requires an exemption from the general prohibition of processing special category data. However, the classification of data as data revealing political opinions recalls much of the discussion earlier in the book surrounding health-related inferences.[15]

The GDPR does not provide a legal definition of political opinion. The phrase used in the GDPR ('revealing [...] political opinions') suggests that the legislators intended for a broad interpretation of the term. The distinction between data revealing political opinion and data that does not is increasingly blurred. One of the biggest challenges is that, with sufficient data and the right algorithm, seemingly random non-sensitive data points can be used to infer political opinions, thus transforming into sensitive data.

For years, Sarah and Drew have been members of a movement advocating for actions to stop the climate crisis. Given the urgency of the cause, the movement wants to participate in the next communal elections. Being a small, local movement, they do not have substantial financial resources. Sarah and Drew have an idea: They could develop a software similar to the one described above for scenario (b) in use case 2, Chapter 5, *this time fine-tuned for political microtargeting.*

> **Scenario (d)**: *a software collecting information about individuals who frequently like and share articles or documentaries about environmental-friendly topics (e.g. nature, animals), and push dislike buttons/angry emojis on non-environmental-friendly issues (e.g. traffic jams, long-distance flights). The software is enhanced with keystroke dynamics analysis. In moments when the users appear most angry and upset, they will be displayed targeted ads featuring the movement, its cause, and the up-coming elections.*

---

[14] EDPB, Guidelines 8/2020, 6.

[15] See use case 1, Chapter 4, on mental health and well-being.

In principle, non-verbal indicators such as social media likes can qualify as data revealing political opinions if they enable a reliable and secure inference of an individual's political views.[16] Hence, the likes/dislikes, emojis, shares, and also the keystroke dynamics in Sarah and Drew's scenario (d) could be classified as data revealing political opinions – provided they allow for a secure inference. For a clear categorisation, the circumstances and context of each individual case must be taken into account.[17] In scenario (d), the likes, shares, emojis for articles, and documentaries on nature, animals, traffic jams, or long-distance flights, as well as the keystroke dynamics, all considered separately and without additional context or substance, do not enable a reliable and secure inference. By themselves, these original data points (also referred to as 'input data') – the single likes/dislikes, shares, emojis, and the keyboard dynamics – are not specific enough to be classified as data revealing political opinions. However, when combined and observed over a longer period of time, an algorithm will be able to infer one's political opinion from these data points. Data analytics can thus transform the non-sensitive data points into sensitive inferences (referred to as 'output data'). Additionally, the purpose of processing ought to be considered. The purpose of merging and processing all these data points in scenario (d) is to reveal and influence data subjects' political opinion and affiliation.

Processing of data revealing political opinions, including for targeted advertising, can only be lawful if it meets one of the exemptions to the general prohibition of processing according to Article 9(2) GDPR, in addition to having a legal basis pursuant to Article 6(1) GDPR. Relevant exemptions in the context of political advertising include explicit consent (lit a), legitimate activities by a foundation, association or any other not-for-profit body with a political aim (lit d), data manifestly made public (lit e), and substantial public interest (lit g).[18] Once more, the analysis will at first explore all options other than (explicit) consent.

Article 9(2)(d) GDPR stipulates that processing of special category data is lawful if 'carried out in the course of its legitimate activities with appropriate safeguards by a foundation, association or any other not-for-profit body with a political, philosophical, religious or trade union aim'. The provision could be relevant as it applies to controllers who are a political party, including non-profit foundations or similar groups with a purpose to permit the exercise of fundamental freedoms.[19] Sarah and Drew's movement aims to participate in the next communal elections, it therefore falls under this provision. The movement might even argue that the processing is carried out in connection with the broader purpose of the organisation. However, the exception is limited to processing that 'relates solely to the members or to former

[16] Alexander Schiff, Article 9, Margin Number 20-23 in Eugen Ehmann and Martin Selmayr (eds.), *DS-GVO Datenschutz-Grundverordnung, Beck'sche Kurz-Kommentare* (3rd edn, C. H. Beck 2024).

[17] Schiff, Article 9, Margin Number 20–23 in Ehmann and Selmayr, *DS-GVO*.

[18] See also EDPS, Opinion 3/2018 on online manipulation and personal data, 5–6.

[19] Recital 51 GDPR.

members of the body or to persons who have regular contact with it in connection with its purposes and that the personal data are not disclosed outside that body without the consent of the data subjects'.[20] Thus, the scope is restricted to internal data processing by the organisation; any disclosure of the data that goes beyond the organisation to another controller requires a different legal basis. Consequently, lit d is not an appropriate legal basis for inferring and processing mind data in the context of unsolicited political microtargeting of random strangers. In Sarah and Drew's scenario (d), the users whose data is collected are not members of the movement. The processing is not for internal data processing by the organisation. Hence, mind data in scenario (d) cannot be inferred and processed based on lit d.

Article 9(2)(g) GDPR allows processing of special category data for public interest. Considering that democratic formation of opinion, democratic procedures, and elections are, broadly speaking, all in the public interest, this legal basis could potentially be applicable for Sarah and Drew's scenario (d). For Article 9(2)(g) GDPR to serve as a valid legal basis, the public interest needs to be 'substantial'.[21] Recital 46 GDPR mentions humanitarian emergencies and disasters as examples of a substantial public interest, but neither of these apply to scenario (d). Recital 56 GDPR is more closely related to political procedures and refers to electoral activities where the operation of the democratic system requires political parties to collect personal data on people's political opinions. Provided appropriate safeguards are in place, such processing would mean a substantial public interest. The substantial public interest would have to pass a balancing test between these public interests and the risks for the data subject.[22] The threshold for the balancing test is high; less intrusive means must be considered for the exception to be valid.

However, scenario (d) does not match the example provided in Recital 56. Even when arguing that the processing occurs, albeit very broadly, 'in the course of electoral activities', it is not the operation of a democratic system, which requires that 'political parties compile personal data on people's political opinions'. Moreover, the employment of MDTs for political microtargeting would not pass the balancing test due to severe infringements of data subjects' fundamental rights and freedoms, including privacy, data protection, and freedom of thought. These infringements are serious, with no safeguards mentioned by Sarah and Drew and less intrusive means available. For instance, there are less intrusive forms of targeted advertising, such as segmented or contextual advertising, alongside a multitude of offline forms of advertising that do not necessitate building an online profile including mind data. Therefore, lit g is not an appropriate legal basis for processing mind data in scenario (d).

20 Article 9(2)(d) GDPR.

21 Article 6(e) GDPR only requires normal public interest.

22 Ludmila Georgieva and Christopher Kuner, Article 9 in Kuner and others, *The EU General Data Protection Regulation (GDPR)*.

Pursuant to Article 9(2)(e), special category data may be processed when the data subject has manifestly made the data public. Examples for 'making public' include publishing data in the mass media, posting data on social network platforms, or similar. However, for the data to be 'manifestly' made public, an affirmative act is required by the data subject, and they must realise that this would be the result.[23] The mere existence or presence of certain data in public space does not qualify as a publication in the sense of lit e.[24] Attention has to be placed on whether the data is indeed accessible for an unlimited number of people (or just a limited number of friends or members of a group) and without significant admission barrier.[25] For publications on social media, the default settings of the platform, as well as its nature and scope, hold particular relevance.[26]

The previously discussed case *Meta Platforms Inc and Others* v *Bundeskartellamt* (C-252/21) brings more detail to the interpretation of lit e. Upon the question whether it falls within the scope of this provision when a user of an online social network visits websites or apps, enters information into those sites or apps, or clicks integrated 'Like' or 'Share' buttons, the CJEU recalls that this provision has to be interpreted strictly (section 74). Overall, the court takes a remarkably nuanced position, depending on whether the settings (if and to what extent the interaction is public) may be determined by the individual (section 81).

> When the users concerned actually have that choice, they can be regarded, when they voluntarily enter information into a website or app or when they click or tap on buttons integrated into them, as manifestly making public, within the meaning of Article 9(2)(e) of the GDPR, data relating to them only in the circumstance where, on the basis of individual settings selected with full knowledge of the facts, those users have clearly made the choice to have the data made accessible to an unlimited number of persons, which it is for the referring court to ascertain.[27]
>
> Where he or she enters information into such websites or apps or where he or she clicks or taps on buttons integrated into those sites and apps, such as the 'Like' or 'Share' buttons or buttons enabling the user to identify himself or herself on those sites or apps using login credentials linked to his or her social network user account, his or her telephone number or email address, that user manifestly makes public, within the meaning of Article 9(2)(e), the data thus entered or resulting from the clicking or tapping on those buttons only in the circumstance where he or she has explicitly made the choice beforehand, as the case may be on the basis of individual settings selected with full knowledge of the facts, to make the data relating to him or her publicly accessible to an unlimited number of persons.[28]

[23] Georgieva and Kuner, Article 9 in Kuner and others, *The EU General Data Protection Regulation (GDPR)*.

[24] Schiff, Article 9, Margin Number 46–47 in Ehmann and Selmayr, *DS-GVO*.

[25] Sebastian Schulz, Article 9, Margin Number 32–33 in Peter Gola and Dirk Heckmann (eds), *Datenschutz-Grundverordnung VO EU 2016/679 Bundesdatenschutzgesetz* (3rd ed. C.H. Beck 2022).

[26] Andras Jori, Article 9, Margin Number 58 in Spiecker gen. Döhmann and others, *General Data Protection Regulation. Article-by-Article Commentary*.

[27] C-252/21 *Meta Platforms Inc and Others* v *Bundeskartellamt*, section 82.

[28] C-252/21 *Meta Platforms Inc and Others* v *Bundeskartellamt*, section 85.

As regards scenario (d), it would be for a court to assess, on a case-by-case basis, whether the platform offers the necessary individual settings and, additionally, whether the data subjects 'on the basis of individual settings selected with full knowledge of the facts [...] have clearly made the choice to have the data made accessible to an unlimited number of persons'.[29] Predefined design settings on social media platforms that favour options where everything is set to 'public' unless pro-actively changed would not fall in this category. On the contrary, the data subject has to explicitly make the choice beforehand, otherwise the data cannot be considered made public. Moreover, the court requires the shares and likes to be made available to an unlimited number of people. Preferences where users decide to make their shares, likes, emojis, or posts available only to their friends, or to a selected group of friends, would therefore not fall within the scope of lit e.

But even if the users in Sarah and Drew's scenario (d) were found to have pro-actively and explicitly chosen, with full knowledge of the facts, to make their likes, shares, and so on, available to an unlimited number of people, the court restricts the applicability of the provision to 'the data thus entered or resulting from the clicking or tapping on those buttons'. Therefore, the court is only referring to the data originally entered (input data). The original data points in scenario (d) consist merely of individual likes, shares, emojis, and keyboard dynamics. The input data in scenario (d), considered separately and bare of additional context, does not reveal political opinions. Only the inferred data (output data) does.

As regards the keyboard dynamics, this data is not made publicly available by the data subject at all. It is observed data, but not data that is made public with an affirmative act. The data subjects are likely not aware that this data is collected, nor are they aware of the results, that is to say, that their allegedly aggressive keyboard dynamics will be used to enhance the impact of political microtargeting. In sum, lit e is not applicable for the processing in scenario (d).

Following the analysis, the only remaining legal basis for processing mind data for political microtargeting in scenario (d) is explicit consent. This ultimately aligns with what the WP29 already concluded in 2010 in their opinion on behavioural advertising in the context of another type of special category, namely sexual preference:

> [I]f an ad network provider processes individual behaviour in order to 'place him/her' in an interest category indicating a particular sexual preference they would be processing sensitive data under Article 8 of Directive 95/46/EC. This Article prohibits the processing of sensitive data except in certain, specific circumstances. In this context, the only available legal ground that would legitimize the data processing would be explicit, separate prior opt-in consent ex Article 8(2)(a). [...] To lawfully collect and process this type of information, ad network providers would have

[29] C-252/21 *Meta Platforms Inc and Others* v *Bundeskartellamt*, section 82.

to set up mechanisms to obtain explicit prior consent, separate from other consent obtained for processing in general.[30]

Finally, Article 22 GDPR on profiling in the context of solely automated decision-making must be revisited. Regarding commercial practices, the main concern was that ads are commonly not perceived as having a legal or similarly significant effect on the data subject. However, this aspect must be re-examined in the context of political microtargeting. The formation of political opinion and the influence on people's voter behaviour are crucial for our democratic procedures. As illustrated by the Cambridge Analytica scandal, the manipulation of large numbers of voters can result in outcomes that jeopardise the resilience of our democratic systems. The EDPB notes in their Statement on the use of personal data in the course of political campaigns that, indeed, '[p]rofiling connected to targeted campaign messaging may in certain circumstances cause "similarly significant effects" and shall in principle only be lawful with the valid explicit consent of the data subject'.[31] The Commission argues accordingly in their Guidance on the application of Union data protection law in the electoral context that, '[g]iven the significance of the exercise of the democratic right to vote, personalised messages which have for instance the possible effect to stop individuals from voting or to make them vote in a specific way could have the potential of meeting the criterion of significant effect'.[32]

For special category data under Article 22 GDPR, only explicit consent and substantial public interest qualify as legal basis. Since substantial public interest has already been ruled out as an option, explicit consent is the only remaining option, both pursuant to Article 9 and Article 22 GDPR.

In conclusion, processing mind data for the purpose of political advertising requires the data subject's explicit consent. Processing operations for political advertising without such consent are not in compliance with the GDPR and thus unlawful.

6.2 UCPD: COMMERCIAL FAIRNESS IS NO CRITERION FOR POLITICAL ADS

Unlike commercial advertising, political advertising does not lie within the scope of the UCPD. Pursuant to Article 3(1) UCPD, the Directive only applies to business-to-consumer commercial practices. These practices involve commercial communication by a trader, directly connected with the promotion, sale, or supply of a

30 WP 171, 20.

31 EDPB, Statement 2/2019 on the Use of Personal Data in the Course of Political Campaigns, Adopted on 13 March 2019, 2 <https://edpb.europa.eu/sites/default/files/files/file1/edpb-2019-03-13-statement-on-elections_en.pdf> accessed 8 January 2025.

32 EU Commission, Guidance on the Application of Union Data Protection Law in the Electoral Context, COM(2018) 638 final <https://eur-lex.europa.eu/legal-content/EN/TXT/HTML/?uri=CELEX:52018DC0638&from=DE> accessed 8 January 2025.

product to consumers. Political advertising is not about business-to-consumer activities. Moreover, unfair commercial practices need to materially distort the economic behaviour of consumers, while political advertising does not involve economic decisions or distort the economic behaviour of a person. The UCPD is therefore not applicable.

Instead, the EU legislators have adopted a new sector-specific law, addressing online political advertising: the Regulation on the Transparency and Targeting of Political Advertising (TTPA).

6.3 TTPA: LIMITED PRACTICAL EFFECT

The stakes and implications of online political advertising are more profound than those of commercial advertising, as they can undermine the democratic process and influence political opinion. However, legislators must tread carefully when they consider regulating this sector, given that online political advertising falls within the scope of the fundamental right to freedom of expression and information.[33] Any limitations on political practices must therefore be approached with greater nuance compared to solely commercial practices, due to potential infringements of this fundamental right and other fundamental rights aimed at ensuring and safeguarding our democratic rights and freedoms.

The European Court of Human Rights (ECtHR) in Strasbourg has affirmed that Article 10 of the European Convention on Human Rights (ECHR) protects the freedom of expression of political parties, consistently emphasising that limitations on political speech are subject to the most rigorous standard of scrutiny, which leaves minimal leeway for restrictions.[34] Any such restriction must undergo a narrow interpretation, and its necessity must be convincingly established. As a consequence, legislators at both national and Union level have shown a very cautious approach towards setting limits on political practices. Until now, harmonised EU legislation in the domain of political targeting and advertising has primarily consisted of general frameworks like the GDPR, complemented by specific guidance and soft law.[35]

33 See Zuiderveen Borgesius and others, 'Online Political Microtargeting'. For an overview of ECHR's case law, see Research and Library Division, 'Article 10 Expression and Advertising of Political Positions through the Media/Internet in the Context of Elections/Referendums', (2018) <https://web.archive.org/web/20210205175235/> and <www.echr.coe.int/Documents/Research_report_expression_advertising_media_elections_ENG.pdf> accessed 8 January 2025.

34 Zuiderveen Borgesius and others, 'Online Political Microtargeting'.

35 EU Commission, Guidance on the Application of Union Data Protection Law in the Electoral Context, COM(2018) 638 final; EU Commission, Communication Tackling Online Disinformation: A European Approach COM(2018) 236 final <https://eur-lex.europa.eu/legal-content/EN/TXT/?uri=CELEX:52018DC0236> accessed 8 January 2025; EU Code of Practice on Disinformation (2018) <https://ec.europa.eu/newsroom/dae/document.cfm?doc_id=54454> accessed 8 January 2025; EU Commission, Guidance on Strengthening the Code of Practice on Disinformation COM(2021) 262 final <https://eur-lex.europa.eu/legal-content/EN/ALL/?uri=COM%3A2021%3A262%3AFIN>

At the national level, Member States have implemented diverse measures, ranging from complete bans on political advertising on television during electoral periods (e.g. Germany) to legal frameworks that allow for significant self-regulation or remain largely unregulated (e.g. the Netherlands).[36]

Regulatory scrutiny at Union level was particularly heightened following controversies related to online political advertising practices during the Brexit referendum and the first election of Donald Trump. The breakdown of open public discourse and the deprivation of information rights for individuals that were not specifically targeted by advertisements called for more harmonised rules. In 2024, EU legislators adopted the Regulation on the Transparency and Targeting of Political Advertising (TTPA), representing the very first attempt to implement EU-wide rules on political practices.[37]

The TTPA introduces modest constraints on data utilisation for targeting and enhanced transparency obligations. The Regulation aims to address disinformation agencies, restrict targeting in political advertising, and de-amplify disinformation in platform recommender systems, mitigating the viral spread of borderline content and conspiracies.

The TTPA is intended to complement the Digital Services Act, which will be discussed in Section 6.4:

> Compared to the DSA, it [the TTPA, comment added] expands the categories of information to be disclosed in the context of political advertising, as well as the scope of the relevant service providers concerned. While the DSA imposes transparency requirements on online platforms, this initiative covers the entire spectrum of political advertising publishers, as well as other relevant service providers involved in the preparation, placement, promotion, publication and dissemination of political advertising. There is complementarity and synergies with the requirement under the DSA to have assessments of systemic risks by very large online platforms stemming from the functioning and use of systems for selecting and displaying advertisement, with actual or foreseeable effects related to electoral processes.[38]

accessed 8 January 2025; EU Strengthened Code of Practice on Disinformation (2022) <https://digital-strategy.ec.europa.eu/en/library/2022-strengthened-code-practice-disinformation> accessed 30 January 2025. This 2022 Strengthened Code of Practice is meant to become part of a broader regulatory framework, particularly in combination with the Regulation on Transparency and Targeting of Political Advertising and the Digital Services Act.

36 See Max Zeno van Drunen and others, 'The Beginning of EU Political Advertising Law: Unifying Democratic Visions through the Internal Market', (2022) 30(2) *International Journal of Law and Information Technology*, 181–199 <https://doi.org/10.1093/ijlit/eaac017>.

37 Regulation (EU) 2024/900 of the European Parliament and of the Council of 13 March 2024 on the Transparency and Targeting of Political Advertising, OJ L 2024/900.

38 European Commission, Explanatory Memorandum on the Proposal for a Regulation of the European Parliament and of the Council on the Transparency and Targeting of Political Advertising, (2021) <https://eur-lex.europa.eu/legal-content/EN/TXT/HTML/?uri=CELEX:52021PC0731> accessed 8 January 2025.

Within the political context, the TTPA has a broader scope than the DSA, not only addressing online media but also traditional offline media, such as newspapers, television, and radio.[39] The definition of political advertising in the TTPA is remarkably expansive, covering the 'preparation, placement, promotion, publication, delivery or dissemination, by any means, of a message, normally provided for remuneration or through in-house activities or as part of a political advertising campaign'.[40] Remuneration is considered the norm for political advertising, but not entirely indispensable; for instance, Recital 1 TTPA mentions that: '[p]olitical advertising can take many forms, including paid content, sponsored search results, paid targeted messages, promotion in rankings, promotion of something or someone integrated into content, such as product placement, influencers and other endorsements. Related activities can involve [...] the publication of content against payment or other forms of remuneration, including benefits in kind.'[41]

Primarily, the TTPA's transparency requirements bind providers of political advertising services. In addition, the regulation also puts disclosure obligations on sponsors of political ads. One main point of critique is that the TTPA places the responsibility to identify a political ad on sponsors and providers of advertising services, pursuant to Article 7 and 8 TTPA and enhanced by Article 15 TTPA, which outlines procedures for potentially unlawful political ads and requirements for very large online platforms and search engines. This leaves considerable leeway for sponsors and providers of advertising services who take their responsibilities lightly or wish to circumvent the obligations.

Concerning the use of MDTs for political practices, Chapter 3 TTPA focuses on the targeting and ad delivery of online political advertising. Ad delivery techniques are defined in Article 3(12) TTPA as 'optimisation techniques that are used to increase the circulation, reach or visibility of a political advertisement on the basis of the automated processing of personal data and that can serve to deliver the political advertisement to a specific person or group of persons only'. The use of MDTs for targeting political ads, such as in Sarah and Drew's scenario (d), is an optimisation technique relying on automated processing, used to deliver ads to a specific person or group of persons. It therefore falls within the scope of the respective provisions.

Article 18 TTPA restricts the targeting and ad delivery techniques to the following conditions:

(a) the controller collected the personal data from the data subject
(b) the data subject has provided explicit consent
(c) those techniques do not involve profiling as defined in Article 4(4) GDPR using special categories of personal data.[42]

39 Recital 2 TTPA.
40 Article 3(2) TTPA.
41 Recital 1 TTPA.
42 Article 18(1) TTPA.

Notably, the TTPA limits the legal basis for processing to explicit consent. Thus, data manifestly made public or any of the other options discussed above are no longer a possible legal basis. The exception for internal communication by political parties and non-profits is kept up by Article 18(3) TTPA. The details surrounding explicit consent are outlined in Article 18(4) TTPA. Article 18(2) provides a full ban for targeting and ad delivery for data subjects at least one year under the voting age.

Unfortunately, the TTPA will have only limited impact on pervasive forms of tracking and ad delivery, in particular the deployment of MDTs as a stand-alone practice or as part of political microtargeting. The ban in Article 18(1)(c) TTPA is restricted to profiling based on special category data. The ban does not address inferred or observed data that is sensitive as a result of the profiling. Any form of a more comprehensive ban discussed before and during the legislative process has failed to succeed in the negotiations for a political agreement. The critical point is, however, that data brokers or big social media providers do not require profiling that relies on special category data. With the necessary computational capacity and data analytics, sensitive inferences can easily be drawn based on normal personal data. The EDPS itself states:

> More advanced profiling practices allow scoring or assessing people against benchmarks of predefined patterns of normal behaviour. An example of such applications is a hiring software that analyse an applicant's voice in order to evaluate 'language proficiency, fluency, critical thinking, and active listening'. Another example is how typing patterns on a computer keyboard serve as a ground for predicting person's confidence, nervousness, sadness, and tiredness. A particular feature of such inference is that highly sensitive data like a person's emotional state can be predicted from seemingly non-sensitive information, such as his keystroke dynamics.[43]

Mind data qualifies only in specific cases as special category input data. The effect of the introduced ban on the deployment of MDTs as a stand-alone political practice therefore will be only minimal. Similarly, political microtargeting that includes MDTs as part of the psychographic profile will not be affected unless the profiling uses special category input data. In both cases, the TTPA falls short of significant improvements. Applied to scenario (d), the input data, the likes/dislikes, shares, emojis, and keyboard dynamics by themselves are not special category data. Only when combined, tracked over a longer period of time, and considering additionally the purpose of processing, does the non-sensitive input data transform into sensitive output data.

Based on the rationale of unfair commercial practices law and the preceding analysis, legislators could have opted for an approach analogous to the UCPD, introducing a blacklist for political practices within the TTPA. The parallels between political and commercial practices, especially regarding the prohibition of unfair

[43] EDPS, Opinion 3/2018 on Online Manipulation and Personal Data, 8.

political practices, have been previously explored in scholarly discussions.[44] The EPDS similarly noted that 'activities which amount to manipulating persons with misinformation, personalising political arguments based on intrusive personal profiles' bear clear resemblances to malpractices addressed in consumer law.[45] Unfair commercial practice law has a long-standing tradition in delineating the conditions distinguishing unlawful manipulation from lawful persuasion. Building upon this experience, certain persuasive political practices could have been argued to necessitate a ban akin to the blacklist in the UCPD.

In their Opinion on the TTPA, the EDPS recommended a ban on political microtargeting, which would prohibit targeted advertising based on 'pervasive tracking, i.e. the processing of information concerning an individual's behaviour across websites and services with a view of advertising on the basis of profiling'.[46] The EDPS's call to end political microtargeting aligns with surveys regarding this practice. A majority of people disapprove of political microtargeting when they are aware of it. In the UK, a 2019 YouGov survey commissioned by the pro-privacy group Open Rights Group (ORG) revealed that 58 per cent of the national sample opposed tailoring election ads based on personal data analysis to categorise people into groups.[47] In the US, an even higher percentage, 72 per cent, expressed opposition to internet companies providing information about users to political campaigns for targeted online ads, according to a poll conducted by Knight Foundation-Gallup in December 2019; only 20 per cent of US adults support allowing campaigns access to limited, broad details like gender, age, or postal code.[48] In the EU, according to a public consultation in the context of the European Democracy Action Plan (EDAP), microtargeting of political content is an important topic for most respondents, 83 per cent would like to see clear criteria for microtargeting (e.g. public disclosure, transparency), with 69 per cent of the respondents favouring strict limitations for these criteria.[49]

If EU legislators had implemented the ban as requested by the EDPS, using MDTs to enhance political microtargeting would no longer comply with the law. Additionally, prohibiting the use of MDTs as stand-alone political practice, similar to the proposed ban under the UCPD, could have been considered pro-actively.

44 Natali Helberger and others, 'Towards Unfair Political Practices Law: Learning Lessons from the Regulation of Unfair Commercial Practices for Online Political Advertising', (2021) 12(3) *Journal of Intellectual Property, Information Technology and E-Commerce Law*, 273–296.

45 EDPS, Opinion 3/2018 on Online Manipulation and Personal Data, 17.

46 EDPS, Opinion 2/2022 on the Proposal for Regulation on the Transparency and Targeting of Political Advertising (20 January 2022), 10.

47 Bakir, 'Psychological Operations', 11.

48 Bakir, 'Psychological Operations'.

49 Report on the Public Consultation for the European Democracy Action Plan (EDAP), (2 December 2020), 8–9 <https://commission.europa.eu/system/files/2020-12/report_edap_public_consultation_final.pdf> accessed 8 January 2025.

However, as matters are, the impact of the TTPA on the regulation of MDTs used for political practices is very limited. Section 6.4 on the DSA, which follows, shows additional safeguards are implemented in horizontal legislation, potentially restricting the employment for MDTs in this domain.

6.4 DSA: DIFFICULTIES IN MEETING THE HIGH EXPECTATIONS

Over the last legislative period, the EU has introduced several new pieces of legislation in a comprehensive effort to modernise and strengthen the regulatory framework for the evolving digital landscape. In response to societal challenges that are going beyond the protection of individual personal data and informational self-determination, the EU adopted new flagship legislations, aiming to establish conceptual regulatory benchmarks. Among these, the Digital Services Act (DSA) and the Digital Markets Act (DMA) are instrumental.

The DSA and the DMA are crafted as a unified set of rules, regulating the responsibilities of digital services that act as intermediaries to connect consumers with goods, services, and content. Together they form the Digital Services Act Package. Their main goal is to make the internet a safer digital space, in which the fundamental rights of all users of digital services are respected and protected, while fostering innovation and competitiveness in the European Single Market. The DSA focuses on enhancing accountability for digital services, particularly for large online platforms. The Act introduces new obligations to combat illegal content, protects users' fundamental rights, and ensures transparency in content moderation practices. The DMA tackles concerns related to the market power of certain large online platforms, often referred to as 'gatekeepers'. The aim is to promote fair competition, prevent unfair practices, and create a level playing field for businesses operating in the digital market.

One of the key aspects in both legal acts is their commitment to strengthening consumer protection in the digital age. The EU Commission has expressed strong ambitions to strengthen consumer rights by adopting the European consumer agenda as a strategic vision on consumer policy.[50] Hence, the adopted acts include measures to improve transparency in online advertising, in particular personalised advertising, and to enhance users' control over their online experience. Due to its practical relevance for the use of MDTs in targeted online advertising, the following analysis will focus on the Digital Services Act.

The DSA was published on 27 October 2022 and came into force on 16 November 2022.[51] For very large online platforms and very large online search engines it came

[50] EU Commission, 'New Consumer Agenda: European Commission to Empower Consumers to Become the Driver of Transition', (Press Release 13 November 2020) <https://ec.europa.eu/commission/presscorner/detail/en/ip_20_2069> accessed 8 January 2025.

[51] Regulation (EU) 2022/2065 of the European Parliament and of the Council of 19 October 2022 on a Single Market For Digital Services and amending Directive 2000/31/EC (Digital Services Act). OJ L 277/1.

into effect on 25 August 2023, to other entities it became fully applicable on 17 February 2024. The DSA is directly applicable across the EU,[52] and aims to ensure a safe and innovative online environment, harmonising rules for intermediary services in the internal market and protecting fundamental rights. The DSA amends but does not replace the e-Commerce Directive (2000/31/EC).[53] One of the main objectives of the DSA is consumer protection, highlighted prominently in Article 1(1) DSA. The regulation establishes rules to regulate social media, online marketplaces, very large online platforms (VLOPs) and very large online search engines (VLOSEs). Larger intermediary services with a substantial societal impact, that is to say, VLOPs and VLOSEs, are subject to stricter rules.

Digital services governed by the DSA include a large category of online services, from simple websites to internet infrastructure services and online platforms. Most relevant for MDTs, the DSA applies to advertising on online intermediaries and platforms, such as online marketplaces, social networks, content-sharing platforms, app stores, online travel and accommodation platforms, or collaborative economy platforms.

Recalling Sarah and Drew's ideas for MDTs in the context of commercial and political practices:

Scenario (a): *a text-based chatbot for a medium-sized ticketing platform. The chatbot handles ticket sales, facilitates access to content, provides notifications of events as well as updates on postponements and cancellations, and infers people's emotional state and their emotional reaction from the written interaction to target ads;*

Scenario (b): *a software for a very large social media platform, which combines mind data from written posts and likes/dislikes/emojis with other information from across websites (if and how long users watch certain videos/ads, what they click, what they search for, etc.) for personalising the content of the users' social media feed and displaying targeted ads in the timeline. Additionally, the algorithm gives preference to sad/controversial posts to increase people's social media engagement and the time they stay on the platform;*

Scenario (c): *EEG-based earbuds as a special promotional tie-in for subscriptions to a music streaming platform. The earbuds personalise the music playlist and target ads based on users' inferred emotions.*

Scenario (d): *a software similar to scenario (b) for political micro-targeting. The software collects information about individuals who frequently like and share environmental-friendly content, and push dislike buttons/angry emojis on non-environmental-friendly content. It is enhanced with keystroke dynamics analysis. In moments when the users appear most angry and upset, they will be displayed targeted political ads.*

---

52 Article 2 (1) DSA provides that the regulation applies to 'intermediary services offered to recipients of the service that have their place of establishment or are located in the Union, irrespective of where the providers of those intermediary services have their place of establishment'.

53 Article 2(3) in conjunction with Article 89 DSA.

6.4.1 *Targeted Advertising*

Targeted online advertising is largely disseminated through online intermediaries. According to Article 3(g) DSA, intermediary services means information society services, including mere conduit services, caching services, and hosting services. An 'online platform' is a sub-category of hosting services,[54] legally defined by Article 3(i) DSA as a hosting service that stores and disseminates information to the public, excluding minor and purely ancillary features or functionalities that are integrated into another service for objective and technical reasons. All deployments in Sarah and Drew's scenarios are designed for online platforms. Scenario (a) is designed for a medium-sized ticketing platform; scenario (b) is for a very large social media platform; scenario (c) is for a music streaming platform; and scenario (d) is again for a very large social media platform. All four scenarios are therefore within the scope of the DSA.

Article 3(r) DSA defines advertisement as: 'information designed to promote the message of a legal or natural person, irrespective of whether to achieve commercial or non-commercial purposes, and presented by an online platform on its online interface against remuneration specifically for promoting that information'. This definition is remarkably broad, it is not limited to purely commercial promotion but applies also to non-commercial promotional information, including political practices. Key point is an explicit link between the platform and the remuneration for the promotion. This required direct link to remuneration may be problematic with regard to influencer marketing,[55] but it is of negligible relevance for MDTs, which are typically embedded in classical online advertising tools.

The DSA provides several rules that are applicable to targeted advertising. Particularly relevant is Article 26 DSA, which addresses advertising on online platforms. Paras 1 and 2 require the platform to put enhanced transparency rules in place in real time. Para 1 stipulates that platform providers must ensure that: (a) the information is clearly marked as an advertisement, that (b) information is given on whose behalf the advertisement is presented, and (c) who paid for it, and that (d) meaningful information is provided about the parameters used to determine the recipient of the advertisement and how to change them. Recital 68 DSA elaborates on the details, stating that providers of online platforms

> should ensure that the recipients of the service have certain individualised information necessary for them to understand when and on whose behalf the advertisement is presented. They should ensure that the information is salient, including through standardised visual or audio marks, clearly identifiable and unambiguous for the

[54] Recital 13 DSA.

[55] See Bram Duivenvoorde and Catalina Goanta, 'The Regulation of Digital Advertising under the DSA: A Critical Assessment', (2023) 51 *Computer Law & Security Review* <https://doi.org/10.1016/j.clsr.2023.105870>.

> average recipient of the service, and should be adapted to the nature of the individual service's online interface. In addition, recipients of the service should have information directly accessible from the online interface where the advertisement is presented, on the main parameters used for determining that a specific advertisement is presented to them, providing meaningful explanations of the logic used to that end, including when this is based on profiling.[56]

These requirements complement and enhance existing rules, mandating that advertisements are clearly marked as such. Moreover, they aim to increase the transparency of online advertising for the consumers.

Admittedly, the new requirements mean considerable additional compliance efforts for the platform providers. Alas, the benefit for individual consumers may not be as significant as hoped – consumer research suggests that information duties generally have a limited effect in empowering consumers, as these often neglect to read, use, or comprehend the provided information.[57] Even if consumers were to read the information, it is doubtful whether it would be clear enough for them to fully understand the complex functioning of the targeting mechanisms. It is also uncertain whether this information would enable a detailed analysis of why a specific ad is being displayed to a particular individual.[58] In contrast, the information is considered crucial for research by academia and civil rights organisations to investigate certain phenomena and their causes. Furthermore, it has the potential to serve as an important prerequisite for future policymaking.[59]

For very large online platforms and online search engines, the transparency requirements will be even stricter. Pursuant to Article 33(1) DSA, platforms with a number of average monthly active recipients of the service in the Union equal to or higher than 45 million are classified as very large online platforms (VLOPs) or very large online search engines (VLOSEs). On 17 February 2023, the Commission designated the first 17 VLOPs and 2 VLOSEs.[60] This list has since been extended.[61] For illustration purposes, we assume that Sarah and Drew's scenarios (b) and (d) are used by VLOPs under the DSA.

Pursuant to Article 39 DSA, the providers in scenario (b) and (d) shall, additionally to the previously mentioned requirements, compile and make publicly available a repository until one year after the advertisement was presented for the last

[56] Recital 68 DSA.

[57] See Duivenvoorde and Goanta, 'The Regulation of Digital Advertising under the DSA', 8.

[58] Karina Grisse, Artikel 26 Margin Number 72, in Franz Hofmann and Benjamin Raue (eds.), *Digital Services Act. Gesetz über digitale Dienste* (Nomos 2023).

[59] Grisse, Artikel 26 Margin Number 72 in Hofmann and Raue, *Digital Services Act. Gesetz über digitale Dienste*.

[60] EU Commission, 'Digital Services Act: Commission Designates First Set of Very Large Online Platforms and Search Engines', (Press Release 25 April 2023) <https://ec.europa.eu/commission/presscorner/detail/en/IP_23_2413> accessed 8 January 2025.

[61] 'Supervision of the Designated Very Large Online Platforms and Search Engines under DSA' <https://digital-strategy.ec.europa.eu/en/policies/list-designated-vlops-and-vloses> accessed 3 January 2025.

time. The information to be displayed in the repository is outlined in Article 39(2) DSA and includes: (a) the content of the advertisement (name of the product, subject matter of the advertisement); (b) the natural or legal person on whose behalf the advertisement is presented; (c) the natural or legal person who paid for the advertisement (if different from point b); (d) the period during which the advertisement was presented; (e) whether the advertisement was intended to be presented specifically to one or more particular groups of recipients of the service and if so, the main parameters used; (f) the commercial communications published on the VLOPs and identified pursuant to Article 26(2); and (g) the total number of recipients reached and numbers for the group or groups of recipients that the advertisement specifically targeted. Once more, this information will likely be significant for research, policymaking, and consumer protection organisations, but less so for individual consumers.

Returning to Article 26 DSA, para 3 thereof applies not only to Sarah and Drew's scenario (b) and (d), but also to all examples. Article 26(3) DSA has often been marketed as a ban on personalised advertising, but this gives it too much credit. A granular look at the provision's small print reveals the disappointing details. Article 26(3) DSA provides that online platforms shall not present advertisements 'based on profiling as defined in Article 4, point (4), of Regulation (EU) 2016/679 using special categories of personal data referred to in Article 9(1) of Regulation (EU) 2016/679'. In other words, just like in the TTPA, the provision only bans ads where the input data of the profiling is already special category data, not the inferred data (output data).[62] Neither does Article 26(3) DSA prohibit ads based on special category data as such (not associated with profiling techniques), nor does it prohibit ads based on inferred special category data, which is sensitive as a result of the profiling.

For the limited number of cases where Article 26(3) applies, the provision does, however, mark a notable difference: The prohibition of Article 26(3) DSA is absolute; it cannot even be circumvented by consumers' consent. Hence, users cannot provide legally effective consent to being profiled and targeted with personalised ads by platforms when the input data is sensitive. Neither can the making publicly available of special category data legitimise their profiling for personalised advertisement.[63]

In Sarah and Drew's vignettes, scenario (a) is a chatbot employing text-based techniques to infer mind data. Text-based data, as specified before, is not considered biometric data. There is no association with any other special category. The input data used for profiling is therefore not special category. The general prohibition in Article 26(3) DSA has no consequence for the employment of MDTs in scenario (a).

Scenario (b) is the very large social media platform using mind data drawn from written posts, likes, dislikes, emojis, and information from across websites for

[62] Grisse, Artikel 26 in Hofmann and Raue, *Digital Services Act. Gesetz über digitale Dienste.*

[63] Grisse, Artikel 26 in Hofmann and Raue, *Digital Services Act. Gesetz über digitale Dienste.*

personalising the content of the user's social media feed and displaying targeted ads. The input data is text-based and not sensitive. The analysis yields the same result as in scenario (a). The general prohibition in Article 26(3) DSA has no consequence for the employment of MDTs in scenario (b), either. Being a VLOP, Article 39 DSA requires the platform provider to publish information about the ads in an ad repository.

Scenario (c) is a music streaming platform inferring users' emotions via EEG-based earbuds to personalise music playlists and target audio ads. By classifying brain data as special category data, Article 26(3) DSA applies. Ads based on profiling of this type of data are prohibited.

Scenario (d) is different in that the advertisement is political and not commercial. The software, Sarah and Drew want to develop, is to be employed by a very large social media platform. As outlined before, considered separately before profiling, the input data does not qualify as special category data. The prohibition of targeted advertising in Article 26(3) DSA is again not evoked. Similar to scenario (b), the social media provider is required to publish information about the ads in an ad repository pursuant to Article 39 DSA.

Regrettably, the widely but imprecisely promoted 'ban of personalised advertising' pursuant to Article 26(3) in the DSA is of very limited use for the employment of MDTs. According to reports, left-wing political groups in the European Parliament had pushed for a full ban of online microtargeting.[64] In the LIBE opinion on the draft DSA there had been a newly proposed Article 2b stipulating that '[p]roviders of information society services shall not collect or process personal data as defined in Article 4, point (1), of Regulation (EU) 2016/679 for the purpose of targeting the recipients to whom advertisements are displayed'.[65] This would have meant a full ban of collecting and processing personal data for the purpose of ad targeting. With regard to behavioural advertising, the Parliament had recommended for a stricter regulation of targeted advertising 'in favour of less intrusive forms of advertising that do not require any tracking of user interaction with content'.[66] Moreover, the Parliament had called for clear boundaries and transparency rules concerning the accumulation of data, the functioning and accountability of such targeted advertisements, a new framework for platform-to-consumer relations addressing digital

[64] Clothilde Goujard, 'European Parliament Pushes to Ban Targeted Ads Based on Health, Religion or Sexual Orientation', (*Politico* 20 January 2022) <www.politico.eu/article/european-parliament-bans-use-of-sensitive-personal-data-for-targeted-ads/> accessed 8 January 2025.

[65] EU Parliament, A9-0356/2021, Opinion of the Committee on Civil Liberties, Justice and Home Affairs <www.europarl.europa.eu/doceo/document/A-9-2021-0356_EN.html#_section5> accessed 8 January 2025.

[66] EU Parliament Resolution of 20 October 2020 with Recommendations to the Commission on a Digital Services Act: Adapting Commercial and Civil Law Rules for Commercial Entities Operating Online (2020/2019(INL)), para 15 <https://eur-lex.europa.eu/legal-content/EN/TXT/?uri=CELEX%3A52020IP0273> accessed 8 January 2025.

nudging and preferential treatment, and it had invited the Commission 'to assess options for regulating targeted advertising, including a phase-out leading to a prohibition'.[67] The EDPS had seconded this recommendation by the Parliament in their Opinion on the draft DSA, urging the legislators to consider a phase-out leading to a prohibition of targeted advertising on the basis of pervasive tracking.[68]

However, the result of the trilogue negotiations is Article 26(3) DSA in its existing wording, which only prohibits targeted advertising based on profiling of sensitive input data. Neither behavioural advertising nor pervasive tracking techniques are prohibited. Emotional targeting or emotion-based advertising is not addressed separately by the DSA.[69]

Sarah and Drew recall the biometric detection system that infers the mood of customers or passersby in a shopping mall. Based on the detected moods, the algorithm targets ads accordingly.

Article 26(3) DSA fails to address this type of deployment as well. The ban in Article 26(3) DSA addresses only the profiling of personal data. Unless the data is classified as personal data, the example falls beyond the scope of the provision before even reaching the crucial threshold distinguishing sensitive from non-sensitive data.

To a certain degree, the new legislation brings about a sense of disappointment with regard to MDT-based advertising. The DSA could have been an excellent opportunity to enhance and supplement the capabilities of the GDPR. While the GDPR's binary classifications of personal versus non-personal and sensitive versus non-sensitive data serve their purpose, they reach their limit when confronted with the challenges posed by big data and data analytics. Large platforms with vast data pools can effectively exploit consumer vulnerabilities for targeted advertising without necessarily relying on sensitive input data. This is where the DSA could have stepped in. A decisive ban on pervasive forms of personalised advertising within the DSA would have represented a more robust stance by the EU, aligning formidably with the regulation's core goals of safeguarding fundamental rights, especially bolstering consumer protection. A remaining hope lies in Article 46 DSA, specifically in the introduction of a voluntary code of conduct for online advertising at the Union level. Yet, this hope is limited by the fact that these code of conduct are to be drafted by the online platform providers themselves.

Given that the provisions addressing targeted advertising will likely have little impact on the employment of MDTs, different approaches should be explored within the DSA.

67 EU Parliament Resolution of 20 October 2020 with Recommendations to the Commission on a Digital Services Act (2020/2019(INL)), para 17.

68 EDPS, Opinion 1/2021 on the Proposal for a Digital Services Act (10 February 2021), 16.

69 See also Grisse, Artikel 26 in Hofmann and Raue, *Digital Services Act. Gesetz über digitale Dienste*.

6.4.2 *Content Moderation: Illegal Content*

Content moderation is a widely debated issue, especially for online platforms. Content moderation, legally defined by Article 3(t) DSA, encompasses a multitude of activities aimed at: 'detecting, identifying and addressing illegal content or information incompatible with their terms and conditions, [...] including measures taken that affect the availability, visibility, and accessibility of that illegal content or that information'.[70]

Essentially, the DSA adheres to the approach already outlined in the e-Commerce Directive. The service provider is not liable for any information on their platform, provided they lack actual knowledge of illegal activity or content.[71] In cases of knowledge or awareness, the provider must promptly remove or disable access to the illegal content to maintain immunity from liability. There is no general obligation for providers to monitor or actively seek indications of illegal activity in the information they transmit or store.[72] However, The DSA aims to establish clearer guidelines and obligations for online platforms regarding the monitoring and removal of illegal content. It seeks to address issues such as hate speech, terrorist content, and other illegal materials on their platforms, emphasising the importance of transparency, user empowerment, and cooperation between platforms and relevant authorities.

The extremely broad definition of illegal content in the DSA could turn out as a possible gateway for the regulation of MDTs in advertising contexts. Illegal content is defined in the DSA as: 'any information that, in itself or in relation to an activity, including the sale of products or the provision of services, is not in compliance with Union law or the law of any Member State which is in compliance with Union law, irrespective of the precise subject matter or nature of that law'.[73] Illegal content therefore extends to any information or activity that is not in compliance with EU law. Recital 12 DSA highlights that illegal content should be interpreted broadly and gives illustrative examples, including 'the sale of products or the provision of services in infringement of consumer protection law'. Unfair commercial practices are infringing consumer protection law and can therefore be considered illegal content under the DSA.[74]

Building on the previous analysis concerning the employment of MDTs in Sarah and Drew's scenarios (a), (b), and (c), their usage for targeted advertising can be

[70] Article 3(t) DSA.

[71] Article 6(1) DSA.

[72] Article 8 DSA.

[73] Article 3(h) DSA.

[74] See Duivenvoorde and Goanta, 'The Regulation of Digital Advertising under the DSA'; Franz Hofmann, Article 3(h) Margin Number 71, in Hofmann and Raue, *Digital Services Act. Gesetz über digitale Dienste*: 'Jedweder Inhalt, der im konkreten Fall in Widerspruch zu Rechtsvorschriften steht, ist rechtswidrig. Die Definition stellt dabei nicht nur auf für sich genommen rechtswidrige Inhalte ab; erfasst werden auch rechtswidrige Tätigkeiten (zB die Erbringung von Dienstleistungen unter Verstoß gegen das Verbraucherschutzrecht).'

considered as aggressive commercial practices. All three examples would therefore initiate the regime for taking down illegal content. Article 9(1) DSA on the orders to act against illegal content upon receipt of an order would be induced; Sarah and Drew's scenarios (a), (b), and (c) would cause an obligation for the online platforms to act against unfair personalised advertising, upon the receipt of an order issued by relevant national judicial or administrative authorities. Such a relevant national authority could, with regard to unfair commercial practices, be a national consumer protection authority.[75] However, the notable downside of Article 9(1) DSA is that it is subject to a case-by-case assessment. In practice, consumer authorities would have to notify platforms about individual commercial practises, which utilise MDTs. This restricts the practicability of relying on illegal content to fight the use of MDTs for targeted advertising significantly.

In addition, Article 16(1) DSA mandates that providers put mechanisms in place, which allow any individual to notify them of information that the individual considers to be illegal content. These notices are intended to give rise to actual knowledge or awareness for the purposes of Article 6 DSA on liability. Individual consumers can flag a specific content as (allegedly) illegal. Pursuant to Article 16(6) DSA, providers have to process the notices and take a decision 'in a timely, diligent, non-arbitrary and objective manner'.[76] In contrast to Article 9 DSA, Article 16 DSA gives providers a margin of discretion in their response.[77] Concerning MDTs for targeted advertising, however, Article 16 DSA provides only little assistance: Typically, consumers are neither informed nor aware that MDTs are employed for targeting. In the absence of such knowledge, they would not be able to flag the practice.

Sarah and Drew's scenario (d), the software targeting political ads, will not be affected by the provisions for illegal content under the DSA. Although the definition of advertisement under the DSA does cover political advertising, political practices are not within the scope of the UCPD. Consequently, the employment of MDTs for political advertising cannot be considered an infringement of the UCPD. The sector-specific law for political practices, the TTPA, does not entail similar provisions, which could be applied to initiate the regime for illegal content under the DSA.

Referring back to Sarah and Drew's scenarios, there was yet another issue that exceeded the current scope of the UCPD: the personalisation of content. In scenario (b), Sarah and Drew wanted their algorithm to prioritise sad or controversial posts in order to enhance users' social media engagement and increase their time spent on the platform. The UCPD does not apply to the personalisation of content, rendering it impossible to deem the practice as unfair commercial practice. In contrast, the DSA may offer alternative legal instruments that are better equipped to address these practices.

75 Duivenvoorde and Goanta, 'The Regulation of Digital Advertising under the DSA'.

76 Article 16(6) DSA.

77 Benjamin Raue, Article 16 Margin Number 3 in Hofmann and Raue, *Digital Services Act. Gesetz über digitale Dienste*.

6.4.3 *Recommender Systems*

The concept of tailoring content to resonate with individuals' emotional states, aiming to prolong their stay on a platform, is not a novel idea. As outlined before, Facebook conducted a significant psychological study in 2012, involving nearly 700,000 users.[78] In this study, Facebook intentionally manipulated the content and emotions displayed on users' timelines. Some were exposed to content containing optimistic words, while others encountered sadder content. After one week, these users exhibited a higher tendency to post words reflecting either positive or negative sentiments, corresponding to the emotional contagion they experienced on their timelines. In the media industry, it is widely acknowledged that negative news are considered more attention-worthy. Stories that disturb or provoke individuals elicit stronger reactions and higher engagement; they make people stay longer on platforms.

The personalisation of content is intricately intertwined with a larger context. Big social media platforms typically use diverse groups of content to personalise the user feeds:

- organic content: this type of content includes posts by friends, fan pages, groups or similar the user is following;
- ads (sponsored posts): paid content that is targeted according to an algorithm;
- content described as 'suggested for you': this type consists of non-sponsored posts by unfamiliar people and pages that the algorithm believes attract the attention of the user.[79]

In order to find the right mix, the providers use a recommender system. Pursuant to Article 3(s) DSA, recommender system means 'a fully or partially automated system used by an online platform to suggest in its online interface specific information to recipients of the service or prioritise that information, including as a result of a search initiated by the recipient of the service or otherwise determining the relative order or prominence of information displayed'. Sarah and Drew's algorithm to personalise user content in scenario (b), including the feature to prioritise sad or upsetting content, matches this description of a recommender system.

The DSA tackles recommender systems through a multitiered approach. Article 27 DSA provides enhanced transparency for recommender systems of online platforms. The provision stipulates that online platform providers 'shall set out in their terms and conditions, in plain and intelligible language, the main parameters used in their recommender systems, as well as any options for the recipients of the service

[78] Kramer and others, 'Experimental Evidence'.

[79] Panopytkon Foundation, 'Anxious about Your Health? Facebook Won't Let You Forget', (7 December 2023) <https://en.panoptykon.org/algorithms-of-trauma-2-anxious-about-health> accessed 8 January 2025.

to modify or influence those main parameters'.[80] Importantly, the providers are only required to disclose the main parameters, not all parameters.[81] Recital 70 DSA outlines that the parameters to be presented shall cover the key criteria in determining the information suggested to the recipient and the 'reasons for their respective importance, including where information is prioritised based on profiling and their online behaviour'. Simply put, platforms such as the platform in scenario (b) should transparently disclose the main parameters of their personalisation practices in their terms and conditions.

At first sight, the transparency requirements in Article 27 DSA appear to bring more clarity with regard to the opaque practices of recommender systems. Yet, there are notable concerns regarding their effectivity. One concern relates to the potential for information overload. The worry is that providing additional information may exacerbate information fatigue, particularly considering the intricate nature of algorithmic functioning, which can be challenging for laypersons to fully grasp.[82] Another concern is that the provider could simply decide that MDTs are not among the main parameters and is therefore not obliged to disclose their employment. Even in cases where disclosure occurs, the guidelines for providing options to influence these parameters are vague. The provider may present methods for altering the recommender system, while retaining MDTs as an integral part of it.

Equally problematic, or possibly more so, is the potential disregard by platforms for users' attempts to influence the recommender system. A case study investigating the effectiveness of features offered by Facebook to shape the recommender system revealed exactly this outcome:[83] Despite users actively employing all available tools to modify their 'preferences', such as hiding content, adjusting advertising preferences, and selecting the option 'Hide post – See fewer posts like this', the content persisted in appearing in their feed. To exacerbate matters, after a few weeks, users were confronted with even more of the content they sought to minimise.

For VLOPs, such as the one in Sarah and Drew's scenario (b), Article 38 DSA stipulates that, additionally to the requirements in Article 27 DSA, they have to provide at least one option that is not based on profiling. However, it is at the discretion of the provider to determine whether to offer users the choice of using the service entirely devoid of any personalisation – an option that may not be very user-friendly – or to provide an alternative for users that excludes the use of MDTs specifically for personalisation.

80 Article 27(1) DSA.

81 Grisse, Article 27 Margin Number 20 in Hofmann and Raue, *Digital Services Act. Gesetz über digitale Dienste*.

82 Grisse, Article 27 Margin Number 32, 33 in Hofmann and Raue, *Digital Services Act. Gesetz über digitale Dienste*.

83 Panopytkon Foundation, 'Algorithms of Trauma: New Case Study Shows That Facebook Doesn't Give Users Real Control over Disturbing Surveillance Ads', (28 September 2021) <https://en.panoptykon.org/algorithms-of-trauma> accessed 8 January 2025; Panopytkon Foundation, 'Anxious about Your Health? Facebook Won't Let You Forget', (2 December 2023).

Overall, when evaluated on a case-by-case basis, the transparency requirements for recommender systems in the DSA strike again as somewhat toothless with regard to the employment of MDTs.

A different perspective could emerge when considering the issue within a systemic context.

6.4.4 *Assessment and Mitigation of Systemic Risks*

Against the backdrop of big social media platforms and their significant influence on disseminating information and fostering public debate, coupled with the inadequacy of an individual's power to address broader structural risks, the DSA transcends the conventional GDPR approach aimed at safeguarding the subjective rights of individuals. While the GDPR predominantly concentrates on bolstering individual control over personal information and the concept of informational self-determination, the DSA introduces a novel concept to the tech sector: systemic risks. A noteworthy illustration of this novel approach can be found in Article 34 DSA.

Article 34 DSA addresses the societal risks highlighted in Recital 1 DSA. These risks stem from the ongoing digital transformation and the escalating reliance on information society services, not just impacting individual users but also society at large. Recital 79 DSA delves deeper into the influence of VLOPs and VLOSEs on shaping public opinion and discourse, emphasising how the design of these services 'is generally optimised to benefit their often advertising-driven business models and can cause societal concerns'.[84]

The term 'systemic risk' is not legally defined in the DSA and no common methodology exists yet to define systemic risks. While the term is a familiar notion in the context of financial markets, its concept and implications still demand further development for applications within the DSA.[85] The categories of systemic risks listed in Article 34 DSA are non-exhaustive. They encompass the dissemination of illegal content, adverse effects on the exercise of fundamental rights, electoral processes, and issues related to gender-based violence, mental health, and well-being.

Article 34(1) DSA outlines a three-step procedure, including the identification, analysis, and assessment of any systemic risks stemming from the design or functioning

[84] Recital 79 DSA.

[85] See Katharina Kaesling, Article 34 Margin Number 56 in Hofmann and Raue, *Digital Services Act. Gesetz über digitale Dienste*. For preliminary considerations, see also Sally Broughton Micova and Andrea Calef, 'Elements for Effective Systemic Risk Assessment under the DSA: Report', (July 2023) <https://cerre.eu/wp-content/uploads/2023/07/CERRE-DSA-Systemic-Risk-Report.pdf> accessed 8 January 2025. For a study examining a systemic risk measurement approach in the context of disinformation and the war in Ukraine, see European Commission, Directorate-General for Communications Networks, Content and Technology, Digital Services Act – Application of the Risk Management Framework to Russian Disinformation Campaigns, Publications Office of the European Union, 2023 <https://data.europa.eu/doi/10.2759/764631> 8 January 2025.

of a service and its related systems or from the use made of a service. The obligation is a lifecycle requirement, applying to the provider at least once every year, ex ante and ex post.[86] Article 34(1)(a) DSA lists illegal content as a potential systemic risk, with the legal definitions pursuant to Article 3(h) DSA applying.[87] Literature has suggested that the scale of underdisclosed advertising may amount to a systemic risk.[88]

However, Article 34 DSA also requires a proportionality test, taking into consideration the severity and probability of the systemic risk. Possible indicators for this severity and probability include 'whether the potential negative impact can affect a large number of persons, its potential irreversibility, or how difficult it is to remedy and restore the situation prevailing prior to the potential impact'.[89] Article 34(2) DSA encompasses a non-exhaustive list of criteria that shall be taken into account for the risk assessment, inter alia it lists the design of the recommender systems and any other relevant algorithmic system (lit a), the content moderation systems (lit b), and the systems for selecting and presenting advertisements (lit d).

Recital 80 DSA illustrates the specific types of illegal content that the EU legislators intended to be regarded as a systemic risk. The examples given by Recital 80 DSA include 'the dissemination of child sexual abuse material or illegal hate speech or other types of misuse of their services for criminal offences, and the conduct of illegal activities, such as the sale of products or services prohibited by Union or national law, including dangerous or counterfeit products, or illegally-traded animals'. The Recital explains further that 'such dissemination or activities may constitute a significant systemic risk where access to illegal content may spread rapidly and widely through accounts with a particularly wide reach or other means of amplification'.[90] Arguably, the examples provided by Recital 80 DSA are of a different quality and scope than the mere utilisation of MDTs by a recommender system for advertising or for personalising content, with the protective goods carrying a more distinct level of gravitas. Considering these examples, there is reason to question whether the employment of MDTs would withstand the proportionality test. Moreover, it is unclear whether the 'risk' caused by the use of MDTs would satisfy the potential for harm implicitly required by the term 'systemic risk'.

The second category of systemic risks, outlined in Article 34(1)(b) DSA, addresses users' fundamental rights. In addition to the right to human dignity, the right to respect for private life and the right to data protection, Article 34(1)(b) explicitly lists the right to a high-level of consumer protection enshrined in Article 38 CFR. The provision serves as an initial, rudimentary prototype of the fundamental rights

86 Kaesling, Article 34 Margin Number 47 in Hofmann and Raue, *Digital Services Act. Gesetz über digitale Dienste*.

87 Kaesling, Article 34 Margin Number 14 in Hofmann and Raue, *Digital Services Act. Gesetz über digitale Dienste*.

88 See Duivenvoorde and Goanta, 'The Regulation of Digital Advertising under the DSA'.

89 Recital 79 DSA.

90 Recital 80 DSA.

impact assessment introduced subsequently by the AIA. How exactly this new legal instrument will be implemented and applied in practice has yet to unfold. The exact threshold for evoking the provision is still in the dark, and judicature is not yet available. Recital 81 DSA does not provide any additional details on the specific process, either. Potentially, the personalisation of content based on MDTs could fall under this provision.

Similarly vague are the specifications regarding the third category of systemic risks related to any actual or foreseeable negative effects on civic discourse and electoral processes, and public security in Article 34(1)(c) DSA. Recital 82 DSA does not provide any further clarifications. Potentially, the use of MDTs for political advertising, such as in scenario (d), could fall under this category, depending on the exact features, the functioning, and how they are employed. The exact parameters and measures for the risk assessment are yet to be defined.[91] Nevertheless, it has to be reiterated that unfair political practices could have been easily addressed by the sector-specific TTPA. If prohibited under the TTPA, such practices would qualify as illegal content under the DSA, subject to the ban outlined in Article 9(1) DSA and initiating content moderating requirements. Importantly, the obligations would be applicable to all online platforms and not be limited to VLOPs and VLOSEs.

The last category of systemic risks, addressed in Article 34(1)(d), focuses on 'any actual or foreseeable negative effects in relation to gender-based violence, the protection of public health and minors and serious negative consequences to the person's physical and mental well-being'. In contrast to the other three categories, lit d includes a threshold of severity. Pursuant to Recital 83 DSA, the consequences to a person's physical and mental well-being or on gender-based violence have to be 'serious'. The assessment of the severity threshold should not only be made in the context of the entire society but also take into account the impact on the affected individual.[92] The Recital further clarifies that the systemic risks may also relate to the online interface design 'that may stimulate behavioural addictions' of users.

Article 34(1)(d) DSA could potentially serve as a basis for addressing the broader risks of the recommender system in Sarah and Drew's scenario (b). A study by the Panoptykon Foundation on the Facebook recommender system presents facts for potential legal arguments.[93] The study provides a real-world illustration through the case of Joanna (name changed for privacy), who was grappling with

[91] For a first approach, see Sofia Calabrese and Orsolya Reich, 'Identifying, Analysing, Assessing and Mitigating Potential Negative Effects on Civic Discourse and Electoral Processes: A Minimum Menu of Risks Very Large Online Platforms Should Take Heed of' (January 2024) <https://dq4n3btxmr8c9.cloudfront.net/files/mpdgy5/DSA_Risk_Analysis_LibertiesxEPDfin.pdf> accessed 8 January 2025.

[92] Kaesling, Article 34 Margin Number 108 in Hofmann and Raue, *Digital Services Act. Gesetz über digitale Dienste*.

[93] Panopytkon Foundation, 'Algorithms of Trauma'; Panopytkon Foundation, 'Anxious about Your Health?'.

the distress of losing a loved one and concerns about her baby's health. As Joanna researched symptoms related to illness, Facebook's algorithm began presenting her predominantly content with distressing health information, ranging from cancer to genetic disorders. The content included crowdfunding campaign ads for seriously ill children, interspersed with offers for paid screening for the very genetic diseases affecting these children. Mental health experts verified that the volume of negative health-related posts shown to Joanna was substantial enough to unsettle even individuals in good health. Despite Joanna's efforts to reduce this type of content, the recommender system ignored her attempts. Joanna's mental health deteriorated, and the algorithmic decisions exacerbated her anxieties. What happened to Joanna is a casebook example of how the functioning and design of a VLOP service negatively impacts a person's mental well-being.

A Resolution on addictive design of online services and consumer protection in the EU single market by the European Parliament supports the argument. In particular, the European Parliament:

> 3. Is alarmed that certain platforms and other tech companies exploit psychological vulnerabilities to design digital interfaces for commercial interests that maximise the frequency and duration of user visits, so as to prolong the use of online services and to create engagement with the platform; stresses that addictive design can cause harm to physical and psychological health as well as material harm to consumers; calls on the Commission to urgently assess and, where appropriate, close existing regulatory gaps with regard to consumer vulnerabilities, dark patterns and addictive features of digital services;[94]

The Resolution directly links addictive designs intended to maximise the frequency and duration of user visits – 'so as to prolong the use of online services and to create engagement with the platform' – to physical and psychological health as well as to material harm to consumers.

A personalisation algorithm, such as the one in Sarah and Drew's scenario (b), utilising MDTs to exploit users' emotional vulnerabilities and displaying sad/upsetting content with the intention of prolonging their time on the platform, could be argued to have a similarly detrimental impact on users' mental well-being. Joanna's case, her deteriorated mental health, and the expert opinion by mental health professionals could potentially build the basis for arguing that such a recommender system surpasses the severity threshold and amounts to a systemic risk.

Putting an end to this type of recommender systems would also align with consumers' preferences and desires. According to a study by BEUC, most consumers are not receptive to AI technologies attempting to elicit emotional reactions from

94 EU Parliament Resolution of 12 December 2023 on Addictive Design of Online Services and Consumer Protection in the EU Single Market (2023/2043(INI)).

them, such as recommender systems proposing unsettling content to grab attention. A majority, around 59 per cent, view it as unjust for apps and websites to employ artificial intelligence in triggering intense emotional responses like fear or anger.[95] In contrast, only 15 per cent of individuals deem this approach fair.

Once a systemic risk is positively identified by the providers, they are obliged to put in place reasonable, proportionate, and effective mitigation measures. Inter alia, Article 35 DSA lists adapting the features or functioning of the services (lit a), adapting content moderation (lit c), testing and adapting their algorithmic systems, including the recommender systems (lit d), and adapting the advertising systems (lit e) as possible mitigation measures.[96]

6.4.5 *Dark Patterns Evolve into Deceptive and Manipulative Practices*

Article 25(1) DSA on online interface design and organisation mandates that platform providers 'shall not design, organise or operate their online interfaces in a way that deceives or manipulates the recipients of their service or in a way that otherwise materially distorts or impairs the ability of the recipients of their service to make free and informed decisions'. While clearly referring to dark patterns, the provision does not specifically mention the term 'dark patterns'. Instead, Recital 67 DSA provides the additional context and description:

> Dark patterns on online interfaces of online platforms are practices that materially distort or impair, either on purpose or in effect, the ability of recipients of the service to make autonomous and informed choices or decisions. Those practices can be used to persuade the recipients of the service to engage in unwanted behaviours or into undesired decisions which have negative consequences for them. Providers of online platforms should therefore be prohibited from deceiving or nudging recipients of the service and from distorting or impairing the autonomy, decision-making, or choice of the recipients of the service via the structure, design or functionalities of an online interface or a part thereof. This should include, but not be limited to, exploitative design choices to direct the recipient to actions that benefit the provider of online platforms, but which may not be in the recipients' interests, presenting choices in a non-neutral manner, such as giving more prominence to certain choices through visual, auditory, or other components, when asking the recipient of the service for a decision.[97]

Difficulties are expected to arise in determining which online interfaces are deceptive or manipulative and how these should be distinguished from those that are

[95] BEUC, 'Connected, but Unfairly Treated', 10.

[96] In April 2024, the Commission adopted guidelines on the mitigation of systemic risks for electoral processes under Article 35 DSA: EU Commission, Guidelines for Providers of Very Large Online Platforms and Very Large Online Search Engines on the Mitigation of Systemic Risks for Electoral Processes Pursuant to Article 35(3) of Regulation (EU) 2022/2065 (C/2024/3014).

[97] Recital 67 DSA.

acceptable. Although Article 25(3) DSA stipulates that the Commission has the authority to issue guidelines on the matter, there is a concern that platform providers could feel encouraged to become more creative in finding ways to bypass the prohibition.

In April 2024, the Commission has opened formal proceedings against Facebook and Instagram under the Digital Services Act for infringements relating, inter alia, to deceptive advertising and political content.[98] The outcome of the proceedings may give clarifications on the implications of the relevant provisions in practice, in particular on Article 24, 25, 34 and 35 DSA. They may also provide guidance on whether the provisions will be useful in the context of MDTs.

While the DSA is still putting a clear emphasis on design choices for the interface ('via the structure, design or functionalities of an online interface or a part thereof' Recital 67 DSA), it is evident that the traditional concept of dark patterns has begun expanding. In response to the sophisticated forms in which digital platforms engage with their users, it started evolving into a more comprehensive notion of deceptive or manipulative practices.[99] Additionally, the attention is shifting notably towards the users' inability to make autonomous and informed choices or decisions. Both developments are reflected further in the AIA and its prohibitions for subliminal, manipulative, and deceptive practices.

6.5 AIA: PROHIBITION OF SUBLIMINAL, MANIPULATIVE, OR DECEPTIVE TECHNIQUES

During the legislative process of the AIA, there have been consistent warnings that, in its proposed form, the Regulation risks falling short of adequate protection for consumers and regulatory instruments for individuals.[100] The Parliament Amendments responded to the critique by introducing 'affected persons' as a subject and suggesting the implementation of direct remedies, such as the right to lodge a complaint, the right to an effective judicial remedy, and the right to an explanation of individual decision-making.[101] The final version of the AIA integrates some of these suggestions, granting natural persons the right to lodge a complaint with

[98] EU Commission, Commission Opens Formal Proceedings against Facebook and Instagram under the Digital Services Act (Press release 30 April 2024). <https://ec.europa.eu/commission/presscorner/detail/en/ip_24_2373> accessed 8 January 2025.

[99] Leiser, 'Psychological Patterns and Article 5 of the AI Act, 8'.

[100] See, for instance, Christiane Wendehorst, 'The Proposal for an Artificial Intelligence Act COM(2021)206 from a Consumer Policy Perspective (2021)' <www.sozialministerium.at/dam/sozialministeriumat/Anlagen/Themen/Konsumentenschutz/Konsumentenpolitik/The-Proposal-for-an-Artificial-Intelligence-Act-COM2021-206-from-a-Consumer-Policy-Perspective_dec2021__pdfUA.pdf> accessed 30 January 2025. BEUC, 'EU Rules on AI Lack Punch to Sufficiently Protect Consumers (Press Release 9 December 2023) <www.beuc.eu/press-releases/eu-rules-ai-lack-punch-sufficiently-protect-consumers> accessed 8 January 2025.

[101] Article 3(8a) and Articles 68 (a)-(c) new AIA Parliament Amendments.

a market surveillance authority,[102] and affected persons a right to explanation of individual decision-making for high risk systems.[103]

The AIA does not include specific provisions for consumers on targeted advertising. However, the prohibitions of AI systems according to Article 5 AIA deserve a more detailed analysis with regard to MDTs for commercial and political practices. The list in Article 5 AIA includes:

(a) AI systems that deploy subliminal, purposefully manipulative or deceptive techniques;
(b) AI systems that exploit vulnerabilities related to age, disability, social or economic circumstances;
(c) AI systems that evaluate or classify individuals or groups based on social behaviour or personal traits;
(d) AI systems that assess the risk of an individual committing criminal offenses solely based on profiling or personality traits;
(e) AI systems that create or expand facial recognition databases by untargeted scraping from the internet or CCTV footage;
(f) AI systems to infer emotions in workplaces or educational institutions;
(g) Biometric categorisation systems that infer sensitive attributes (race, political opinions, trade union membership, religious or philosophical beliefs, sex life, or sexual orientation);
(h) 'Real-time' remote biometric identification in publicly accessible spaces for law enforcement.

In particular, the prohibition of AI systems deploying subliminal, purposefully manipulative, or deceptive techniques (Article 5(1)(a) AIA) may be relevant for the employment of MDTs in the context of commercial and political practices.[104]

Since being first proposed by the Commission, Article 5(1)(a) AIA has suffered a lot of critique and considerable transformation.[105] For a better understanding of the rationale behind the finally adopted version, it is worth comparing the different approaches to this provision.

Arguably, the provision is complex. The version proposed by the Parliament is the one most granularly developed compared to the original proposal. It is the first to incorporate purposefully manipulative or deceptive techniques within its scope. It is the first to integrate groups of people that may be affected by these. It is the first to include the ability of making an informed decision as criteria. It is the first to

[102] Article 85 AIA.

[103] Article 86 AIA.

[104] For the eventual overlap and interplay between Article 5(1)(a) and 5(1)(b) AIA, see Helberger and others, 'Digital Fairness for Consumers', 17. EU Commission, Annex to the Communication to the Commission, Approval of the Content of the Draft Communication from the Commission – Commission Guidelines on Prohibited Artificial Intelligence Practices, section 122 subsequential.

[105] Rostam J. Neuwirth, *The EU Artificial Intelligence Act: Regulating Subliminal AI Systems* (Routledge 2023).

	Commission Proposal	Council Position	Parliament Amendments	Adopted Act
Article 5(1)(a)	the placing on the market, putting into service or use of an AI system that deploys subliminal techniques beyond a person's consciousness in order to materially distort a person's behaviour in a manner that causes or is likely to cause that person or another person physical or psychological harm;	the placing on the market, putting into service or use of an AI system that deploys subliminal techniques beyond a person's consciousness *with the objective to or the effect of* materially distorting a person's behaviour in a manner that causes or is *reasonably* likely to cause that person or another person physical or psychological harm;	the placing on the market, putting into service or use of an AI system that deploys subliminal techniques beyond a person's consciousness *or purposefully manipulative or deceptive techniques, with the objective to or the effect of* materially distorting a person's or *a group of persons' behaviour by appreciably impairing the person's ability to make an informed decision, thereby causing the person to take a decision that that person would not have otherwise taken* in a manner that causes or is likely to cause that person, another person or *group of persons significant* harm; *The prohibition of AI system that deploys subliminal techniques referred to in the first sub-paragraph shall not apply to AI systems intended to be used for approved therapeutical purposes on the basis of specific informed consent of the individuals that are exposed to them or, where applicable, of their legal guardian;*	the placing on the market, the putting into service or the use of an AI system that deploys subliminal techniques beyond a person's consciousness *or purposefully manipulative or deceptive techniques, with the objective, or the effect of* materially distorting the behaviour of a person or *a group of persons by appreciably impairing their ability to make an informed decision, thereby causing them to take a decision that they would not have otherwise taken* in a manner that causes or is reasonably likely to cause that person, another person or *group of persons significant* harm;

Article 5(1)(a) across different versions of the AIA (emphasis added).

introduce the specification that the harm caused has to be significant. In the final version of the AIA, the legislators adopted all these proposed changes.[106]

The prohibition consists of a number of criteria, which have to apply cumulatively. According to lit a, an AI system is prohibited if:

- it deploys subliminal techniques (beyond a person's consciousness) or purposefully manipulative or deceptive techniques;
- the technique must have the objective or the effect of materially distorting the behaviour of a person or a group of persons; the distortion must appreciably impair their ability to make an informed decision, resulting in a decision that they would not have otherwise taken;
- the distorted behaviour must cause or be reasonably likely to cause that person, another person, or a group of persons significant harm.

Some of the components sound familiar and resemble the wording in the DSA. However, legislators have developed the concept further in the AIA. Recital 29 AIA aims to provide comprehensive guidance on the broader notion of Article 5(1)(a) AIA:

> AI-enabled manipulative techniques can be used to persuade persons to engage in unwanted behaviours, or to deceive them by nudging them into decisions in a way that subverts and impairs their autonomy, decision-making and free choices. The placing on the market, the putting into service or the use of certain AI systems with the objective to or the effect of materially distorting human behaviour, whereby significant harms, in particular having sufficiently important adverse impacts on physical, psychological health or financial interests are likely to occur, are particularly dangerous and should therefore be prohibited. Such AI systems deploy subliminal components such as audio, image, video stimuli that persons cannot perceive, as those stimuli are beyond human perception, or other manipulative or deceptive techniques that subvert or impair person's autonomy, decision-making or free choice in ways that people are not consciously aware of those techniques or, where they are aware of them, can still be deceived or are not able to control or resist them. This could be facilitated, for example, by machine-brain interfaces or virtual reality as they allow for a higher degree of control of what stimuli are presented to persons, insofar as they may materially distort their behaviour in a significantly harmful manner. In addition, AI systems may also otherwise exploit the vulnerabilities of a person or a specific group of persons due to their age, disability within the meaning of Directive (EU) 2019/882 of the European Parliament and of the Council, or a specific social or economic situation that is likely to make those persons more vulnerable to exploitation such as persons living in extreme poverty, ethnic or religious minorities. Such AI systems can be placed on the market, put into service or used with the objective to or the effect of materially distorting the behaviour of a person and in a manner that causes or is reasonably likely to cause significant harm to that

[106] The Parliament Amendments' exception for therapeutic purposes has been integrated into Recital 29 AIA.

> or another person or groups of persons, including harms that may be accumulated over time and should therefore be prohibited. It may not be possible to assume that there is an intention to distort behaviour where the distortion results from factors external to the AI system which are outside the control of the provider or the deployer, namely factors that may not be reasonably foreseeable and therefore not possible for the provider or the deployer of the AI system to mitigate. In any case, it is not necessary for the provider or the deployer to have the intention to cause significant harm, provided that such harm results from the manipulative or exploitative AI-enabled practices. The prohibitions for such AI practices are complementary to the provisions contained in Directive 2005/29/EC of the European Parliament and of the Council, in particular unfair commercial practices leading to economic or financial harms to consumers are prohibited under all circumstances, irrespective of whether they are put in place through AI systems or otherwise. The prohibitions of manipulative and exploitative practices in this Regulation should not affect lawful practices in the context of medical treatment such as psychological treatment of a mental disease or physical rehabilitation, when those practices are carried out in accordance with the applicable law and medical standards, for example explicit consent of the individuals or their legal representatives. In addition, common and legitimate commercial practices, for example in the field of advertising, that comply with the applicable law should not, in themselves, be regarded as constituting harmful manipulative AI-enabled practices.[107]

First, a prohibited AI system needs to deploy a subliminal or a purposefully manipulative or deceptive technique. Manipulative techniques or manipulation are not legally defined by the AIA. Similar to the DSA, manipulation is understood in the AIA as a form of influence that can impair the ability for decision-making capabilities.[108] Recital 29 AIA outlines that manipulative techniques include techniques used to persuade people to engage in unwanted behaviours or to deceive them into decisions that infringe their autonomy, their decision-making and their free choices. The Commission Guidelines on prohibited AI practices specify manipulative techniques further:

> (67) 'Purposefully manipulative techniques' are not defined in the AI Act, but they should be understood as techniques that are designed or objectively aim to influence, alter, or control an individual's behaviour in a manner that undermines their individual autonomy and free choices. Manipulative techniques are typically designed to exploit cognitive biases, psychological vulnerabilities, or situational factors that make individuals more susceptible to influence. Because of their adaptability, AI systems are also able to respond well to a person's individual circumstances or vulnerabilities and increase the effectiveness and impact of manipulation at scale.[109]

107 Recital 29 AIA.

108 See Helberger and others, 'Digital Fairness for Consumers', 17.

109 EU Commission, Annex to the Communication to the Commission, Approval of the Content of the Draft Communication from the Commission – Commission Guidelines on Prohibited Artificial Intelligence Practices, section 67.

MDT-based targeting practices aim to deliver highly tailored ads by exploiting psychological vulnerabilities that make users more susceptible to influence, thereby maximising the ads' effectiveness. Thus, MDT-based targeting practices align with the description of manipulative techniques.

The Commission Guidelines recognise that there may be overlaps between different types of techniques.[110] Neurotechnology is specifically referred to under subliminal techniques, stating that: 'big data analytics, neuro technologies, brain–computer interfaces and virtual reality, heightens the risk of sophisticated subliminal manipulation and its capability to effectively influence human behaviour in a subconscious manner'.[111] Additionally, the Guidelines mention emerging machine-brain interfaces and advanced techniques like dream-hacking and brain spyware.[112] Manipulative techniques can therefore also be subliminal.

Distinguishing between manipulation and mere persuasion is especially challenging in the context of commercial practices. Recital 29 AIA clarifies that legitimate commercial practices, such as advertising, shall not be considered harmful manipulative AI-enabled practices. The Guidelines offer additional explanation on this issue:

> (128) Manipulation involves, in most cases, covert techniques undermining autonomy, leading individuals to make decisions they might not have otherwise made if they were fully aware of the influences at play. These techniques often exploit psychological weaknesses or cognitive biases. By contrast, persuasion operates within the bounds of transparency and respect for individual autonomy. It involves presenting arguments or information in a way that appeals to reason and emotions, but explains the AI system's objectives and functioning, provide relevant and accurate information to ensure informed decision-making and supports the individual's ability to evaluate the information and make free and autonomous choices.[113]

The explanatory example provided for differentiating between manipulative and persuasive practices is particularly relevant to the use of MDTs:

> For example, an AI system which operates in a transparent manner and analyses customers' emotions to improve customer interactions and provide support with the knowledge of the users engages in persuasion and aligns with their interests. By contrast, an emotion recognition system used for targeted advertising that infers emotions of consumers in a hidden manner to offer products of higher prices at a

[110] EU Commission, Annex to the Communication to the Commission, Approval of the Content of the Draft Communication from the Commission, section 68.

[111] EU Commission, Annex to the Communication to the Commission, Approval of the Content of the Draft Communication from the Commission, section 66.

[112] EU Commission, Annex to the Communication to the Commission, Approval of the Content of the Draft Communication from the Commission, section 66.

[113] EU Commission, Annex to the Communication to the Commission, Approval of the Content of the Draft Communication from the Commission – Commission Guidelines on Prohibited Artificial Intelligence Practices, section 128.

specific moment when the user is more likely to buy them engages in manipulation and is to the detriment of the consumers.[114]

According to the Guidelines, ERS that covertly infer consumers' emotions to offer higher-priced products at moments when they are more likely to purchase are considered manipulative techniques. Arguably, the same reasoning should apply to AI systems that do not rely on biometric data (and thus are not classified as ERS) but instead use text, as the manipulative technique remains fundamentally the same.

Second, these techniques must have the objective or the effect of materially distorting the behaviour of a person or a group. In contrast to the original proposal, both the Council Position as well as the Parliament Amendments insisted that AI systems should be included in the provision not only if they have the specific objective to distort people's behaviour but also if they have simply this effect.[115] More specifically, these techniques must be 'appreciably impairing their ability to make an informed decision' and cause 'them to take a decision that they would not have otherwise taken' (Article 5(1)(a) AIA). For an interpretation of the concept of 'material distortion of the behaviour', the Commission Guidelines refer to the UCPD as a source of inspiration, particularly Articles 5 to 9 UCPD, stating that there is 'no need to prove that a consumer's economic behaviour has been distorted, it suffices to establish that a commercial practice is "likely" (i.e. capable) of impacting an average consumer's transactional decision'.[116]

Building on the detailed discussion under the UCPD, in particular Articles 5 to 9 UCPD, Sarah and Drew's scenarios (a), (b), and (c) should all be considered an unfair commercial practice: Scenario (a), the ticketing chatbot using mind data for targeted advertising; scenario (b), the VLOP enhancing their online behavioural advertising with mind data; and scenario (c), the music streaming platform inferring mind data through EEG-based earbuds for targeted advertising, they all constitute aggressive commercial practices. Complementing the UCPD, they should be considered as manipulative techniques with the objective or the effect of materially distorting consumers' behaviour under the AIA as well.

Finally, the distorted behaviour must cause or be reasonably likely to cause significant harm. In contrast to the original proposal, the final version of the AIA has a broad notion of harm, including not only physical but also psychological health and financial interests.[117] The AIA even acknowledges harm that accumulates

[114] EU Commission, Annex to the Communication to the Commission, Approval of the Content of the Draft Communication from the Commission – Commission Guidelines on Prohibited Artificial Intelligence Practices, section 129.

[115] Recital 29 AIA seconds that the intention to cause significant harm is not required, as long as it is a result of the manipulative or exploitative practices.

[116] EU Commission, Annex to the Communication to the Commission, Approval of the Content of the Draft Communication from the Commission – Commission Guidelines on Prohibited Artificial Intelligence Practices, section 80.

[117] Recital 29 AIA.

over time.[118] In the context of commercial practices, such as in Sarah and Drew's scenario (a), (b), and (c), financial and economic harm emerges as the most relevant form of harm.[119] Initial clarifications on the notion of harm have been provided through the Commission Guidelines. However, the Guidelines stress with emphasis that the prohibition in Article 5(1)(a) AI Act only applies if the harm is 'significant'.[120]

Neither the AIA nor the Guidelines offer a precise definition of the concept of 'significant harm'.[121] The Guidelines note that the concept 'should be understood as implying significant adverse impacts on physical, psychological health or financial and economic interests of persons and groups of persons' and that its determination is 'fact-specific, requiring careful consideration of each case's individual circumstances and a case-by-case assessment'.[122] Factors to be considered for establishing the significance of harm include severity of harm, context and cumulative effects, scale and intensity, affected persons' vulnerability and duration, and reversibility. The Guidelines expressly note that there will be many cases where the required threshold of significant harm will likely not be met even if the systems may be deploying subliminal, purposefully manipulative, or deceptive techniques.[123] Therefore, questions arise as to whether Sarah and Drew's scenarios would meet the threshold for significant harm. Notably, in the example cited above on the manipulative use of ERS for targeted advertising, the Guidelines amplify the impact – and, consequently, the harm – by introducing the element of higher prices.

Sarah and Drew's scenario (d), the VLOP enhancing their online political microtargeting with mind data, may also face challenges in meeting the final criterion of harm, though for different reasons. Here, the difficulty already lies in establishing the very notion of harm itself. Article 5(1)(a) AIA lists main categories of harm, including physical and psychological health as well as financial interests. It remains

[118] For a granular discussion on consumer harm in this context, see Helberger and others, 'Digital Fairness for Consumers', 192 subsequential.

[119] The Guidelines specify that financial and economic harm include a range of adverse effects, such as financial loss, financial exclusion, economic instability. (EU Commission, Annex to the Communication to the Commission, Approval of the Content of the Draft Communication from the Commission – Commission Guidelines on Prohibited Artificial Intelligence Practices, section 89).

[120] EU Commission, Annex to the Communication to the Commission, Approval of the Content of the Draft Communication from the Commission – Commission Guidelines on Prohibited Artificial Intelligence Practices, section 91.

[121] On the notion of significant harm, see EU Commission, Annex to the Communication to the Commission, Approval of the Content of the Draft Communication from the Commission – Commission Guidelines on Prohibited Artificial Intelligence Practices, section 85 subsequential.

[122] EU Commission, Annex to the Communication to the Commission, Approval of the Content of the Draft Communication from the Commission, section 85 subsequential.

[123] EU Commission, Annex to the Communication to the Commission, Approval of the Content of the Draft Communication from the Commission – Commission Guidelines on Prohibited Artificial Intelligence Practices, section 93.

unclear whether the notion of harm under the AIA extends to encompass also democratic or electoral harms.[124]

Moving forward, regulatory authorities could clarify that the notion of harm in Article 5(1)(a) AIA does in fact include adverse impacts on democracy or electoral processes. This would transform the provision and its complex set of requirements into a nuanced regulatory instrument against manipulative online political practices, addressing not only MDTs but also other emerging practices in the future.

> Clarification that 'harm' in Article 5(1)(a) AIA includes adverse impacts on democracy or electoral processes could transform the provision into a nuanced regulatory tool against manipulative political practices.

Article 5(1)(a) AIA could potentially even be invoked to advocate a ban to the recommender system in scenario (b), which prioritises sad or controversial content to increase user engagement. It could be argued that the AI system in scenario (b) uses purposefully manipulative techniques – specifically, an algorithm covertly using emotional contagion and exploiting psychological vulnerabilities to increase users' susceptibility and undermine their individual autonomy and free choices. This can have the effect of distorting users' behaviour, making them stay longer than intended and possibly fostering addictive patterns. It impairs their ability to make informed decisions, such as leaving the service, leading them to take actions they otherwise would not take – like continuing to engage with distressing content, which harms their mental health. A substantial deterioration of people's mental health can be considered a significant adverse impact, meeting the threshold for significant psychological harm. Notably, the Commission Guidelines highlight that psychological harm is especially relevant when AI systems exploit emotional and cognitive vulnerabilities.[125]

124 In the interest of thoroughness, it should be noted that the Commission Guidelines briefly mention references to Union values of respect for democracy and rule of law in Recital 28 AIA and Article 1 AIA in the context of harm (EU Commission, Annex to the Communication to the Commission, Approval of the Content of the Draft Communication from the Commission – Commission Guidelines on Prohibited Artificial Intelligence Practices, footnote 76.)

125 EU Commission, Annex to the Communication to the Commission, Approval of the Content of the Draft Communication from the Commission – Commission Guidelines on Prohibited Artificial Intelligence Practices, section 88.

7

Use Case 4: Employment Monitoring

Is My Boss Allowed to Spy on My Mind?

The increasing digitalisation within the employment context had already begun years before the COVID-19 pandemic, but the pandemic surely exacerbated this trend.[1] While today's employees enjoy the benefits of remote working and technological assistance, companies rely increasingly on continuous and low-cost forms of digital management. The large amounts of data that are processed together with advancements in data analytics have enabled unprecedented levels of surveillance:

> The systems involved differ from existing approaches in three fundamental ways: the collection and organisation of data, including both digital and real-world information, as well as its preparation in machine-readable formats; their processing, relying on machine learning and other 'artificial intelligence' techniques, which – broadly speaking – focus on identifying patterns and correlations in data sets; and the way control is exercised at a highly granular level, and sometimes even in the absence of clear orders.[2]

The omnipresence of digital technologies has brought about a new era of employee monitoring practices.[3] Employers gather information through mobile devices,

[1] The WP29 has established a very broad scope of employment within the data protection context, covering 'all situations where there is an employment relationship, regardless of whether this relationship is based on an employment contract', including also 'new business models served by different types of labour relationships, and in particular employment on a freelance basis' (Article 29 Data Protection Working Party, Opinion 2/2017 on Data Processing at Work, Adopted on 8 June 2017. (WP 249), 4). The terms employment/work, employee/worker are therefore being used interchangeably here, despite the fact that they may have different legal implications under national labour laws.

[2] Jeremias Adams-Prassl, 'Regulating Algorithms at Work: Lessons for a "European Approach to Artificial Intelligence"', (2022) 13(1) *European Labour Law Journal*, 30–50, 36 <https://doi.org/10.1177/20319525211062558>.

[3] For the following examples in this paragraph, see ICO, 'Data Protection and Monitoring Workers' (4 October 2023) <https://ico.org.uk/for-organisations/uk-gdpr-guidance-and-resources/employment/monitoring-workers/data-protection-and-monitoring-workers/> accessed 8 January 2025; European Agency for Safety and Health at Work (EU-OSHA), Policy Brief, Impact of Artificial Intelligence

wearables, or embedded monitoring software. They deploy digital technologies to monitor timekeeping or to assess productivity, they take webcam shots at regular intervals confirming the availability or mere presence of employees, they make audio recordings, they mine text messages, and they collect information from social media. They use bossware to capture and log keyboard activities, they trace browsing histories, they record the number and content of telephone calls, they scan emails and files, they track locations, body movements, and other vital signs, they look for indicators of stress and fatigue in micro-facial expressions or tone of voice. They use sophisticated data analytics, people analytics,[4] and gamification to evaluate or improve performance and productivity, to streamline the organisation of work and production, to limit the cost of monitoring and surveillance itself, to support the employees' physical and mental well-being, to create profiles of workers, to influence their behaviours, to discipline them, or to enhance HR management.

The use of MDTs for monitoring practices at work aligns with this general development. MDTs can be deployed to evaluate employees' personal characteristics, their productivity, their emotional attitude towards their work, their company, their clients, their colleagues, their boss. For example, MDTs can be used to flag recruitment candidates as potentially temperamental, impulsive, self-obsessed, thrill-seeking, disinterested, or a good team-worker.[5] In other instances, MDTs are utilised to guide employees on adjusting their language and tone of voice to enhance client mood and facilitate more effective complaint resolution.[6] In Australia, the USA, China, South America, and Africa, companies require workers to wear EEG-sensors embedded in headsets or helmets to monitor their fatigue level in sectors such as mining, aviation, construction, trucking, or high-speed railway.[7] As soon as the wearer reaches a certain level of drowsiness, the wearer and the manager are notified. The warning can come as an auditive signal; alternatively, a haptic trigger like vibrations could be initiated to increase the alertness of the wearer when they show a decrease in engagement.[8]

on Occupational Safety and Health (2021) <https://osha.europa.eu/sites/default/files/Policy_brief_Impact_AI_OSH.pdf> accessed 8 January 2025; Eurofound, 'Employee Monitoring and Surveillance: The Challenges of Digitalisation', Publications Office of the European Union, Luxembourg, and Eurofund, Monitoring and Surveillance of Workers in the Digital Age, (2020) <www.eurofound.europa.eu/en/monitoring-and-surveillance-workers-digital-age> accessed 8 January 2025; Wolfie Christl, 'Surveillance and Algorithmic Control in the Call Center: A Case Study on Contact and Service Center Software, Automated Management and Outsourced Work', (2023) <https://crackedlabs.org/dl/CrackedLabs_Christl_CallCenter.pdf> accessed 8 January 2025.

4 'People analytics' or 'Big Data HR' are both terms referring to algorithmic management in the employment context (see Adams-Prassl, 'Regulating Algorithms at Work', 31).

5 Vidushi Marda, 'Not Just Privacy: The Dangers of Emotion Recognition Technology', (14 August 2024) <https://casi.sas.upenn.edu/iit/vidushimarda> accessed 8 January 2025.

6 Christl, 'Surveillance and Algorithmic Control in the Call Center'.

7 Farahany, *The Battle for Your Brain*, 40 subsequential; Article 19, Emotional Entanglement: China's Emotion Recognition Market and Its Implications for Human Rights (2021) <www.article19.org/wp-content/uploads/2021/01/ER-Tech-China-Report.pdf> accessed 8 January 2025.

8 Farahany, *The Battle for Your Brain*, 49.

The use of MDT-based monitoring practices within the employment context raises a multitude of questions. Among the most pressing are those concerning data protection. In their Opinion 8/2001, the WP29 stipulated that monitoring or surveillance activities in the employment context involving personal data must comply with EU data protection requirements.[9] The GDPR therefore applies to the processing of personal data by MDT-based monitoring practices in the context of work.

7.1 GDPR: FRAGMENTED PROTECTION IN THE EMPLOYMENT CONTEXT

The GDPR has been designed as a piece of horizontal legislation, providing harmonised rules for data protection across the entire EU. Nevertheless, the GDPR contains several opening clauses that permit Member States to delineate the application of the GDPR in specific areas. These areas typically pertain to domains where Member States either struggled to reach a political consensus or necessitated greater flexibility to accommodate national particularities, approaches, and solutions. One such opening clause is Article 88 GDPR, concerning data protection within the employment context.

Compared to other data processing contexts, the employer–employee relationship is characterised by a power asymmetry that is existential. This specificity has caused repeated calls for harmonised, sector-specific legislation regulating data processing.[10] The EU attempted several times to adopt such rules, but all attempts have failed so far.[11] Consequently, EU legislators made Article 88 GDPR on data processing within the employment context an opening clause, allowing Member States the liberty to adopt and tailor their national solutions.

Finding a comprehensive EU-wide approach to regulate data protection in the context of work has proven to be a significant challenge for multiple reasons. Too big are the discrepancies between key stakeholders, too different the interests, too adamant the political disagreements. To some extent it is the side of the employers rejecting more harmonised regulation, in other cases workers and trade unions with strong guarantees in their national legislation, hesitant to agree to political deals that undermine or reduce their existing rights.

[9] Article 29 Data Protection Working Party, Opinion 8/2001 on the Processing of Personal Data in the Employment Context, Adopted on 13 September 2001 (WP 48), 4 and 24.

[10] One of the most prominent calls was written as early as 1999, see Spiros Simitis, 'Reconsidering the Premises of Labour Law: Prolegomena to an EU Regulation on the Protection of Employees' Personal Data' (1999) 5(1) *European Law Journal*, 45–62.

[11] See Halefom H. Abraha, 'A Pragmatic Compromise? The Role of Article 88 GDPR in Upholding Privacy in the Workplace', (2022) 12(4) *International Data Privacy Law*, 276–296, at 280 <https://doi.org/10.1093/idpl/ipac015>. The new Platform Work Directive as a lex specialis in this regard will be discussed further on.

Labour law itself is fragmented within the Union. For data processing in the employment context, this fragmentation is of particular importance as two specificities are generally addressed by labour law:

- Labour law aims to mitigate the power imbalance between employers and employees and the resulting subordinate position of employees through special provisions that, for instance, restrict the contractual freedom by providing certain minimum standards.
- Labour law recognises the collective dimensions through a number of collective rights to information, participation, and co-determination.[12]

Both aspects are crucial for data processing in this context, and both are currently left to fragmented national solutions. Instead of being subject to a harmonised sector-specific EU data protection law for the employment context, relevant data processing is regulated by a multitude of domestic legislation and semi-legislative instruments. The GDPR is applicable and regulates the basics, details are fleshed out in national laws, collective agreements, or a combination thereof.

Opening clause Article 88 GDPR foresees for Member States to provide specific rules to safeguard the rights and freedoms in respect of the processing of employees' personal data in the employment context. The Member States' regulatory freedom is constrained by the minimum standards laid down in the GDPR, which they are not allowed to fall below. Article 88 GDPR establishes a broad scope, including recruitment, performance of the contract, management, planning and organisation, equality and diversity, health and safety, protection of property, rights and benefits related to employment, and the termination of the employment. Although covering a comprehensive field, the list in para 1 is non-exhaustive. Para 2 specifies that the rules ought to include suitable and specific measures to safeguard the employee's human dignity, legitimate interests, and fundamental rights, highlighting the special importance that has to be given to the transparency of the processing.

The transposition of Article 88 GDPR varies significantly among Member States, with notable differences in the level of detail provided. Two aspects are particularly interesting for the use of MDTs within the employment context: the regulation of data processing, including monitoring practices, through collective agreements and the adoption of special regulations for certain monitoring practices, such as technologies using biometrics. Both options have been explored to varying degrees by the Member States.

Some Member States, such as Germany, Greece, and Spain, utilise the freedom granted by the opening clause extensively and are remarkably detailed in their rules on data processing; others, like Croatia, France, and Luxembourg, address only particular issues (e.g. biometric data or practices surrounding monitoring

[12] See Abraha, 'A Pragmatic Compromise?', 279.

and surveillance).[13] Some Member States have adopted provisions that allow trade unions, work councils, workplace employee representatives, or employees' associations to counterfight the power asymmetry and negotiate comprehensive collective agreements on national, industry, or company level; others have limited their role to a merely consultative body.[14] In addition to national solutions, there are also examples of collective agreements at a national intersectoral level, for example in Belgium and Norway.[15]

Austrian labour law, for instance, is known for allowing employee representative bodies to take on a strong role. The Austrian Labour Constitution Act provides works councils with a wide range of competencies related to data protection,[16] taking a multilayered approach consisting of participatory, co-determining, and informational rights. The introduction and maintaining of any control measures or technical systems affecting human dignity in Austria requires the works council's approval. The works council's consent is mandatory, it can neither be replaced by an arbitration board nor by the court. The works council thus enjoys veto powers against any monitoring practices and technologies touching upon human dignity.

Regulations on the use of biometrics for monitoring also vary.[17] In Cyprus, the use of biometrics for monitoring purposes is generally prohibited, whereas in France, specific requirements apply to the use of biometric systems. In Greece, biometrics are only allowed to ensure workplace safety. In Hungary, biometric entry systems are only allowed in exceptional cases. In Malta, a privacy impact assessment is recommended before using biometric systems. The Netherlands prohibit video monitoring and surveillance, including facial recognition technologies, to establish patterns of behaviour. Portugal has prohibited the use of biometric devices for monitoring employees.

7.1.1 *Monitoring Must Be Necessary, Lawful, Proportionate, Transparent, and Fair*

Given the complexities of this fragmented landscape at the national legislative level, the only unified layer of comprehensive guidance regarding the legitimate use of MDTs for monitoring purposes remaining is the general data protection framework. Article 88(2) GDPR provides the broad basics, mandating the implementation of

[13] See Abraha, 'A Pragmatic Compromise?', 283.

[14] See Abraha, 'A Pragmatic Compromise?', 287. On the issue of co-determination in the context of algorithmically managed work, see also Zoe Adams and Johanna Wenckebach, 'Collective Regulation of Algorithmic Management' (2023) 14(2), *European Labour Law Journal*, 211–229 <https://doi.org/10.1177/20319525231167477>.

[15] Eurofound, 'Employee Monitoring and Surveillance', 23.

[16] Bundesgesetz vom 14, Dezember 1973 betreffend die Arbeitsverfassung (Arbeitsverfassungsgesetz – ArbVG) BGBl, 22/1974 idF I 60/2023.

[17] For a detailed overview, among them the following examples, see Eurofound, 'Employee Monitoring and Surveillance', 8–16.

suitable and specific measures to protect human dignity, legitimate interests, and fundamental rights of data subjects. Notably, a specific emphasis is placed on ensuring transparency in the processing procedures. Further details and a more granular understanding are outlined in additional guidance documents by the WP29.

The WP29 established in their Opinion 8/2001 that any form of monitoring and surveillance within the employment context, be it email use, Internet access, video cameras, location data, or similar, has to comply with data protection requirements. For the monitoring to be compliant, it must be:

> a proportionate response by an employer to the risks it faces taking into account the legitimate privacy and other interests of workers. Any personal data held or used in the course of monitoring must be adequate, relevant and not excessive for the purpose for which the monitoring is justified. Any monitoring must be carried out in the least intrusive way possible.[18]

The reiterated emphasis put on transparency is supported by a call to respect the principle of data minimisation ('any data held or used [...] must be adequate, relevant and not excessive for the purpose'), and to ensure that the monitoring is targeted on the area of risk and takes into account the principle of secrecy of correspondence, where necessary.[19] The WP29 further stipulates that transparency shall be achieved by informing the employees of the existence of surveillance and of the purposes for which their data will be processed.[20]

Opinion 8/2001 is complemented by a Working document on the surveillance of electronic communications in the workplace. Therein, the WP29 insists that mere convenience to serve the interest of the employers cannot justify the intrusion of employees' privacy for monitoring practices.[21] The WP29 recommends a detailed test before implementing any monitoring measures, elaborating the key points of the previous Opinion:

(a) Is the monitoring activity transparent to the workers?
(b) Is it necessary? Could not the employer obtain the same result with traditional methods of supervision?
(c) Is the processing of personal data proposed fair to the workers?
(d) Is it proportionate to the concerns that it tries to ally?[22]

With regard to the required transparency, the WP29 underscores that the employees must be informed of (i) the presence, use, and purpose of any detection equipment and (ii) of any misuse of the electronic communications detected (email or the

[18] WP 48, 4 and 25.
[19] WP48, 25.
[20] WP48, 25.
[21] Article 29 Data Protection Working Party, Working Document on the Surveillance of Electronic Communications in the Workplace, Adopted on 29 May 2002 (WP55), 4.
[22] WP55, 4.

Internet).[23] Moreover, the WP29 emphasises that the human dignity of an employee takes precedence over any other considerations.[24]

Numerous new technologies have been introduced since the initial release of the first two documents by the WP29, making an adaptation of the guidance documents a necessity. Hence, the WP29 published Opinion 2/2017 on data processing at work, which is intended to complement and update the already existing documents.[25] With its focus on new technologies, Opinion 2/2017 is the most relevant document for the use of MDTs within the employment context. Therein, the WP29 provides instructions on the legitimate use of new monitoring techniques in certain scenarios and elaborates on the suitable and specific measures mentioned in Article 88(2) GDPR. The examples outlined by the WP29 serve as a rough guide for distinguishing between legitimate and illegitimate monitoring practices and allow drawing conclusions regarding the use of MDT-based monitoring practices.

The last resort Sarah and Drew are considering for their MDT-based software is the context of employment. Possible choices are:

Scenario (a): *an online recruitment software that analyses the candidate's voice to draw inferences regarding their teamwork ability, discomfort with certain interview questions, level of emotional engagement when discussing future tasks, and irritation or insecurity with factual questions;*

Scenario (b): *a keylogger software for a customer service, recording the entirety of written online conversations of customer service agents to assess the emotional effectiveness of the agents' responses to clients and their ability to collaborate with colleagues. The outcomes will be discussed during the annual appraisal and will serve as one of the factors taken into account during the subsequent salary negotiations.*

In scenario (a), voice analytics are used to assess and predict the employability and the future performance of a job applicant. As established before, data processing for and during the recruitment process lies within the scope of Article 88 GDPR. The requirements for data processing in the context of employment do therefore apply to scenario (a). In continuation of the WP29's earlier position, Opinion 2/2017 recommends evaluating a set of general criteria before implementing any monitoring practice. The employer should consider whether the processing is necessary (and if so, based on what legal grounds), whether it is fair to the employees, whether it is proportionate to the concerns raised, and whether it is transparent.[26]

23 WP55, 4.
24 WP55, 6.
25 Article 29 Data Protection Working Party, Opinion 2/2017 on Data Processing at Work (WP 249), Adopted on 8 June 2017.
26 WP 249, 11.

With regard to the necessity in scenario (a), the ability to work in a team and the professional competence of a candidate are relevant to the performance of most jobs and thus also relevant for a recruitment decision. It is understandable that recruiters would like to know whether a potential candidate will be able to work well with their colleagues and also which kind of questions make them uncomfortable or where they might lack factual knowledge and therefore feel insecure. In this sense, gathering information about these characteristics can be considered relevant and necessary for an employer.

The question of lawfulness is linked to defining an appropriate legal basis for the processing. By classifying the data in the illustrative scenario (a) as special category data, this leads to a dilemma.[27] Out of the possible exemptions from the general prohibition of processing according to Article 9(2) GDPR, only explicit consent represents a reasonable option. Alas, consent as a legal basis for processing within the employment context is generally problematic. For consent to be valid it must be informed and freely given. Recital 43 GDPR stipulates that consent should not be defined as legal basis when there is a clear imbalance between the data subject and the controller.[28] Employment is one of the primary contexts characterised by a clear structural imbalance between employers and employees. Regulatory guidance considers consent only a fallback position within the employment context, if, indeed, no other option is available. The WP29 has emphasised that consent becomes invalid when there is an actual or potential prejudice resulting from the refusal to consent.[29] Even more specifically, the WP29 does not consider it to be freely given where refusal results in the loss of a job opportunity.[30] Opinion 2/2017 reiterates that: '[e]mployees are almost never in a position to freely give, refuse or revoke consent, given the dependency that results from the employer/employee relationship. Given the imbalance of power, employees can only give free consent in exceptional circumstances, when no consequences at all are connected to acceptance or rejection of an offer'.[31]

Member States have shown a degree of flexibility in accepting consent as a valid legal basis within the employment context. Finland, for instance, does not recognise consent; Portugal excludes consent unless there are economic or legal benefits for the employee; Germany takes the contrasting approach and deems consent as freely given only if there is an economic or legal advantage.[32]

In scenario (a), refusing consent to having one's mind data inferred during the interview carries the risk of either being disinvited from the interview or being

27 For an example based on normal personal data, see scenario (b) further on.

28 Recital 43 GDPR: 'In order to ensure that consent is freely given, consent should not provide a valid legal ground for the processing of personal data in a specific case where there is a clear imbalance between the data subject and the controller […].'

29 WP 48, 23.

30 WP 48, 23.

31 WP 249, 23.

32 See Abraha, 'A Pragmatic Compromise?', 294.

quietly excluded in due process. Both outcomes would lead to a missed job opportunity. The applicant's consent can therefore not be considered freely given. Even if informed about the monitoring practice (a fact which itself is highly unlikely, see the section on transparency further on), their consent would not be valid. In absence of any other suitable exemption for processing, scenario (a) remains without such and would be unlawful.[33]

Furthermore, there are traditional, far less intrusive methods to gather the same information and achieve the same goals. If recruiters suspect factual insecurity or incompetence, they could ask more demanding questions. If they want to know more about whether a candidate fits a team and matches the rest, they could arrange for diverse elements of the recruitment process, including sessions where the applicant meets their potential colleagues or does trial sessions with them. As per regulatory guidance, less intrusive practices would have to be given preference and they would be taken into account when evaluating the proportionality of the practice. The mere fact that using MDTs may be cheaper or more convenient for the employer than arranging for a multifaceted recruitment procedure does not justify the practice.

In scenario (b), an employer wants to use a keylogger software to evaluate employees' effectivity at work and their ability to work together with colleagues. The results will be included in the annual appraisal and be considered for salary negotiations. Regarding the necessity of the monitoring, one can argue that assessing and evaluating employees' performance, discussing the results during the annual appraisal, and considering them in salary negotiations, all lie in the natural interest of an employer. The employees' effectiveness in handling customer wishes and complaints are part of their performance as customer service agents. In this sense, the monitoring could be considered necessary.

The data in scenario (b) is text-based and qualifies as normal personal data. For normal personal data, all options under Article 6(1) GDPR are possible legal grounds. Consent is still the weakest of all possibilities. The WP29 has for instance excluded that the default settings on the employees' device and/or the mere installation of a software package, including keylogger software, can be considered as the employees' consent.[34] Consent needs to be specific and requires an affirmative action that is an expression of will. Both requirements would not be met.

The most appropriate legal basis remaining for scenario (b) is legitimate interest. As shown in the Chapter 5, legitimate interest requires a balancing test prior to putting the technology in place – the processing needs to be strictly necessary for a legitimate purpose, proportionate, and not overridden by the fundamental rights and interests of the data subject. This is reiterated by the WP29 in Opinion 2/2017.[35]

33 For exceptions, such as health and safety reasons, see below.

34 WP 249, 7.

35 'The legitimate interest of employers can sometimes be invoked as a legal ground, but only if the processing is strictly necessary for a legitimate purpose and the processing complies with the principles of

Additionally, data processing based on legitimate interest can be objected by the employee pursuant to Article 21 GDPR.

The most obvious fundamental right that could override the interest of the employer in scenario (b) is the employees' right to privacy. Monitoring and surveillance are in a natural tension with people's right to privacy. However, the question arose whether or not the right to respect for people's private life actually extends to people's work life. In a pivotal decision, the European Court of Human Rights (ECtHR) clarified that Article 8 ECHR is indeed applicable to people's work life.

> The Court does not consider it possible or necessary to attempt an exhaustive definition of the notion of 'private life'. However, it would be too restrictive to limit the notion to an 'inner circle' in which the individual may live his own personal life as he chooses and to exclude therefrom entirely the outside world not encompassed within that circle. Respect for private life must also comprise to a certain degree the right to establish and develop relationships with other human beings.
>
> There appears, furthermore, to be no reason of principle why this understanding of the notion of 'private life' should be taken to exclude activities of a professional or business nature since it is, after all, in the course of their working lives that the majority of people have a significant, if not the greatest, opportunity of developing relationships with the outside world. This view is supported by the fact that, as was rightly pointed out by the Commission, it is not always possible to distinguish clearly which of an individual's activities form part of his professional or business life and which do not.[36]

In *Bărbulescu* v *Romania*, the ECtHR sets the bar for ensuring the respect for private life and correspondence in an employment context by outlining general principles for monitoring practices. The Court puts special emphasis on transparency and adequate safeguards and gives a number of criteria, limiting the discretion of employers with regard to the monitoring of employees. The list of criteria includes:

(i) whether the employee has been notified (notification due in advance);
(ii) the extent of the monitoring and the degree of intrusion into the employee's privacy (distinction should be made between monitoring of the flow of communications versus the content, whether all communications or only part are monitored, and whether the monitoring was limited in time and number of people who had access);
(iii) whether the employer has provided legitimate reasons to justify monitoring and accessing their actual content (the Court emphasises that the monitoring

proportionality and subsidiarity. A proportionality test should be conducted prior to the deployment of any monitoring tool to consider whether all data are necessary, whether this processing outweighs the general privacy rights that employees also have in the workplace and what measures must be taken to ensure that infringements on the right to private life and the right to secrecy of communications are limited to the minimum necessary.' (WP 249, 23).

[36] ECtHR, Case *Niemietz* v *Germany* (Application no. 13710/88), 16 December 1992, section 29.

of content is by nature a distinctly more invasive method and thus requires weightier justification);

(iv) whether less intrusive methods would have been possible (case-by-case assessment);

(v) the consequences of the monitoring for the employee and the use made by the employer of the results;

(vi) whether adequate safeguards have been put in place, especially when the monitoring operations were intrusive.[37]

Returning to scenario (b) and considering the criteria outlined by the ECtHR in *Bărbulescu* v *Romania* for the monitoring of employees, two elements stand out: the extent of the monitoring and the degree of intrusion. The Court specifically differentiates between monitoring only the flow of conversation versus the content itself and between the monitoring of all communications versus only parts of it. In scenario (b), the employer intends to continuously monitor the entirety of the communication, which sets the levels of intensity of monitoring very high. As to the degree of intrusiveness, the practice of inferring mind data from written content is very intrusive. Both arguments weigh heavily against the legitimate interests of the employer in the balancing test.

In addition, the Court stresses that in a case-by-case assessment, less intrusive methods have to be considered and that the consequences of the monitoring have to be taken into account. In scenario (b), the performance of the employees can be evaluated also by traditional, less intrusive means, such as the total rate of successfully solved complaints/cases and the time spent on them, or by offering/implementing feedback features for clients on how satisfied they were with the service/their agent. Moreover, the results of the monitoring in scenario (b) would be used for decisions regarding the professional and financial future of the employee, the consequences would therefore be severe.

Questions surrounding the (dis)proportionality of monitoring practices enabled by emerging digital technologies have also been subject to discussions by national DPAs and courts. The debates and decisions reflect the fragmented picture of data protection within the employment context and support the call for more harmonised sector-specific data protection legislation. While some DPAs appear to apply a strict approach, this approach is not always seconded by the courts. For instance, CNIL, the French DPA, fined Amazon €32 million for setting up an excessively intrusive system for monitoring employee activity and performance, stressing that the exhaustiveness of the data processing and the detailed monitoring of the work of the employees led to such a high fine.[38] Similarly, the DPA in Niedersachsen, Germany,

[37] ECtHR, Case *Bărbulescu v Romania* (Application no. 61496/08), 5 September 2017, section 121.

[38] CNIL, 'Employee Monitoring: CNIL Fined Amazon France Logistique €32 million', (23 January 2024) <www.cnil.fr/en/employee-monitoring-cnil-fined-amazon-france-logistique-eu32-million> accessed 8 January 2025.

banned the excessive collection and processing of monitoring data by Amazon. The administrative court in Hannover, however, took an opposing stance and decided that the legitimate interests of the employer outweigh possible infringements of the fundamental rights of the data subject.[39] What stands out in the reasoning of the court's decision in Hannover, especially with regard to the MDT-based monitoring in scenario (b), is the notable emphasis placed on two factors: (i) Amazon did not primarily collect and process the data for evaluating the performance of the employees but for improving the logistical process; and (ii) Amazon did not collect and process data concerning behavioural and personality traits, such as whether an employee is 'communicative', motivates or demotivates colleagues, their behaviour in conflicts, or whether they display an uplifting mood at the office.[40] The monitoring practice in scenario (b) would do exactly that, it would collect and process the data primarily for performance evaluation and it would infer data on behavioural and personality traits.

The WP29 has a very clear stance on forms of monitoring similar to the one in scenario (b) and on their proportionality:

> [E]mployers may think there is a justification for deploying software packages (either on-premise or in the cloud) that have the capabilities of, for example, logging keystrokes and mouse movements, screen capturing (either randomly or at set intervals), logging of applications used (and how long they were used for), and, upon compatible devices, enabling webcams and collecting the footage thereof. Such technologies are widely available including from third parties such as cloud providers. However, the processing involved in such technologies are disproportionate and the employer is very unlikely to have a legal ground under legitimate interest, e.g. for recording an employee's keystrokes and mouse movements.[41]

39 Verwaltungsgericht Hannover Urteil vom 09.02.2023, Az.: 10 A 6199/20.

40 'Was sich aus der hiesigen Auswertung der Leistungsdaten hingegen nicht ergibt, sind Anhaltspunkte zur Persönlichkeitsstruktur der Mitarbeiterinnen und Mitarbeiter, beispielsweise ob eine Mitarbeiterin oder ein Mitarbeiter 'kommunikativ' ist und andere zur Arbeit motiviert oder von der Arbeit abhält, ob eine Mitarbeiterin oder ein Mitarbeiter am Arbeitsplatz Konflikte schürt oder auflöst, ob eine Mitarbeiterin oder ein Mitarbeiter zu bestimmten Arbeitszeiten stets gute oder schlechte Laune verbreitet usw. Die Beschäftigten werden durch die Beschäftigtendatenverarbeitung bei der Klägerin aus der Sicht des erkennenden Gerichts – und anders als die Beklagte meint – deshalb nicht 'gläsern'. Dies wird (möglicherweise) anhand der begrenzten Kennziffern und lediglich in diesem Umfang die von ihnen erbrachte Arbeitsleistung. Daran ist aus Sicht des erkennenden Gerichts aber nichts auszusetzen. Jedenfalls verkommen hierdurch – anders als die Beklagte meint – die Menschenwürde und das allgemeine Persönlichkeitsrecht in der sozialen Marktwirtschaft und bei der Klägerin nicht zu reinen 'Lippenbekenntnissen'. Die Klägerin hat vielmehr ausreichend dargelegt, dass es ihr gar nicht primär um die Erfassung der Leistungen der Mitarbeiterinnen und Mitarbeiter geht, sondern darum, die bei ihr ablaufenden Logistikprozesse reibungsfrei steuern zu können. Dass die Klägerin aufgrund der erhobenen Leistungsdaten darüber hinaus und mithin – sekundär – durch Qualifizierung und Feedback ihrer Mitarbeiterinnen und Mitarbeiter versucht, dieses primäre Ziel zu erreichen, ist aus der Sicht des erkennenden Gerichts nicht zu beanstanden.' (Verwaltungsgericht Hannover Urt. v. 09.02.2023, Az.: 10 A 6199/20 <https://voris.wolterskluwer-online.de/browse/document/568c3088-f56c-4cea-a91c-d417e7b7cc6f> accessed 8 January 2025).

41 WP 249, 16.

Following the rationale of relevant DPAs and court decisions as well as regulatory guidance, the practice in scenario (b) does not withstand the balancing test. As a result, legitimate interests cannot be used as a legal basis for processing in scenario (b). Since no other legal basis but consent is available, and consent is not a suitable legal basis for these cases, the processing in scenario (b) would be unlawful.

In addition to violating the right to privacy and data protection, monitoring practices like the one in scenario (b) infringe also upon human dignity. Along with inducing stress and exerting pressure on employees, they can have chilling effects and limit the employees' independent thinking, identity, agency, and autonomy. They could even infringe Article 12 CFR, the freedom of assembly and of association, as indicated by the WP29:

> Technologies that monitor communications can also have a chilling effect on the fundamental rights of employees to organise, set up workers' meetings, and to communicate confidentially (including the right to seek information). Monitoring communications and behaviour will put pressure on employees to conform in order to prevent the detection of what might be perceived as anomalies, in a comparable way to the way in which the intensive use of CCTV has influenced citizens' behaviour in public spaces.[42]

For the sake of completeness, Article 22 GDPR on profiling should be considered, too, when discussing legal grounds for processing. However, the provision is unlikely to play a significant role here. In scenario (a), the recruiter holding the interview would likely be involved in the decision-making, the decision would therefore not be solely based on automated decision-making. Similarly, in scenario (b), the supervisor leading the annual appraisal and the salary negotiations would have a say in the outcome of the talks. But unless the decision is solely based on profiling, the rights/restrictions in Article 22 GDPR are not invoked.[43]

As a result of the analysis, neither scenario (a) nor scenario (b) have a valid legal basis. Both of Sarah and Drew's scenarios would be considered unlawful.

As regards transparency, Article 12 and 13 GDPR outline the modalities for complying with the transparency principle, which serves as the primary basis for exercising data subjects' rights. Recital 39 GDPR specifies that for compliance with the transparency principle, data subjects need to be informed about the collection or processing of their data, including to what extent their data is or will be processed. In addition, the Recital underscores that data should only be processed if the purpose of the processing cannot be achieved by other means.[44] The inference and processing of mind data during an online interview is usually not

[42] WP 249, 9–10.

[43] Article 22 GDPR could become relevant in examples where an algorithm preselects and excludes, for instance, CVs from further processing. However, this is not the typical scenario where MDTs are employed.

[44] Recital 39 GDPR.

revealed pro-actively by recruiters. In scenario (a), the candidate would typically not be informed comprehensively about the precise kind of data that is collected, even less so what information is inferred from it. Unless that is the case, the inference and processing of mind data in scenario (a) is not transparent.[45] Similarly, it is unlikely that the employer in scenario (b) would reveal the full information about the monitoring practice to their employees. But unless this requirement is met, scenario (b) would also fail to comply with the transparency principle.

Transparency is closely linked to fairness. The procedural aspect of fairness requires the processing to be transparent and lawful. The fairness principle stipulates that data cannot be obtained or processed through unfair means, by deception or without the data subject knowing about the processing.[46] Any form of hidden surveillance or data collection can be considered to violate fair processing. In addition, there is the element of substantive fairness, which is inherent to the fairness principle.[47] The fairness principle aims to protect data subjects from abuse by the controller and from unjust infringements of their fundamental rights, in particular their right to the protection of personal data. The principle encompasses a balancing of interests between data controller and data subject, striving to mitigate forms of unfair imbalances.[48] The notion of 'fair' processing requires to include the likelihood of unjustified adverse impacts of the processing on the data subject. Considerations on how the processing affects the interests of a data subject or data subjects must therefore be taken into account.

In scenario (a), mind data is inferred and processed in a situation as stressful as a job interview, without the candidate's knowledge, in an unpredictable manner, contributing to an eventually detrimental decision with major implications (whether or not the applicant will be offered a position and be hired). Even if informed that MDTs will be employed during the interview and that mind data will be inferred and processed, it is very unlikely that the candidate could stop or refuse the practice without facing severe consequences, such as being disinvited or not being further considered. Both the lack of transparency and the inherent power asymmetry between the recruiter and the applicant in the situation lead to the conclusion that the processing is unfair. The described monitoring practice in scenario (a) is therefore in contradiction with the principle of fairness.

45 The legal basis and its legitimacy will be discussed separately in Section 7.1.2.

46 Cécile de Terwagne, Article 5 in Kuner and others, *The EU General Data Protection Regulation (GDPR)*.

47 On the substantive aspect of the fairness principle in the GDPR, complementing the procedural aspect, see, for instance, Andreas Häuselmann and Bart Custers, 'Substantive Fairness in the GDPR: Fairness Elements for Article 5.1a GDPR', (2024) 52 *Computer Law & Security Review*, 105942 <https://doi.org/10.1016/j.clsr.2024.105942>.

48 Gianclaudio Malgieri, 'The Concept of Fairness in the GDPR: A Linguistic and Contextual Interpretation', in Mireille Hildebrandt and Carlos Castillo (eds.), ACM *Proceedings of the 2020 Conference on Fairness, Accountability, and Transparency* (Association for Computing Machinery 27 January 2020), 154–166, at 154 <https://doi.org/10.1145/3351095.3372868>.

In scenario (b), it is equally unlikely that the employees are fully and comprehensively informed about the practice. Even if informed about the practice, the power asymmetry would still be inherent to the relationship and the employees will unlikely have the option of rejecting the monitoring. The inferences would further be used to assess and evaluate the employees' performance and be reflected in performance reviews (annual appraisals), they would also contribute to the salary decisions and determine the future finances of the employees. Considering this imbalance between employer and employees, the employees' specific vulnerability and the severeness of the consequences, the practice in scenario (b) would also be unfair.

The legal analysis concludes that employing MDT-based monitoring practices in contexts and ways like the ones considered by Sarah and Drew in scenario (a) and (b) would not be compliant with Article 88 GDPR.

7.1.2 *Can Health and Safety Grounds Justify 'Neurosurveillance'?*

One field of deployment that has been gaining particular attention, not only in the media but also among regulators and scholars, is 'neurosurveillance' at work.[49] The notion refers to coerced or forced surveillance practices involving neurotechnology in the employment context. The previous analysis already established that monitoring or surveillance practices like the ones in scenario (a) and (b) at work are not compliant with prevailing EU laws. Using a BCI instead of any other type of MDT would not alter the result of the analysis. However, some of the practices described at the beginning of the chapter, such as the use of BCIs in sectors like mining, aviation, construction, trucking, or high-speed railways raise the question whether it is possible to justify surveillance under EU law on grounds of safety and health.

In addition to the scenarios above, Sarah and Drew develop an idea for a new BCI in the employment context:

> **Scenario (c):** *a headset with embedded EEG sensors for overland truck drivers. The sensors initiate a strong vibration whenever a certain level of fatigue is reached. The drivers have to wear the headset mandatorily as long as they actively steer the vehicle. If the drivers take a break or while charging/discharging the vehicle, they are allowed to switch off the headset.*

---

49 See, for instance: ICO, 'ICO Tech Futures: Neurotechnology (Version 01 June 2023)' <https://ico.org.uk/about-the-ico/research-reports-impact-and-evaluation/research-and-reports/technology-and-innovation/ico-tech-futures-neurotechnology/> accessed 28 January 2025; Ekaterina Muhl and Roberto Andorno, 'Neurosurveillance in the Workplace: Do Employers Have the Right to Monitor Employees' Minds?', (19 September 2023) 5 *Frontiers in Human Dynamics*, Sec. Digital Impacts <https://doi.org/10.3389/fhumd.2023.1245619>.

Considering the situation described in scenario (c), the choices for a legal basis under the GDPR are broader than for the previous vignettes in this chapter. By classifying the data as special category data, all exemptions listed in Article 9(2) GDPR are potentially available. As discussed, consent/explicit consent is not a favourable option in the employment context as it is only appropriate if circumstances allow workers to have a genuine choice and control over the monitoring. In contrast to scenario (a), here, two alternative options emerge prominently: Article 9(2)(c) vital interest and (h) assessment of the working capacity of the employee.

Article 9(2)(c) provides that special category data can be processed if the processing is necessary to protect the vital interests of the data subject or of a third person. Initially, this legal basis seems to fit scenario (c) perfectly. To ensure the safety and protect the health of both the driver and all other road users, it is important that the driver remains awake and attentive. Monitoring the driver's level of fatigue and keeping them awake while driving is a way to safeguarding everyone's vital interests. The ICO, for instance, provides a scenario in their guidance document on data protection and the monitoring of workers, which is similar: When listing the legal basis of vital interest, the ICO gives the example of a test pilot who is monitored for heart rate, blood pressure, and brain activity.[50]

Yet, upon closer examination of the provision, it becomes apparent that it is less appropriate than expected. This is because the provision continues to state that processing on the grounds of vital interest in Article 9(2)(c) GDPR is restricted to cases where the data subject is physically or legally incapable of giving consent. Noteworthy, this particular restriction only applies to special category data. Article 6(1)(d), the corresponding provision for processing normal personal data, does not encompass this restriction. The addendum for sensitive data aligns with the rationale that the processing of special category data is subject to stricter regulations compared to the processing of regular personal data. However, in Sarah and Drew's scenario (c), the driver is capable of giving consent; there is no physical, mental, or legal reason hindering them. Vital interest is therefore not a suitable legal basis for processing in scenario (c).

Next in line as legal basis is Article 9(2)(h) GDPR. This provision belongs to the exemptions for health care and health purposes. Inter alia, lit (h) allows processing of special category data that is necessary for the assessment of the working capacity of the employee. It could be argued that the brain activity of the driver needs to be monitored to assess whether the driver has the capacity to drive a large and heavy motor vehicle. Alas, the remaining parts of the provision are again not suitable for the scenario described. According to the provision, the processing needs to be based

50 ICO, 'Employment Practices and Data Protection: Monitoring Workers: Data Protection and Monitoring Workers', (4 October 2023) <https://ico.org.uk/for-organisations/uk-gdpr-guidance-and-resources/employment/monitoring-workers/data-protection-and-monitoring-workers/#dp4> accessed 8 January 2025.

on Union or Member State law or pursuant to a contract with a health professional; additionally, Article 9(3) GDPR requires the data to be processed 'by or under the responsibility of a professional subject to the obligation of professional secrecy'. The employer in scenario (c) is not a professional subject in health-related matters and they are not bound by any relevant professional secrecy. The applicability of Article 9(2)(h) for scenario (c) is therefore not convincing.

Rather, Article 9(2)(b) GDPR emerges as a possible option. The exemption allows for the processing of sensitive data if it is necessary 'for the purposes of carrying out the obligations and exercising specific rights of the controller or of the data subject in the field of employment and social security and social protection law'. Literature suggests that the processing of biometric data for access control can be based on this provision; moreover, the provision is also used for the processing of health data and genetic data by employers.[51] One could argue that ensuring their driver is fit to operate the large vehicle and does not endanger themselves or any other road user gives the employer a specific right to apply the monitoring practice while driving. Similar to Article 88 GDPR, Article 9(2)(b) can be authorised by collective agreements (other than Union or Member State law). In scenario (c), the truck company could, for instance, enter into such an agreement with the collective representatives of the drivers. These representatives would then negotiate the terms and conditions for the monitoring practice and co-determine the details on behalf of the drivers.

Article 9(2)(b) thus emerges as a suitable legal basis to make the processing lawful in scenario (c), provided it is authorised by law or collective agreement and provided appropriate safeguards for the fundamental rights and the interests of the data subject are in place. Such safeguards would include, for instance, a Data Protection Impact Assessment. Pursuant to Article 35(1) GDPR, a controller has to carry out a DPIA '[w]here a type of processing in particular using new technologies, and taking into account the nature, scope, context and purposes of the processing, is likely to result in a high risk to the rights and freedoms of natural persons'. BCIs for the monitoring of brain activity would meet the description of a new technology. Para 3 lit b provides that a DPIA is particularly required when special category data is processed on a large scale. Para 9 allows again to integrate the collective dimension of the employment context and to seek the view of worker representatives.[52]

For scenario (c) to be fully compliant, the processing must be transparent, fair, and proportionate. Moreover, it is imperative that the same goal cannot be achieved by less intrusive methods. In accordance with the principle of transparency, it is

[51] Georgieva and Kuner, Article 9 in Kuner and others, *The EU General Data Protection Regulation (GDPR)*; Eike Michael Frenzel, Article 9(2)(b) Margin Number 26 in Paal and Pauly, *Datenschutz-Grundverordnung Bundesdatenschutzgesetz*; Marion Albers and Raoul-Darius Veit, Article 9 Margin Number 64 in Heinrich A. Wolff and others (eds), *BeckOK Datenschutzrecht* (C.H.Beck 48th ed, 1.5.2024); Schiff, Article 9 Margin Number 41 in Ehmann and Selmayr, *DS-GVO* explicitly mentions that the provision can be relevant for special category data processed by wearables.

[52] Adams-Prassl, 'Regulating Algorithms at Work'.

crucial that drivers are clearly informed that the BCI they are required to wear while manoeuvring the truck is collecting and processing data on their brain activity. In terms of fairness and proportionality, one could argue that although the practice interferes with the fundamental rights and interests of the data subject, the high risks to the health and safety of the driver and others on the road make the practice proportionate. In addition, possible safeguards and mitigating measures are being put in place: The monitoring is only restricted to the time the driver is actively steering the vehicle and not applied on a continuous basis. Depending on the exact circumstances and analysis of actual accident statistics, the requirements could be further refined. For instance, the employer could consider making the devices mandatory only on long overland tours but not in urban traffic, or only during night shifts and not during daylight, while offering the devices as a voluntary safety service to the drivers for the rest of the time. Importantly, however, possible less intrusive methods have to be considered.

Provided the necessary safeguards are in place and no less intrusive methods are available, the monitoring practice in scenario (c) can be considered compliant with the GDPR. Thus, safety and health can be a valid reason to justify monitoring practices that would otherwise contradict data protection, as long as the practice is deemed lawful, transparent, fair, and proportionate, and as long as all other data protection principles are adhered to as well.

The EU Framework Directive for occupational safety and health (Directive on Safety and Health of Workers 89/391/EEC, 'OSH Framework Directive'), a directive introducing obligations for employers to evaluate the safety and health risks of workers and to take protective measures, supports the findings above. The Directive does not address specifically MDTs or any other new technology or surveillance practice, but it does reiterate that the introduction of new technologies has to be subject to consultation with workers and/or their representatives.[53]

Not directly applicable to Sarah and Drew's scenario (c) but eventually to other, more traditional office monitoring practices, the Display Screen Equipment Directive (Directive 90/270/EEC) may additionally have to be considered in matters related to health and safety.[54] The Directive stipulates that workers shall be informed about all aspects of safety and health relating to their workstation.[55] All aspects would include, inter alia, the inference and processing of brain data.[56]

53 Article 6(3)(c) Directive 89/391/EEC (consolidated version 2008).

54 The Directive explicitly excludes drivers' cabs or control cabs for vehicles as well as computer systems on board a means of transport (Article 1(3) Directive 90/270/EEC).

55 Article 6(1) Directive 90/270/EEC.

56 See also European Agency for Safety at Work, Artificial Intelligence for Worker Management: Existing and Future Regulations, 5 <https://osha.europa.eu/sites/default/files/documents/artificial-inteligence-worker-management-regulations_en.pdf> accessed 8 January 2025.

Overall, despite its inherent limitations as an opening clause, Article 88 GDPR stands as a significant and crucial impediment to the adoption of MDT-based monitoring practices in the employment context. Examples discussed regularly in global media would most likely fail to meet the fundamental requirements outlined in Article 88 GDPR. One of the primary challenges lies is establishing a legal basis for such processing. Scenarios such as those illustrated in Sarah and Drew's scenarios (a) and (b) typically lack a valid legal basis. Within the employment context, consent generally proves inadequate as an option. In the absence of consent, processing of normal personal data for monitoring practices is likely to rely on legitimate interests and necessitates a careful balancing test. Such a balancing test is likely to fail for most MDT-based monitoring practices due to their intrusive nature. For special category data, establishing a valid legal basis and a suitable exemption from the general prohibition of processing is even more challenging.

Although providing solid regulatory guardrails, the existing framework remains flexible enough to accommodate specific cases where monitoring practices can be justified, such as for reasons of health and safety. Importantly, adequate safeguards must be implemented, and the processing must adhere to all data protection principles. Depending on national legislation, these practices may require collective agreements and the involvement of worker representatives.

The primary challenge in combatting the unlawful deployment of MDTs for monitoring practices in the EU remains enforcement. Given the generally observed lack of transparency surrounding the use of MDTs and the fragmented transposition of Article 88 GDPR into national legislation, particularly regarding the involvement of collective representative bodies, affected data subjects are either unaware that the practice is applied or left to seek justice for themselves.

7.2 EQUALITY ACQUIS: AN EXTRA LAYER OF PROTECTION

One aspect not yet addressed is the risk of inherent bias in MDT-based monitoring practices and its potential to cause discriminatory effects on data subjects.[57] Facial expressions and body language associated with emotions can differ significantly between geo-cultural regions. Moreover, these characteristics vary across genders and age groups, as well as between individuals or within different contexts. Linguistic differences further contribute to this intricate landscape, with variations in regional accents or socioeconomic linguistic patterns.

Adding to the complexity, the interpretation and decoding of emotions can lead to a dual-layer bias. It is not only the expression of emotion itself that is varying, but the interpretation of emotion also differs across cultures, age groups, and other

[57] See Tessa Verhoef and Eduard Fosch-Villaronga, 'Towards Affective Computing That Works for Everyone', (2023), 11th International Conference on Affective Computing and Intelligent Interaction (ACII), Cambridge, MA (IEEE 2024), 1–8 <https://doi.org/10.1109/ACII59096.2023.10388169>.

factors. In an algorithmic context, differing perception leads to differences in the labelling of the data. Differences in emotional expression as well as perception can lead to biases in multiple respects, resulting in the development of biased algorithms and inferences, ultimately causing discriminatory effects on individuals.[58] Studies suggest that darker faces may be perceived as angrier or as displaying more negative emotions compared to white faces, regardless of their expression.[59] Elderly faces are less likely to be decoded accurately.[60] Key language markers can differ between races, genders, and age groups.[61] In jobs with a clear majority of male/female employees, training data can be predominantly based on the emotional response and engagement features of one gender, the algorithm would then be likely to read the emotions of the underrepresented gender less accurately.[62] Such biases can have serious repercussions in the employment context, including discrimination in recruitment, performance evaluation, and promotion processes.

Concerning the use of neurotechnology, the ICO explicitly points to the risk of discrimination and unfair decisions in the workplace.[63] The ICO stresses particularly that neurodivergent people could suffer discrimination due to inaccurate systems and databases that have been trained on neuro-normative patterns.[64]

In cases of discrimination due to MDT-based monitoring practices, the EU equality acquis provides an additional layer of protection, with solid legal provisions in primary law and several directives supporting them at a secondary law level. Complementing the prohibition of discrimination in Article 14 of the European Convention on Human Rights, Title III of the Charter of Fundamental Rights on equality includes rights to guarantee equality before the law (Article 20 CFR), to non-discrimination (Article 21 CFR), to equality between women and men (Article 23 CFR), and to the integration of persons with disabilities (Article 26 CFR). The secondary law framework includes Directive 2000/43/EC (Racial Equality Directive) against discrimination on grounds of race and ethnic origin, Directive 2000/78/EC (Employment Equality Directive) establishing a general framework for equal treatment in employment and occupation, Directive 2004/113/EC on equal treatment for men and women in the access to and

58 Isabelle Hupont and others, 'Measuring and Fostering Diversity in Affective Computing Research', (2024) 15(01) *IEEE Transactions on Affective Computing*, 63–78 <https://doi.org/10.1109/TAFFC.2023.3244041>.

59 See Rhue, 'Racial Influence'.

60 Mara Fölster and others, 'Facial Age Affects Emotional Expression Decoding', *Frontiers in Psychology* (4 February 2014) <www.frontiersin.org/articles/10.3389/fpsyg.2014.00030/full#h4> accessed 8 January 2025.

61 Sunny Rai and others, 'Key Language Markers of Depression on Social Media Depend on Race', *Proceedings of the National Academy of Sciences*, (26 March 2024) <https://doi.org/10.1073/pnas.2319837121>.

62 Mark Purdy and others, 'The Risks of AI to Interpret Human Emotions', *Harvard Business Review* (18 November 2019) <https://hbr.org/2019/11/the-risks-of-using-ai-to-interpret-human-emotions> accessed 8 January 2025.

63 ICO, 'Tech Futures', 3.

64 ICO, 'Tech Futures', 19.

supply of goods and services, and Directive 2006/54/EC (Gender Equality Directive) on the implementation of the principle of equal opportunities and equal treatment of men and women in matters of employment and occupation (recast).[65]

The comprehensive list of directives and their scope of application underscore the EU's robust tradition of anti-discrimination rights in the context of employment.[66] Assuming hypothetically that Sarah and Drew's scenarios were compliant with data protection law, affected individuals could still rely on the equality framework if they were discriminated against due to biases in MDT-based monitoring practices.

Scenario (a_1) *The employer using voice analytics for recruitment has removed an older applicant from the shortlist because the algorithm qualified their voice as less spirited and engaged compared to younger applicants.*

Scenario (b_1) *The employer using the keylogger software has denied a male customer service agent a long-anticipated promotion because the algorithm has classified this agent as being little empathetic and emotionally effective. The algorithm was trained with data predominantly from female agents.*

Scenario (c_1) *The truck driver wearing the EEG headset is neurodiverse. The algorithm interprets his brain activity as indicating constant fatigue. Consequently, the employer assigns the truck driver fewer and shorter tours, resulting in reduced pay.*

The Employment Equality Directive (EED), Directive 2000/78/EC, is the most relevant legislation to combat the discrimination in scenario (a_1). The purpose of the Employment Equality Directive is to combat discrimination on the grounds of religion or belief, disability, age, or sexual orientation as regards employment and occupation.[67] Following prevailing opinion, discrimination by an algorithm is considered to be within the scope of indirect discrimination as in Article 2(2)(b) EED.[68] Article 3(1)(a) EED extends the scope of the Directive to access to employment, including selection criteria and recruitment conditions. The EED therefore applies to the recruitment situation in scenario (a_1). The EED aims to combat discrimination at work on grounds of certain protected characteristics. Scenario (a_1) describes discrimination based on age. Article 6(1) EED lists several reasons for the justification of differences of treatment on grounds of age, but none of the reasons apply

65 In addition, the Commission has proposed the Directive Proposal (COM(2008)462) against discrimination based on age, disability, sexual orientation, and religion or belief beyond the workplace, which has not been adopted.

66 For a justification for less favourable treatment under European non-discrimination law, see European Union Agency for Fundamental Rights and Council of Europe, Handbook on European Non-discrimination Law (Publications Office of the European Union 2018), 91–109.

67 Article 1 EED.

68 For arguments to possibly consider algorithmic bias a direct discrimination, see Jeremias Adams-Prassl and others, 'Directly Discriminatory Algorithms', (2022) *Modern Law Review* <https://doi.org/10.1111/1468-2230.12759>; Aislinn Kelly-Lyth, 'Algorithmic Discrimination at Work', (2023) 14(2) *European Labour Law Journal*, 152–171 <https://doi.org/10.1177/20319525231167300>.

to scenario (a_1). The rejected candidate in scenario (a_1) could therefore pursue the case further against the employer based on age-based discrimination against them.

Scenario (b_1) could be argued to fall within the scope of Directive 2006/54/EC (recast Gender Equality Directive), pursuant to the principle of equal treatment in relation to access to employment, including promotion, in Article 1(a). Article 14(1)(a) prohibits any direct or indirect discrimination on grounds of sex in relation to conditions for access to employment at all levels of the professional hierarchy, including promotion. The affected agent could claim that male agents have reduced access to promotion compared to women, given that the algorithm was trained primarily on female training data, therefore categorising male data as being less empathetic. This led to the male agent being denied a promotion. The agent could pursue the case further based on discrimination, too.

As a result of the analysis, both MDT-based monitoring practices could be fought in court on grounds of discrimination. Once more, the crucial challenge in both scenarios lies however in enforcement. In real-life scenarios beyond the vignettes, it is highly probable that the affected individuals would never learn about the categorisation parameters or the biased algorithm; they would remain unaware they were even subject to discrimination. In addition, the limited access for potential plaintiffs to the necessary evidence to initiate legal proceedings poses a significant hurdle. Initially, the burden falls on the plaintiff to provide evidence suggesting possible discrimination; employers are not directly mandated by EU law to disclose such information.[69] Given these circumstances, while non-discrimination laws theoretically offer robust protection, they are nearly unenforceable at the individual level when it comes to algorithmic discrimination, including MDT-based discrimination.

Scenario (c_1) is different to scenarios (a_1) and (b_1) in that it is unclear whether the discrimination even concerns a legally protected characteristic. One possible option lies in the EED. The EED applies to discrimination on grounds of disability. However, the EED does not define the term disability. The UN Convention on the Rights of Persons with Disabilities (UN CRPD), being an overarching point of reference behind the EED, does not provide an exact definition of disability either, it rather offers an evolving concept of disability.[70] For invoking the EED in scenario (c_1), it would be necessary to determine whether there is national legislation clarifying the status of this specific neurodiversity as a disability. If so, the full catalogue of obligations and prohibitions outlined in the EED would apply. Inter alia, Article 5 EED mandates that reasonable accommodation shall be provided for disabled persons, including that employers must take appropriate measures 'to enable a person

[69] See also Aislinn Kelly-Lyth, 'Algorithmic Discrimination at Work', 168.

[70] See Irmgard Anglmayer, 'Implementation of the Employment Equality Directive in light of the UN CRPD' European Implementation Assessment, Study European Parliamentary Research Service, (2020) <www.europarl.europa.eu/RegData/etudes/STUD/2020/654206/EPRS_STU(2020)654206_EN.pdf> accessed 8 May 2025.

with a disability to have access to, participate in, or advance in employment [...] unless such measures would impose a disproportionate burden on the employer'. Consequently, Article 5 EED could be used as an argument to mandate the implementation of alternative monitoring practices for neurodiverse persons. Negotiating such measures may be facilitated by collective representatives.

However, if the specific neurodiversity is not classified as a disability and it is not associated with any other recognised protected characteristic, then discrimination as per the EED does not occur, rendering the case likely outside the scope of equality law. This could potentially create a legal loophole in the future, as mentioned by the ICO. Alternatively, a harmonised piece of legislation on data protection in the employment context could, de lege ferenda, include specific guidelines with respect to neurodiversities.

7.3 PWD: PROTOTYPE FOR AN EMPLOYMENT-SPECIFIC DATA PROTECTION LAW

After intense political debates, marked by several setbacks along the way, EU legislators were able to reach a political agreement on the Platform Work Directive (PWD) in spring 2024.[71] The legal presumption of employment for platform workers proposed in the Commission draft had sparked major controversies, as it aimed to combat the widespread false attribution of self-employment in the sector. Highly debated and contested by various stakeholders, the finally adopted version includes a rebuttable legal presumption, leaving the details to be defined by the Member States.[72] In general, the PWD provides minimum standards that have to be applied by digital labour platforms across the Union. However, Member States are free to adopt laws or provisions that go beyond the PWD and that are more favourable to platform workers, including to encourage or permit the application of collective agreements.[73]

The PWD aims not only to enhance the working conditions of people performing platform work but also to improve the protection of personal data processed by digital labour platforms.[74] Although its applicability is restricted to the narrow

[71] Directive (EU) 2024/2831 of the European Parliament and of the Council of 23 October 2024 on Improving Working Conditions in Platform Work, OJ L, 2024/2831.

[72] Article 5 PWD.

[73] Article 26 PWD.

[74] See Article 1 PWD, Recital 16 PWD ('This Directive aims to improve the working conditions of platform workers and to protect the personal data of persons performing platform work. Both objectives are pursued simultaneously and, while mutually reinforcing and inseparably linked, one is not secondary to the other.') and Recital 38 PWD ('This Directive provides for more specific safeguards concerning the processing of personal data by means of automated systems in the context of platform work, thereby providing for a higher level of protection of the personal data of persons performing platform work. In particular, this Directive establishes more specific rules in relation to Regulation

domain of digital labour platforms, the PWD represents the first piece of unified legislation tackling data protection challenges in a digitalised world of employment.[75] The approaches and regulatory measures introduced by the PWD merit therefore a discussion, especially in the context of monitoring practices.

As regards data protection, the PWD explicitly excludes consent as a legal basis in the context of platform work, stating that: 'the consent of persons performing platform work to the processing of their personal data cannot be assumed to be freely given. [...] Therefore, digital labour platforms should not process the personal data of persons performing platform work on the basis that a person performing platform work has given consent to the processing of his or her personal data.'[76] Any attempt to base data processing on consent is bound to fail under the PWD.

Chapter 3 PWD on algorithmic management is certainly the most revolutionary chapter in this context. Although limited to the specific sector of platform work, Chapter 3 PWD is noteworthy beyond this realm, as it introduces the first-ever EU rules on algorithmic management in the workplace.[77] The PWD addresses the concerns related to algorithmic management and the need for regulatory measures already in its Recitals, reiterating some of the main challenges: Persons performing platform work 'do not have access to information on how the algorithms work, which personal data are used or how the behaviour of those persons affects decisions taken by automated systems', and they 'do not know the reasons for decisions taken or supported by automated systems and are not able to obtain an explanation for those decisions, to discuss those decisions with a human contact person, to contest those decisions or to seek rectification or, where relevant, redress'.[78]

Article 8 PWD establishes a general legal assumption that the processing by a digital labour platform by means of automated monitoring and decision-making

(EU) 2016/679 concerning the use of and transparency with regard to automated decision-making. This Directive also establishes additional measures in relation to Regulation (EU) 2016/679 in the context of platform work to safeguard the protection of the personal data of persons performing platform work, in particular where decisions are taken or supported by the automated processing of personal data. Terms relating to the protection of personal data in this Directive should be understood in light of the definitions set out in Regulation (EU) 2016/679.').

75 For a discussion on regulatory gaps with regard to algorithmic management and an analysis of the draft PWD, see Jeremias Adams-Prassl and others, 'Regulating Algorithmic Management: A Blueprint', (2023) 14(2) *European Labour Law Journal*, 124–151 <https://doi.org/10.1177/20319525231167299>; Michael Veale and others, 'Fortifying the Algorithmic Management Provisions in the Proposed Platform Work Directive', (2023) 14(2) *European Labour Law Journal*, 308–332 <https://doi.org/10.1177/20319525231167983>.

76 Recital 39 PWD.

77 For earlier discussions on algorithmic management in the domain of platform work, see, for instance, Jeremias Prassl, *Humans As a Service: The Promise and Perils of Work in the Gig Economy* (Oxford University Press 2018); Jeremias Adams-Prassl, 'What If Your Boss Was an Algorithm? The Rise of Artificial Intelligence at Work', (2019) 41(1) *Comparative Labor Law & Policy Journal*, 123.

78 Recital 8 PWD.

systems is a type of processing likely to result in a high risk to the rights and freedoms of natural person, requiring a GDPR Data Protection Impact Assessment. Going beyond GDPR standards and specifically tailored for the employment context, this DPIA shall specifically involve persons performing platform work themselves and their representatives.

In response to existing power asymmetries and to enforcement weaknesses previously discussed, the PWD strengthens the transparency requirements that already exist in the GDPR. Again, the requirements go further, compared to the GDPR, and are better tailored to the employment context:

> Article 9: Transparency with regard to automated monitoring systems and automated decision-making systems
>
> 1. Member States shall require digital labour platforms to inform persons performing platform work, platform workers' representatives and, upon request, national competent authorities, of the use of automated monitoring systems or automated decision-making systems.
>
> That information shall concern:
>
> (a) as regards automated monitoring systems:
>   (i) the fact that such systems are in use or are in the process of being introduced;
>   (ii) the categories of data and action monitored, supervised or evaluated by such systems, including evaluation by the recipient of the service;
>   (iii) the aim of the monitoring and how the system is to carry out that monitoring;
>   (iv) the recipients or categories of recipient of the personal data processed by such systems and any transmission or transfer of such personal data, including within a group of undertakings;
>
> (b) as regards automated decision-making systems:
>   (i) the fact that such systems are in use or are in the process of being introduced;
>   (ii) the categories of decision that are taken or supported by such systems;
>   (iii) the categories of data and the main parameters that such systems take into account and the relative importance of those main parameters in the automated decision-making, including the way in which the personal data or behaviour of the person performing platform work influence the decisions;
>   (iv) the grounds for decisions to restrict, suspend or terminate the account of the person performing platform work, to refuse the payment for work performed by them, as well as for decisions on their contractual status or any decision of equivalent or detrimental effect;
>
> (c) all categories of decision taken or supported by automated systems that affect persons performing platform work in any manner.[79]

[79] Article 9 PWD.

Furthermore, Article 9 PWD provides that the information shall be given in a transparent, intelligible, and easily accessible form, using clear and plain language (para 2), at the latest on the first working day, prior to the introduction of changes (para 3), and that workers' representatives shall receive comprehensive and detailed information about all relevant systems and their features (para 4). These transparency requirements also apply to persons undergoing a recruitment or selection procedure (para 5).

Particularly with regard to automated decision-making systems, the PWD goes substantially beyond GDPR requirements. While Article 22 GDPR is only invoked when the decision is based solely on automated processing and produces legal effects concerning him or her or similarly significantly affects him or her, the PWD provisions have a much broader scope, addressing systems 'which are used to take or support, by electronic means, decisions that significantly affect persons performing platform work, including the working conditions of platform workers'.[80] Hence, support systems are also included and the decisions are not restricted to those having legal or similar effects on the individuals themselves; instead, it is sufficient that they affect their working conditions. The non-exhaustive catalogue of what can affect the working conditions is comprehensive, including recruitment, access to and organisation of assignments, earnings, safety and health, working time, access to training, promotion, and contractual status including restriction, suspension, or termination of account. It is also noteworthy that the main parameters and their relative importance in automated decision-making must be disclosed.

Moreover, Article 10 PWD on human oversight prohibits that platforms take certain important decisions, for example decisions to restrict, suspend, or terminate the contractual relationship, without human intervention (para 5). Article 11 PWD on human review guarantees a right to obtain an explanation and a right to request the digital labour platform to review the decisions and to eventually rectify the decision.

Most relevant for MDT-based monitoring practices is Article 7 PWD. In Article 7, the PWD introduces a blacklist similar to the one we have seen in the UCPD. But while the UCPD prohibits specific commercial practices, the PWD does not ban specific monitoring practices. Instead, the PWD prohibits the processing of specific types of personal data by means of automated monitoring or decision-making systems. The provision is applicable to any person performing platform work (not only platform workers) – and the prohibition is absolute. It also applies to the recruitment or selection procedure (para 2), and not only applies to automated monitoring and decision-making systems but also to support systems and systems taking decisions that affect persons performing platform work in any manner (para 3).

The exhaustive list in Article 7(1) PWD bans the processing of any personal data in relation to private conversations, the processing to predict the exercise of

[80] Article 2(1)(i) PWD.

fundamental rights (in particular the right of association, the right of collective bargaining and action, and the right to information and consultation), and the collection of any personal data while not offering or performing platform work.

Importantly, Article 7(1)(a) PWD prohibits the processing of any personal data on the emotional or psychological state of the person performing platform work by means of automated monitoring systems or automated decision-making systems. Processing of any personal data on emotional or psychological states will therefore no longer be permitted. In addition, Article 7(1)(e) bans the processing of 'any personal data *to infer the* racial or ethnic origin, migration status, political opinions, religious or philosophical beliefs, disability, state of health, including chronic disease or HIV status, *emotional or psychological state*, trade union membership, sex life or sexual orientation' (emphasis added). Therefore, the PWD does not only prohibit the processing of output data on the emotional or psychological state but also any processing of input data to infer the emotional or psychological state. Recital 40 PWD reiterates the prohibitions made in Article 7 PWD.

The scope of lit (e) is remarkably broad, not limiting itself to the known special categories in the GDPR but complementing them with specifications and additional types of data that lend themselves to discrimination. New in the list are, for instance, migration status, disability, the explicit mentioning of chronic disease or HIV status, and, among others, the emotional or psychological state. The explicit integration of these categories in Article 7(1)(e) PWD might indicate that the existing list of special categories in the GDPR could undergo a significant overhaul during a potential future reform of the GDPR.

Article 7(1)(a) and (e) PWD are pivotal milestones and will impact the use of MDT-based monitoring practices. In essence, the PWD is banning all monitoring practices that require *processing* of personal data on the emotional or psychological state – albeit, solely within the realm of digital labour platforms. Additionally, the PWD prohibits the *processing* of personal data *to infer* the emotional and psychological states, irrespective of whether the input data is classified as special category or not. Moreover, the PWD does not link emotional or psychological states exclusively to biometric data. Data processing by text-based MDTs should therefore be encompassed within the prohibition of the PWD. The PWD prohibition of processing is absolute, there are no exceptions to this ban in the PWD, not even for reasons of safety and health.

Provided Sarah and Drew's scenario (c) detects only the physical state of fatigue and does not process or infer any personal data on the emotional or psychological state of the driver, the prohibitions in 7(1)(a) PWD will not affect scenario (c). In addition, however, lit (e) strictly prohibits using the data concerning the physical state of fatigue to infer data on emotional and psychological states.

Arguably, the PWD is a sector-specific piece of legislation, in parts a lex specialis for data protection that is applicable solely to the employment context of digital labour platforms. Yet, its provisions regarding data processing, algorithmic management, and algorithmic decision-making, including the prohibitions on processing and inferring personal data on emotional or psychological states, may serve as a foundational framework for other contexts. Through its various provisions and prohibitions, the PWD presents an innovative regulatory framework, offering a potential blueprint for a modern horizontal regulation on data protection in the workplace. Hopes are that the PWD will establish a precedent for addressing data protection in other employment contexts beyond the confines of digital labour platforms.

If EU legislators were able to find an agreement on such a horizontal law for data protection in the employment context, including a blacklist similar to the one in the PWD, it should be aligned with existing legal concepts and proposed adaptations in horizontal law. A possible prohibition for processing mind data in a horizontal data protection regulation for the employment context de lege ferenda could therefore read:

> Employers shall not, by means of automated monitoring or decision-making systems:
> – process and infer mind data.

7.4 AIA: REGULATION REMAINS FRAGMENTED

The employment context is addressed prominently by two provisions in the AIA, both are relevant for MDTs.[81] Article 5(1)(f) AIA prohibits the use of 'AI systems to infer emotions' in the workplace:

> the placing on the market, the putting into service for this specific purpose, or the use of AI systems to infer emotions of a natural person in the areas of workplace and education institutions, except where the use of the AI system is intended to be put in place or into the market for medical or safety reasons;[82]

Sarah and Drew's scenario (a), the online recruitment software relying on voice analytics to draw inferences regarding candidates' teamwork ability, their level of discomfort, emotional engagement, irritation, or insecurity is potentially affected by the Article 5(1)(f) prohibition. The AI system is inferring emotions. Being based on biometric data, scenario (a) also meets the strict interpretation of Article 5(1)(f) in conjunction with Recital 44 AIA.[83]

However, it is reasonable to question whether a recruitment process would fall within the scope of the provision. Article 5(1)(f) AIA itself only refers to 'areas of

[81] For a discussion on algorithmic management in the AIA Commission Proposal, see Adams-Prassl, 'Regulating Algorithms at Work'.
[82] Article 5(1)(f) AIA.
[83] The discrepancies between 'ERS' and 'AI systems to infer emotions' in Article 5(1)(f) AIA have already been discussed earlier, see the Section 3.1 on 'Emotion Recognition Systems'.

workplace'. Like the GDPR, the AIA takes a broad approach to the employment sector. Annex III Section 4, categorising AI systems utilised in the context of employment, worker management, and access to self-employment as high risk AI systems, sets a remarkably expansive scope:

> 4. Employment, workers management and access to self-employment:
> (a) AI systems intended to be used for the recruitment or selection of natural persons, in particular to place targeted job advertisements, to analyse and filter job applications, and to evaluate candidates;
> (b) AI systems intended to be used to make decisions affecting terms of work-related relationships, the promotion or termination of work-related contractual relationships, to allocate tasks based on individual behaviour or personal traits or characteristics or to monitor and evaluate the performance and behaviour of persons in such relationship.[84]

Pursuant to Annex III Section 4 AIA, the areas of workplace encompass recruitment, promotion, termination, task allocation, and performance monitoring or evaluation.[85] By analogy to Annex III Section 4, it can be concluded that the prohibition in Article 5(1)(f) AIA also applies to the recruitment process.

This has been confirmed by the Commission Guidelines on prohibited AI practices.[86] Furthermore, the Guidelines specify that the prohibition in Article 5(1)(f) AIA is closely related to the power imbalance inherent in the employment context. Therefore, the ban on AI systems inferring emotions in the workplace should be understood to only apply to those who are subject to this power imbalance, that is to say, the employees. According to the Guidelines, the ban does not, for instance, extend to the use of ERS for tracking customers' emotions, provided it is ensured that no employees are being tracked and there are sufficient safeguards.[87]

Moreover, the Commission Guidelines on prohibited AI practices clarify that the exceptions for medical and safety reasons should be interpreted narrowly.[88] Therapeutic uses should be understood to refer to the use of CE-marked medical devices. The detection of general aspects of well-being or the general monitoring of stress levels is not permitted under health and safety grounds:

[84] Annex III section 4 AIA.

[85] See also Recital 57 AIA.

[86] EU Commission, Annex to the Communication to the Commission, Approval of the Content of the Draft Communication from the Commission – Commission Guidelines on Prohibited Artificial Intelligence Practices, section 254.

[87] EU Commission, Annex to the Communication to the Commission, Approval of the Content of the Draft Communication from the Commission – Commission Guidelines on Prohibited Artificial Intelligence Practices, section 254.

[88] EU Commission, Annex to the Communication to the Commission, Approval of the Content of the Draft Communication from the Commission – Commission Guidelines on Prohibited Artificial Intelligence Practices, section 256–263.

> (259) It follows from this narrow interpretation of the exception that any use for medical and safety reasons should always remain limited to what is strictly necessary and proportionate, including limits in time, personal application and scale, and should be accompanied by sufficient safeguards. Such safeguards could include, for example, prior written and motivated expert opinion relating to the specific use case. The necessity should be assessed on an objective basis in relation to the medical and safety purpose, and not refer to the employer's or educational institution's 'needs'. This assessment should inquire whether less intrusive alternative means exist which would achieve the same purpose.
>
> (260) Employers and educators should only deploy emotion recognition systems for medical and safety reasons in case of an explicit need. Data collected and processed in this context may not be used for any other purpose. This is particularly important given that the use of AI management software at work has proven to potentially negatively impact workers' health and safety. Continuous monitoring via wearables, for instance, may increase work-stress while affecting productivity.[89]

The Commission Guidelines also highlight that employers shall consult with workers or their representatives when introducing such new technologies and that data protection legislation remains applicable.[90]

Scenario (a) infers emotions in the recruitment process based on biometric data. The exemptions for medical and safety reasons mentioned in Article 5(1)(f) AIA do not apply. Therefore, scenario (a) would be considered an unacceptable risk. Its placing on the market or the putting into service would be prohibited in the EU. Sarah and Drew should rather not invest their time in developing this application further if they want for their software to be available in the EU.

Scenario (c), the EEG-based headset monitoring brain activity of truck drivers while driving their vehicle, meets the workplace requirement. However, the prohibition in Article 5(1)(f) AIA will not be applicable. In the context of ERS, Recital 18 AIA clarifies that the notion of ERS (as defined per Article 3(39) AIA: 'an AI system for the purpose of identifying or inferring emotions or intentions of natural persons on the basis of their biometric data') does not apply to systems used for detecting physical states, such as the state of fatigue of professional drivers:

> The notion of 'emotion recognition system' referred to in this Regulation should be defined as an AI system for the purpose of identifying or inferring emotions or intentions of natural persons on the basis of their biometric data. The notion

[89] EU Commission, Annex to the Communication to the Commission, Approval of the Content of the Draft Communication from the Commission – Commission Guidelines on Prohibited Artificial Intelligence Practices, section 259–260.

[90] EU Commission, Annex to the Communication to the Commission, Approval of the Content of the Draft Communication from the Commission – Commission Guidelines on Prohibited Artificial Intelligence Practices, section 256–263 EU Commission, Annex to the Communication to the Commission, Approval of the Content of the Draft Communication from the Commission – Commission Guidelines on Prohibited Artificial Intelligence Practices, section 259–260, footnote 167.

refers to emotions or intentions such as happiness, sadness, anger, surprise, disgust, embarrassment, excitement, shame, contempt, satisfaction and amusement. *It does not include physical states, such as pain or fatigue, including, for example, systems used in detecting the state of fatigue of professional pilots or drivers for the purpose of preventing accidents.*[91]

Following the rationale of Recital 18 AIA, scenario (c), the EEG-based monitoring system detecting the physical state of fatigue of professional drivers, is not subject to the prohibition in Article 5(1)(f) AIA, which bans 'AI systems to infer emotions', not AI systems to detect physical states.[92] Rather, scenario (c) falls under the classification as high risk system according to Annex III, section 4(b) AIA. The employment of such a system is permitted under the AIA, provided all requirements for high risk AI systems are met.

Sarah and Drew's scenario (b), the keylogger software recording written conversations and inferring mind data for performance monitoring, performance evaluation, and promotion decisions, is not based on biometric data. Applying a strict interpretation of Article 5(1)(f) AIA in conjunction with Recital 44 AIA, scenario (b) is not within the scope of the prohibition.[93] However, it falls within the scope of Annex III, section 4(b) AIA. Promotion and performance monitoring or evaluation are explicitly listed. Thus, scenario (b) is permitted and subject to the requirements for high risk AI systems under the AIA.

Recital 57 AIA provides further guidance on AI systems used in employment contexts for monitoring or evaluation of persons in work-related contractual relationships, stressing the risk of perpetuating historical patterns of discrimination and the risk for fundamental rights, in particular the right to data protection and privacy.

In recognition of the specificities of the employment context, the AIA allows Member States to maintain or introduce laws, regulations, or administrative provisions that are more favourable to workers.[94] This enables legislators to adopt future leges speciales, such as the PWD, which could potentially ban or restrict other types of applications, strengthen collective representation, and balance the existing power asymmetry.

Overall, the regulation of MDTs at work under the AIA remains fragmented. There are positive aspects, such as the prohibition of AI systems to infer emotions in Article 5(1)(f) AIA. However, a strict interpretation of the provision – limiting this prohibition to AI systems based on biometric data, as indicated by Recital 44

[91] Recital 18 AIA (emphasis added). For a discussion on the exemption of physical states from the notion of ERS in Recital 18 AIA, see Section 3.1 on 'Emotion Recognition Systems'.

[92] This has been confirmed by EU Commission, Annex to the Communication to the Commission, Approval of the Content of the Draft Communication from the Commission – Commission Guidelines on Prohibited Artificial Intelligence Practices, section 261.

[93] The Commission Guidelines on prohibited AI practices support such a strict interpretation, see Section 3.1 on 'Emotion Recognition Systems'.

[94] Article 2(11) AIA.

AIA and supported by the Commission Guidelines on prohibited AI practices – leaves many applications unaddressed. Conversely, a broader interpretation of the prohibition would be better aligned with the intentions as expressed in the PWD, which prohibits the processing and inference of data on emotional and psychological states, regardless of whether the AI system relies on biometric data.

Ultimately, the AIA, being general legislation, does not fulfil the urgent need for a sector-specific data protection law addressing AI-based management and monitoring. As outlined earlier, such a Union-wide sector-specific data protection law should include a blacklist similar to the one in the PWD, prohibiting the inference and processing of mind data.

Concluding Remarks

Amidst ongoing global debates on the governance of emerging technologies, this book intended to offer a fresh perspective on regulating emotion technology and neurotechnology, collectively termed 'Mind Datafying Technologies' (MDTs). Rather than treating the challenges posed by these technologies – particularly those arising from their expansion beyond the distinct medical sector – as isolated or distinct, this study framed them as interconnected, advocating for an integrated regulatory framework for MDTs that is both nuanced and multilayered.

Complementing current discussions on potential international governance instruments and the adequacy of existing human rights catalogues in addressing neurotechnology, this study examined the potential of EU secondary law in regulating MDTs. The book adopted a distinctly pragmatic perspective, taking a use case-based approach with semi-fictional vignettes to analyse the complex landscape across specific fields. This approach helped to build a comprehensive picture of the legal environment, highlighting key challenges, legal gaps, and inconsistencies. The insights gained from this detailed analysis formed the basis for potential policy responses within relevant domains.

At the time of its adoption, the GDPR was groundbreaking legislation, with many of its notions and concepts shaping data protection globally. Since then, technology has advanced, revealing several weaknesses therein, some of which affect the employment of MDTs. Under the GDPR, MDTs are most commonly associated with the category of biometric data. However, in its current form, accurately classifying data processed by MDTs under the correct biometric category and ensuring compliance with the appropriate legal regime is highly complex, leaving substantial amounts of data without special protection. Importantly, data processed by text-based MDTs falls completely beyond the scope of special protection, unless the data is associated with another special category. Given the growing use of text-based applications, amplified by the availability of Large Language Models, this raises concerns.

Building on these considerations, this book advocates for a shift away from focusing primarily on the technological or biophysical parameters used to datafy people's minds and mental processes. Instead, the study suggests prioritising the protection of the actual information that needs safeguarding. To this end, it proposes incorporating the category of 'mind data' into the GDPR and defining it as a sui generis special category. The classification of mind data as a sui generis special category aligns seamlessly with the rationale and tradition of special category data in data protection law. Furthermore, the proposed definition is consistent with concepts and approaches already integrated by EU legislators into existing hard law, such as the AIA and the PWD. Assigning mind data this status would have a significant effect across all relevant legislation.

The EU's AI Act is the first legislation specifically addressing Emotion Recognition Systems (ERS). The AIA adopts a multilayered approach to ERS. By categorising all ERS as limited risk AI systems and requiring that all natural persons be informed of their exposure to such a system, EU legislators aim to end the practice of AI systems identifying and inferring the emotions or intentions of individuals without their awareness. Additionally, all ERS must meet the stringent requirements for high-risk AI systems. The high-risk category is the highest category under the AIA, and the requirements are substantial. Notably, the use of AI systems to infer emotions in the workplace and in educational institutions is deemed an unacceptable risk under the AIA and thus prohibited, except for medical and safety reasons. Considering the broader context, the AIA's regulation of ERS emerges as a multifaceted effort by the legislators to foster innovation and development in a nascent sector while imposing significant guardrails. Nonetheless, this book argues that the AIA should not be viewed as the definitive regulation of MDTs. Rather, the AIA serves as a general framework, a baseline that necessitates further legal measures, including additional restrictions or prohibitions, through sector-specific laws.

The definition of ERS under the AIA is strictly linked to biometric data. This is regrettable as it excludes all text-based MDTs. As regards the discrepancies surrounding biometric and special category biometric data under the GDPR, the definition of biometric data in the AIA is detached from its definition in the GDPR, removing problematic parts and not differentiating between biometric and special category biometric data. These adaptations will undoubtedly enhance the regulation of MDTs within the scope of the AIA. However, many laws refer to the GDPR as the general framework for the protection of personal data. Practically all digital laws build upon the GDPR and its definitions. The improvements in the AIA will have no impact on them in this respect.

The analysis of MDT regulation in specific use cases suggests that MDTs do not always present entirely new legal questions or phenomena. In certain instances, they instead highlight and amplify pre-existing deficiencies and weaknesses that have long been recognised. Through strategic adaptations and the utilisation of existing laws and legal instruments, significant improvements could be made to the legal framework governing MDTs. Stricter regulation is urgently needed in some areas, while in others, compliance and enforcement remain the primary challenges. Although recent legislation has provided significant opportunities to address identified shortcomings, and certain approaches will bring improvement, political consensus has not yet been achieved on all necessary aspects.

In the sector of mental health and well-being, data protection problems are not primarily rooted in deficiencies of the law. Rather, the sector suffers from critical compliance weaknesses, especially in applications beyond the distinct medical sector. Consumer mental health and well-being devices would benefit greatly from co-regulatory instruments, such as a sector-specific data protection certificate. Additionally, legislators are called to address the issue of manufacturers circumventing MDR certification due to ambiguities in the classification model. For instance, they could improve device efficacy by reopening risk class I MDR or introducing a 'conditioned exemption' for digital mental health devices within the MDR. As regards the EU's regulatory approach to non-medical BCIs within medical devices legislation, it stands out as a blueprint and deserves to be highlighted in ongoing global policy discussions on neurotechnology.

In the realms of commercial and political advertising, MDTs can be employed to exacerbate practices that have long been concerning from a consumer and citizen perspective. The prohibition of advertising based on profiling of special category input data in both the DSA and the TTPA does not reflect the capabilities of state-of-the-art data analytics. Both the DSA and the TTPA fall short in addressing MDTs as stand-alone techniques or as complements to online behavioural advertising or political microtargeting. An impactful adaptation would be to include the processing and inference of mind data in the blacklist of Annex I UCPD. The UCPD is a frequent point of reference for related laws. Notably, a general ban on processing and inferring mind data for commercial practices according to Annex I UCPD would mean that these practices are automatically prohibited under the DSA. In contrast, a correspondingly powerful tool for political practices is not available within the existing framework of the TTPA, as there is no blacklist for political practices under the TTPA.

As regards MDT-based monitoring practices in the employment context, the most concerning issue is the lack of a sector-specific horizontal data protection law and the fragmented legal landscape that follows from it. In principle, Article 88 GDPR provides a useful foundation, and there is valuable guidance complementing the provision to protect employees from unlawful monitoring practices. However, the details are regulated very differently in various Member States, sometimes with more favourable effects for employees and sometimes with less. In theory, most of the monitoring practices discussed in this book are already prohibited under the GDPR. Additionally, the EU has a robust equality acquis that can help mitigate discrimination in this sector. However, the core issue with monitoring practices in the employment context revolves around transparency and enforcement. Enhancements could be achieved through implementing rigorous transparency obligations and bolstering collective representation. The call to establish a distinct data protection regime for the employment context aligns particularly well with an MDT-based perspective. Such a lex specialis for data protection in the employment context could include a blacklist for prohibited practices or processing operations, similar to the one incorporated in the PWD. Processing and inferring mind data should be among the prohibited practices on this blacklist.

Throughout the book, adaptations de lege ferenda within both established and recently adopted laws have been offered as inspirations. While many of the discussed laws remain in their early stages, requiring further refinement through guidance documents, standards, and case law, this study has demonstrated that the existing legal system offers valuable instruments, well suited to the fast-paced evolution of these technologies. With a combination of technical curiosity, legal creativity, and the political will to enact necessary legislative adaptations, these instruments can help ensure that regulatory mechanisms remain resilient and responsive to the risks arising from neurotechnology and emotion technology.

Bibliography

SECONDARY SOURCES

Abraha, Halefom H, 'A Pragmatic Compromise? The Role of Article 88 GDPR in Upholding Privacy in the Workplace' (2022) 12(4) *International Data Privacy Law* 276–296. https://doi.org/10.1093/idpl/ipac015.

Adams, Zoe and Johanna Wenckebach, 'Collective Regulation of Algorithmic Management' (2023) 14(2), *European Labour Law Journal*, 211–229. https://doi.org/10.1177/20319525231167477.

Adams-Prassl, Jeremias, 'Regulating Algorithms at Work: Lessons for a "European Approach to Artificial Intelligence"' (2022) 13(1) *European Labour Law Journal*, 30–50. https://doi.org/10.1177/20319525211062558.

Adams-Prassl, Jeremias, 'What If Your Boss Was an Algorithm? The Rise of Artificial Intelligence at Work' (2019) 41(1) *Comparative Labor Law & Policy Journal* 123.

Adams-Prassl, Jeremias and others, 'Directly Discriminatory Algorithms' (2022) *Modern Law Review*. https://doi.org/10.1111/1468-2230.12759.

Adams-Prassl, Jeremias and others, 'Regulating Algorithmic Management: A Blueprint' (2023) 14(2) *European Labour Law Journal*, 124–151. https://doi.org/10.1177/20319525231167299.

Alegre, Susie, 'Rethinking Freedom of Thought for the 21st Century' (2017) 3 *European Human Rights Law Review*, 221–233. https://susiealegre.com/wp-content/uploads/2020/04/Alegre%20from%202017_EHRLR_Issue_3_Print_final_0806%5B6745%5D.pdf (accessed 8 January 2025).

Al-Mosaiwi, Mohammed and T Johnstone, 'In an Absolute State: Elevated Use of Absolutist Words Is a Marker Specific to Anxiety, Depression, and Suicidal Ideation' (2018) Jul 6(4) *Clinical Psychological Science*, 529–542. https://doi.org/10.1177/2167702617747074.

Anger, Heike, 'Gesichtsscan im Supermarkt ist unbedenklich' *Handelsblatt* (12 June 2017) www.handelsblatt.com/politik/deutschland/datenschuetzer-zu-real-werbebildschirm-gesichtsscan-im-supermarkt-ist-unbedenklich/19921456.html?ticket=ST-143784-Qpdthm7uM2VsokkEhOHW-ap5 (accessed 8 January 2025).

Anglmayer, Irmgard, 'Implementation of the Employment Equality Directive in light of the UN CRPD' European Implementation Assessment, Study European Parliamentary Research Service (2020). www.europarl.europa.eu/RegData/etudes/STUD/2020/654206/EPRS_STU(2020)654206_EN.pdf (accessed 8 May 2025).

Article 19, Emotional Entanglement: China's Emotion Recognition Market and Its Implications for Human Rights (2021). www.article19.org/wp-content/uploads/2021/01/ER-Tech-China-Report.pdf (accessed 8 January 2025).

Article 29 Data Protection Working Party, Advice paper on special categories of data ('sensitive data') (2011).

Article 29 Data Protection Working Party, Annex – health data in apps and devices (2018).

Article 29 Data Protection Working Party, Guidelines Data Protection Impact Assessment (DPIA) and Determining Whether Processing Is 'Likely to Result in a High Risk' for the Purposes of Regulation 2016/679, as last revised and adopted on 4 October 2017 (WP 248 rev.01).

Article 29 Data Protection Working Party, Guidelines on Automated Individual Decision-making and Profiling for the Purposes of Regulation 2016/679, adopted on 3 October 2017, as last revised and adopted on 6 February 2018 (WP 251 rev.01).

Article 29 Data Protection Working Party, Guidelines on Consent under Regulation 2016/679, adopted on 28 November 2017, as last revised and adopted on 10 April 2018 (WP 259 rev.01).

Article 29 Data Protection Working Party, Guidelines on Data Protection Officers (DPOs), as last revised and adopted on 5 April 2017 (WP 243 rev.01).

Article 29 Data Protection Working Party, Opinion 01/2015 on Privacy and Data Protection Issues Relating to the Utilisation of Drones, adopted on 16 June 2015 (WP 231).

Article 29 Data Protection Working Party, Opinion 06/2014 on the Notion of Legitimate Interests of the Data Controller under Article 7 of Directive 95/46/EC (WP 217).

Article 29 Data Protection Working Party, Opinion 2/2010 on Online Behavioural Advertising, adopted on 22 June 2010 (WP 171).

Article 29 Data Protection Working Party, Opinion 2/2017 on Data Processing at Work, adopted on 8 June 2017 (WP 249).

Article 29 Data Protection Working Party, Opinion 3/2012 on Developments in Biometric Technologies, adopted on 27 April 2012 (WP 193).

Article 29 Data Protection Working party, Opinion 8/2001 on the Processing of Personal Data in the Employment Context, adopted on 13 September 2001 (WP 48).

Article 29 Data Protection Working Party, Working Document on Genetic Data, adopted on 17 March 2004 (WP 91).

Article 29 Data Protection Working Party, Working Document on the Surveillance of Electronic Communications in the Workplace, adopted on 29 May 2002. (WP55).

Article 29 Data Protection Working Party, Working document on biometrics adopted on 1 August 2003. (WP80).

Bakir, Vian, 'Psychological Operations in Digital Political Campaigns: Assessing Cambridge Analytica's Psychographic Profiling and Targeting' (2020) (5)67 *Frontiers in Communication*. doi: 10.3389/fcomm.2020.00067.

Belli, Luca and others, 'Regulating Facial Recognition in Brazil: Legal and Policy Perspectives' In R. Matulionyte, M. Zalnieriute (eds), *The Cambridge Handbook of Facial Recognition in the Modern State*. Cambridge Law Handbooks. (Cambridge University Press 2024), 228–241.

Bertuzzi, Luca, AI Act: EU Parliament's Legal Office Gives Damning Opinion on High Risk Classification "Filters", *Euractiv* (19 October 2023). www.euractiv.com/section/artificial-intelligence/news/ai-act-eu-parliaments-legal-office-gives-damning-opinion-on-highrisk-classification-filters/ (accessed 8 January 2025).

BEUC, 'A European Health Data Space' (2023). www.beuc.eu/sites/default/files/publications/BEUC-X-2023-029_A_European_Health_Data_Space.pdf (accessed 8 January 2025).

BEUC, 'Connected, but unfairly treated. Consumer survey results on the fairness of the online environment' (2023). www.beuc.eu/sites/default/files/publications/BEUC-X-2023-113_Fairness_of_the_digital_environment_survey_results.pdf (accessed 8 January 2025).

BEUC, 'Consumer attitudes to health data sharing' (2023). www.beuc.eu/sites/default/files/publications/BEUC-X-2023-051_consumer_attitudes_to_health_data.pdf (accessed 8 January 2025).

BEUC, 'Consumers need strong safeguards to protect their health data' BEUC position paper on the proposed European Health Data Space (2022). www.beuc.eu/sites/default/files/publications/BEUC-X-2022-104_Position_paper_on_the_proposed_European_Health_Data_Space.pdf (accessed 8 January 2025).

BEUC, 'EU Consumer Protection 2.0. Protecting fairness and consumer choice in a digital economy' (2022). www.beuc.eu/sites/default/files/publications/beuc-x-2022-015_protecting_fairness_and_consumer_choice_in_a_digital_economy.pdf (accessed 8 January 2025).

BEUC, 'EU rules on AI lack punch to sufficiently protect consumers' (Press release 9 December 2023). www.beuc.eu/press-releases/eu-rules-ai-lack-punch-sufficiently-protect-consumers (accessed 8 January 2025).

Biasin, Elisabetta and others, 'New Cybersecurity Requirements for Medical Devices in the EU: The Forthcoming European Health Data Space, Data Act, and Artificial Intelligence Act' (2023) 5(2) *Law, Technology and Humans*, 43–58. https://doi.org/10.5204/lthj.3068.

Biéri, Martin and others, On the Record. Exploring the ethical, technical and legal issues of voice assistants, White Paper Collection No 1. (2020). www.cnil.fr/sites/cnil/files/atoms/files/cnil_white-paper-on_the_record.pdf (accessed 8 January 2025).

Black Dog Institute, The Future Proofing Study. www.blackdoginstitute.org.au/research-centres/future-proofing/ (accessed 8 January 2025).

Boire, RG, 'On Cognitive Liberty I' (1999) 1 *Journal of Cognitive Liberties*, 7–13.

Boire, RG, 'On Cognitive Liberty II' (2000) 2(2), *Journal of Cognitive Liberties*, 7–20.

Boire, RG, 'On Cognitive Liberty III' (2001) 2(1) *Journal of Cognitive Liberties*, 7–22.

Bol, Nadine and others, 'Vulnerability in a Tracked Society: Combining Tracking and Survey Data to Understand Who Gets Targeted with What Content' (2020) 22(11) *New Media & Society*, 1996–2017. https://doi.org/10.1177/1461444820924631.

Booth, Robert, 'Facebook Reveals News Feed Experiment to Control Emotions', *The Guardian* (30 June 2014). www.theguardian.com/technology/2014/jun/29/facebook-users-emotions-news-feeds (accessed 8 January 2025).

Borbón, Diego and Luisa Borbón, 'A Critical Perspective on NeuroRights: Comments Regarding Ethics and Law' *Frontiers in Human Neuroscience* (25 October 2021) https://doi.org/10.3389/fnhum.2021.703121.

Bossewitch, Jonah and others, 'Digital Futures in Mind: Reflecting on Technological Experiments in Mental Health & Crisis Support' (University of Melbourne, 2021) https://automatingmentalhealth.cc/ (accessed 15 January 2025).

Bradford, Anu, *The Brussels Effect: How the European Union Rules the World* (New York, 2020; online ed., Oxford Academic, 19 December 2019). https://doi.org/10.1093/oso/9780190088583.001.0001.

Brazal, Arturo and others, 'TechDispatch – Neurodata', EDPS TechDispatch 2024-1. https://doi.org/10.2804/411725.

Broughton Micova, Sally and Andrea Calef, Elements for effective systemic risk assessment under the DSA. Report. (July 2023). https://cerre.eu/wp-content/uploads/2023/07/CERRE-DSA-Systemic-Risk-Report.pdf (accessed 8 January 2025).

Brożek, Bartosz and others (eds), *Law and Mind. A Survey of Law and the Cognitive Sciences*, (Cambridge University Press 2021).

Bublitz, Jan Christoph, 'Cognitive Liberty or the International Human Right to Freedom of Thought' In J. Clausen and N. Levy (eds), *Handbook of Neuroethics* (Springer 2015). https://doi.org/10.1007/978-94-007-4707-4_166.

Bublitz, Jan Christoph, 'Freedom of Thought as an International Human Right: Elements of a Theory of a Living Right' In M. J. Blitz and J. C. Bublitz (eds), *The Law and Ethics of Freedom of Thought*, 1. Palgrave Studies in Law, Neuroscience, and Human Behavior. (Palgrave Macmillan 2021). https://doi.org/10.1007/978-3-030-84494-3_3.

Bublitz, Jan Christoph, 'Freedom of Thought in the Age of Neuroscience: A Plea and a Proposal for the Renaissance of a Forgotten Fundamental Right' 2014 100(1) *ARSP: Archiv Für Rechts- Und Sozialphilosophie / Archives for Philosophy of Law and Social Philosophy*, 1–25. www.jstor.org/stable/24756752 (accessed 19 April 2024).

Bublitz, Jan Christoph, 'Neurotechnologies and Human Rights: Restating and Reaffirming the Multi-Layered Protection of the Person' (2024) 28(5) *The International Journal of Human Rights*, 782–807. https://doi.org/10.1080/13642987.2024.2310830.

Bublitz, Jan Christoph, 'Novel Neurorights: From Nonsense to Substance' (2022) 15(7) *Neuroethics*. https://doi.org/10.1007/s12152-022-09481-3.

Calabrese, Sofia and Orsolya Reich, 'Identifying, analysing, assessing and mitigating potential negative effects on civic discourse and electoral processes: A minimum menu of risks very large online platforms should take heed of' (January 2024). https://dq4n3btxmr8c9.cloudfront.net/files/mpdgy5/DSA_Risk_Analysis_LibertiesxEPDfin.pdf (accessed 8 January 2025).

Cappello, Maja (ed.), *New Actors and Risks in Online Advertising*, IRIS Special, (European Audiovisual Observatory 2022).

Carta de derechos de la persona en el entorno digital código de buenas práticas. Mexico. www.infocdmx.org.mx/images/biblioteca/2022/Carta_Derechos_Persona_EntornoDigital_Digital.pdf (accessed 11 April 2024).

Carta de los derechos digitales. Spain. www.lamoncloa.gob.es/presidente/actividades/Documents/2021/140721-Carta_Derechos_Digitales_RedEs.pdf (accessed 10 April 2024).

Christl, Wolfie, 'Surveillance and Algorithmic Control in the Call Center. A case study on contact and service center software, automated management and outsourced work' (2023). https://crackedlabs.org/dl/CrackedLabs_Christl_CallCenter.pdf (accessed 8 January 2025).

Civil society urges European Parliament to protect people's rights in the AI Act. (19 April 2023) https://edri.org/our-work/civil-society-urges-european-parliament-to-protect-peoples-rights-in-the-ai-act/ (accessed 8 January 2025).

Clifford, Damian, *Data Protection Law and Emotion*. (Oxford University Press 2024).

CNIL, Employee monitoring: CNIL fined Amazon France Logistique €32 million. (23 January 2024) www.cnil.fr/en/employee-monitoring-cnil-fined-amazon-france-logistique-eu32-million (accessed 8 January 2025).

CNIL, Health data and use of cookies: DOCTISSIMO fined €380,000 (17.5.2023). www.cnil.fr/en/health-data-and-use-cookies-doctissimo-fined-eu380000 (accessed 8 January 2025).

Council of Europe, Consultative Committee of the Convention for the protection of individuals with regard to automatic processing of personal data (Convention 108), Guidelines on facial recognition (2021). https://edoc.coe.int/en/artificial-intelligence/9753-guidelines-on-facial-recognition.html (accessed 8 January 2025).

Council of Europe, Declaration by the Committee of Ministers on the manipulative capabilities of algorithmic processes Decl (13/02/2019)1.

Council of Europe, Strategic Action Plan on Human Rights and Technologies in Biomedicine www.coe.int/en/web/bioethics/strategic-action-plan (accessed 8 January 2025).

D'Aloia, Antonio and Maria Chiara Errigo (eds), *Neuroscience and Law. Complicated Crossings and New Perspectives* (Springer 2020).

D'Amico, Alessia Sophia and others, 'Meta's Pay-or-Okay Model: An analysis under EU Data Protection, Consumer and Competition Law' (2024), *Technology and Regulation*, 254–272. https://doi.org/10.26116/techreg.2024.019.

Daly, Ian, 'Affective Brain–Computer Interfacing and Methods for Affective State Detection', In Chang S. Nam and others (eds), *Brain–Computer Interfaces Handbook. Technological and Theoretical Advances*' (CRC Press 2018), 147–159.

Das, Shanti, 'Mental Health Helpline Funded by Royals Shared Users' Conversations' *The Guardian* (19 February 2022). www.theguardian.com/society/2022/feb/19/mental-health-helpline-funded-by-royals-shared-users-conversations (accessed 8 January 2025).

Davis, Peter AE, 'Facial detection and smart billboards: Analysing the 'identified' criterion of personal data in the GDPR' (2020) Jahr 6 Ausgabe 3 *European Data Protection Law Review*. https://doi.org/10.21552/edpl/2020/3/7.

Maia de Oliveira Wood, Guilherme and others, 'The protection of mental privacy in the area of neuroscience – Societal, legal and ethical challenges' (2024) European Parliament, Directorate-General for Parliamentary Research Services. https://data.europa.eu/doi/10.2861/869928 (accessed 8 January 2025).

De Sourya, Joyee and Abdessamad Imine, 'Consent for Targeted Advertising: The Case of Facebook' (2020) 35 *AI & Society*, 1055.

Dejam, Jubin, *Gefühlsdatenschutz, Eine Untersuchung der datenschutzrechtlichen Rahmenbedingungen von Datenverarbeitungen mittels Affective Computing*, Frankfurter Studien zum Datenschutz 69 (Nomos 2023), doi.org/10.5771/9783748917953.

Duchoňová, Tereza, 'Voice as the Window to the Soul: Analysis of the Level of Protection Granted by the GDPR to Emotions Inferred from One's Voice' (2024) 3/2023 *CompLex*. www.jus.uio.no/ifp/forskning/om/publikasjoner/complex/2023/complex_voice_as_the_window_to_the_soul_analysis-.html (accessed 8 January 2025).

Duivenvoorde, Bram and Catalina Goanta, 'The Regulation of Digital Advertising under the DSA: A Critical Assessment' (2023) 51 *Computer Law & Security Review*. https://doi.org/10.1016/j.clsr.2023.105870.

Dutch Ministry of the Interior and Kingdom Relations, Impact Assessment Fundamental rights and algorithms (März 2022), www.nldigitalgovernment.nl/wp-content/uploads/sites/11/2022/05/Impact-Assessment-fundamental-rights-and-algorithms.pdf (accessed 8 January 2025).

Eccles, Mari and Giedre Peseckyte, 'Why Is It So Hard to Deliver a European Health Data Deal?' *Politico* (8 March 2024). www.politico.eu/article/why-is-it-so-hard-to-deliver-a-european-health-data-deal/ (accessed 8 January 2025).

EDPB, Binding Decision 03/2022 on the dispute submitted by the Irish SA on Meta Platforms Ireland Limited and its Facebook service (Art. 65 GDPR) adopted on 5 December 2022.

EDPB, Binding Decision 4/2022 on the dispute submitted by the Irish SA on Meta Platforms Ireland Limited and its Instagram service (Art. 65 GDPR) adopted on 5 December 2022.

EDPB, Guidelines 03/2022 on Dark patterns in social media platform interfaces: How to recognise and avoid them, version 1.0, adopted on 14 March 2022.

EDPB, Guidelines 03/2022 on Deceptive design patterns in social media platform interfaces: How to recognise and avoid them, version 2.0, adopted on 14 February 2023.

EDPB, Guidelines 2/2019 on the processing of personal data under Article 6(1)(b) GDPR in the context of the provision of online services to data subjects, version 2.0 (8 October 2019).

EDPB, Guidelines 3/2019 on processing of personal data through video devices, version 2.0 adopted on 29 January 2020.

EDPB, Guidelines 8/2020 on the targeting of social media users, version 2.0, adopted on 13 April 2021.

EDPB, Opinion 08/2024 on Valid Consent in the Context of Consent or Pay Models Implemented by Large Online Platforms, adopted on 17 April 2024.

EDPB, Statement 02/2019 on the use of personal data in the course of political campaigns, adopted on 13 March 2019.

EDPB-EDPS, Joint Opinion 03/2022 on the Proposal for a Regulation on the European Health Data Space (2022).

EDPB-EDPS, Joint Opinion 05/2021 on the proposal for a Regulation of the European Parliament and of the Council laying done harmonized rules on artificial intelligence (Artificial Intelligence Act) (18 June 2021).

EDPS, Opinion 01/2021 on the Proposal for a Digital Services Act (10 February 2021).

EDPS, Opinion 02/2022 on the Proposal for Regulation on the transparency and targeting of political advertising (20 January 2022).

EDPS, Opinion 3/2018 on online manipulation and personal data (9 March 2018).

EHCR Research and Library Division, 'Article 10 Expression and advertising of political positions through the media/Internet in the context of elections/referendums' (2018). https://web.archive.org/web/20210205175235/www.echr.coe.int/Documents/Research_report_expression_advertising_media_elections_ENG.pdf (accessed 8 January 2025).

Ehmann, Eugen and Martin Selmayr (eds), *DS-GVO Datenschutz-Grundverordnung*, Beck'sche Kurz-Kommentare (3rd ed. C.H. Beck 2024).

Emotional AI Lab, 'What is emotional AI'. https://emotionalai.org/so-what-is-emotional-ai/ (accessed 8 January 2025).

Empatica, E4 Bytes: 'Predicting aggressive outbursts in people with autism a minute in advance' (10 November 2020). www.empatica.com/blog/e4-bytes-predicting-aggressive-outbursts-in-people-with-autism-a-minute-in-advance.html (accessed 8 January 2025).

EU Agency for Fundamental Rights and Council of Europe, Handbook on European Non-Discrimination Law (Publications Office of the European Union 2018).

EU Agency for Safety and Health at Work (EU-OSHA), 'Impact of Artificial Intelligence on Occupational Safety and Health' (2021). https://osha.europa.eu/sites/default/files/Policy_brief_Impact_AI_OSH.pdf (accessed 8 January 2025).

EU Agency for Safety at Work, 'Artificial Intelligence for Worker Management: Existing and Future Regulations'. https://osha.europa.eu/sites/default/files/documents/artificial-inteligence-worker-management-regulations_en.pdf (accessed 8 January 2025).

EU Code of Practice on Disinformation (2018) https://ec.europa.eu/newsroom/dae/document.cfm?doc_id=54454 (accessed 8 January 2025).

EU Commission, Annex to the Communication to the Commission, Approval of the content of the draft Communication from the Commission – Commission Guidelines on prohibited artificial intelligence practices established by Regulation (EU) 2024/1689 (AI Act), C(2025) 884 final. https://digital-strategy.ec.europa.eu/en/library/commission-publishes-guidelines-prohibited-artificial-intelligence-ai-practices-defined-ai-act (accessed 6 February 2025).

EU Commission, 'Artificial intelligence: Commission kicks off work on marrying cutting-edge technology and ethical standards' (Press Release 8 March 2018). https://ec.europa.eu/commission/presscorner/detail/en/IP_18_1381 (accessed 8 January 2025).

EU Commission, 'Beyond the Horizon. Foresight in support of future EU research and innovation policy (BOHEMIA)'. https://ec.europa.eu/info/research-and-innovation/strategy/support-policy-making/shaping-eu-research-and-innovation-policy/foresight/bohemia_en (accessed 8 January 2025).

EU Commission, Communication from the Commission to the European Parliament, the Council, the European Economic and Social Committee of the Regions Fostering a European approach to Artificial Intelligence (COM/2021/205 final). https://eur-lex.europa.eu/legal-content/EN/TXT/?uri=celex:52021DC0205 (accessed 30 January 2025).

EU Commission, 'Commission opens formal proceedings against Facebook and Instagram under the Digital Services Act' (Press Release 30 April 2024). https://ec.europa.eu/commission/presscorner/detail/en/ip_24_2373 (accessed 8 January 2025).

EU Commission, Communication Tackling Online Disinformation: A European Approach COM(2018) 236 final. https://eur-lex.europa.eu/legal-content/EN/TXT/?uri=CELEX:52018DC0236 (accessed 8 January 2025).

EU Commission, 'Digital Services Act: Commission designates first set of Very Large Online Platforms and Search Engines', (Press Release 25 April 2023). https://ec.europa.eu/commission/presscorner/detail/en/IP_23_2413 (accessed 8 January 2025).

EU Commission, Directorate-General for Communications Networks, Content and Technology, Digital Services Act – Application of the risk management framework to Russian disinformation campaigns, (2023), https://data.europa.eu/doi/10.2759/764631 (accessed 8 January 2025).

EU Commission, Directorate-General for Justice and Consumers, Lupiáñez-Villanueva, F., and others, 'Behavioural study on unfair commercial practices in the digital environment – Dark patterns and manipulative personalisation' – Final report (2022) https://data.europa.eu/doi/10.2838/859030 (accessed 30 January 2025).

EU Commission, 'Emotional Intelligence Online. Targeted scenario N° 7. Glimpses of the future from the BOHEMIA study' (2018). https://research-and-innovation.ec.europa.eu/system/files/2018-06/emotional-intelligence-targeted-scenario-7_2018_en.pdf (accessed 8 January 2025).

EU Commission, European Health Data Space. https://health.ec.europa.eu/ehealth-digital-health-and-care/european-health-data-space_en (accessed 8 January 2025).

EU Commission, Explanatory Memorandum on the Proposal for a Regulation of the European Parliament and of the Council on the transparency and targeting of political advertising (2021). https://eur-lex.europa.eu/legal-content/EN/TXT/HTML/?uri=CELEX:52021PC0731 (accessed 8 January 2025).

EU Commission, Guidance on Strengthening the Code of Practice on Disinformation COM(2021) 262 final. https://eur-lex.europa.eu/legal-content/EN/ALL/?uri=COM%3A2021%3A262%3AFIN (accessed 8 January 2025).

EU Commission, Guidance on the application of Union data protection law in the electoral context, COM(2018) 638 final. https://eur-lex.europa.eu/legal-content/EN/TXT/HTML/?uri=CELEX:52018DC0638&from=DE (accessed 8 January 2025).

EU Commission, Guidance on the interpretation and application of Directive 2005/29/EC of the European Parliament and of the Council concerning unfair business-to-consumer commercial practices in the internal market. (2021/C 526/01). https://eur-lex.europa.eu/legal-content/EN/TXT/?uri=oj:JOC_2021_526_R_0001 (accessed 30 January 2025).

EU Commission, Guidelines for providers of Very Large Online Platforms and Very Large Online Search Engines on the mitigation of systemic risks for electoral processes pursuant to Article 35(3) of Regulation (EU) 2022/2065 (C/2024/3014). https://eur-lex.europa.eu/legal-content/EN/TXT/?uri=CELEX%3A52024XC03014&qid=1714466886277 (accessed 30 January 2025).

EU Commission, Independent HLEG, Assessment List for Trustworthy Artificial Intelligence (ALTAI) for self-assessment (2020). https://digital-strategy.ec.europa.eu/en/library/assessment-list-trustworthy-artificial-intelligence-altai-self-assessment (accessed 8 January 2025).

EU Commission, Independent HLEG on Artificial Intelligence, Ethics guidelines for trustworthy AI (2019). https://digital-strategy.ec.europa.eu/en/library/ethics-guidelines-trustworthy-ai (accessed 8 January 2025).

EU Council, Infographic – Transparency and targeting of political advertising. www.consilium.europa.eu/en/infographics/political-advertising/ (accessed 8 January 2025).

EU Commission, 'New Consumer Agenda: European Commission to empower consumers to become the driver of transition' (Press Release 13 November 2020) https://ec.europa.eu/commission/presscorner/detail/en/ip_20_2069 (accessed 8 January 2025).

EU Commission, Questions and answers – EU Health: European Health Data Space (EHDS) (3 May 2022). https://ec.europa.eu/commission/presscorner/detail/en/qanda_22_2712 (accessed 8 January 2025).

EU Commission, Staff working document impact assessment on the revision of the regulatory framework for medical devices. SWD/2012/0273 final.

EU Commission, Supervision of the designated very large online platforms and search engines under DSA. https://digital-strategy.ec.europa.eu/en/policies/list-designated-vlops-and-vloses (accessed 8 January 2025).

EU Léon Declaration on European Neurotechnology, A Human Centric and Rights-Oriented Approach (2023).

EU Parliament, Resolution of 20 October 2020 with recommendations to the Commission on a Digital Services Act: Adapting commercial and civil law rules for commercial entities operating online (2020/2019(INL)). https://eur-lex.europa.eu/legal-content/EN/TXT/?uri=CELEX%3A52020IP0273 (accessed 8 January 2025).

EU Parliament, Resolution of 12 December 2023 on addictive design of online services and consumer protection in the EU single market (2023/2043(INI)).

EU Parliament, Resolution of 23 October 2024 on the urgent need to revise the Medical Devices Regulation (2024/2849(RSP)). www.europarl.europa.eu/doceo/document/TA-10-2024-0028_EN.html (accessed 8 January 2025).

EU Parliament, A9-0356/2021, Opinion of the Committee on Civil Liberties, Justice and Home Affairs www.europarl.europa.eu/doceo/document/A-9-2021-0356_EN.html#_section5 (accessed 8 January 2025).

EU Parliament, AIA IMCO-LIBE Report (13 June 2023), Article 3(1)(34), Amendment 1031–1037. https://artificialintelligenceact.eu/wp-content/uploads/2022/06/AIA-IMCO-LIBE-Report-All-Amendments-14-June.pdf (accessed 8 January 2025).

EU Strengthened Code of Practice on Disinformation (2022). https://digital-strategy.ec.europa.eu/en/library/2022-strengthened-code-practice-disinformation (accessed 30 January 2025).

Eurofound, Employee monitoring and surveillance: The challenges of digitalisation, Publications Office of the European Union, Luxembourg, and Eurofund, Monitoring and surveillance of workers in the digital age (2020) www.eurofound.europa.eu/en/monitoring-and-surveillance-workers-digital-age (accessed 8 January 2025).

European Parliamentary Research Service, Costica Dumbrava, 'Artificial intelligence at EU borders. Overview of applications and key issues' (2021). www.europarl.europa.eu/RegData/etudes/IDAN/2021/690706/EPRS_IDA(2021)690706_EN.pdf 19 January 2025.

Farahany, Nita, *The Battle for Your Brain: Defending the Right to Think Freely in the Age of Neurotechnology* (St Martin's Press 2023).

Feldman Barrett, Lisa and others, 'Emotional Expressions Reconsidered: Challenges to Inferring Emotion from Human Facial Movements' (2019) 20 *Psychological Science in the Public Interest*, 1–68.

Floridi, Luciano, 'Group Privacy: A Defence and an Interpretation' In L. Taylor and others (eds), *Group Privacy: New Challenges of Data Technologies* (Springer 2016), 83–100.

Floridi, Luciano, 'Open Data, Data Protection, and Group Privacy' (2014) 27(1–3) *Philosophy & Technology*. https://doi.org/10.1007/s13347-014-0157-8.

Fölster, Mara and others, 'Facial Age Affects Emotional Expression Decoding', *Frontiers in Psychology* (4 February 2014) www.frontiersin.org/articles/10.3389/fpsyg.2014.00030/full#h4 (accessed 8 January 2025).

Fourberg, Niklas and others, 'Online advertising: The impact of targeted advertising on advertisers, market access and consumer choice'. Study requested by the European Parliament's committee on the Internal Market and Consumer Protection (IMCO) (2021). www.europarl.europa.eu/RegData/etudes/STUD/2021/662913/IPOL_STU(2021)662913_EN.pdf (accessed 8 January 2025).

Future of Privacy Forum, 'Privacy and the connected mind. Understanding the Data Flows and Privacy Risks of Brain-Computer Interfaces' (2021). https://fpf.org/wp-content/uploads/2021/11/FPF-BCI-Report-Final.pdf (accessed 8 January 2025).

Future of Privacy Forum, 'Privacy and the Rise of "Neurorights" in Latin America' (20 March 2024). https://fpf.org/blog/privacy-and-the-rise-of-neurorights-in-latin-america/ (accessed 8 January 2025).

Garante per la protezione dei dati personali, Installazione di apparati promozionali del tipo 'digital signage (definiti anche Totem) presso una stazione ferroviaria – 21 dicembre 2017 [7496252]. www.garanteprivacy.it/web/guest/home/docweb/-/docweb-display/docweb/7496252 (accessed 8 January 2025).

Gellert, Raphaël, *The Risk-Based Approach to Data Protection* (Oxford University Press 2020).

George, Damian and others, 'GDPR Bypass by Design? Transient Processing of Data under the GDPR' (2019) 9(4) *International Data Privacy Law*, 285–298. https://doi.org/10.1093/idpl/ipz017.

Gola, Peter and Dirk Heckmann (eds), *Datenschutz-Grundverordnung VO EU 2016/679 Bundesdatenschutzgesetz* (3rd ed. C.H. Beck 2022).

Gooding, Piers, 'Mapping the Rise of Digital Mental Health Technologies: Emerging Issues for Law and Society' (2019) 67 *International Journal of Law and Psychiatry*, 101498, https://doi.org/10.1016/j.ijlp.2019.101498.

Goujard, Clothilde, 'European Parliament pushes to ban targeted ads based on health, religion or sexual orientation' *Politico* (20 January 2022) www.politico.eu/article/european-parliament-bans-use-of-sensitive-personal-data-for-targeted-ads/ (accessed 8 January 2025).

Greene, Gretchen, 'The Ethics of AI and Emotional Intelligence. Data sources, applications, and questions for evaluating ethics risk', Partnership on AI (2020). https://partnershiponai.org/paper/the-ethics-of-ai-and-emotional-intelligence/ (accessed 8 January 2025).

Grisse, Karina, 'Recommender Systems, Manipulation and Private Autonomy: How European Civil Law Regulates and Should Regulate Recommender Systems for the Benefit of Private Autonomy' In S. Genovesi and others (eds), *Recommender Systems: Legal and Ethical Issues*. The International Library of Ethics, Law and Technology, vol 40. (Springer 2023). https://doi.org/10.1007/978-3-031-34804-4_6.

Haber, Nick and others, 'Upgraded Google Glass Helps Autistic Kids "See" Emotions', *IEEE Spectrum* (26 March 2023). https://spectrum.ieee.org/upgraded-google-glass-helps-autistic-kids-see-emotions (accessed 8 January 2025).

Hackenburg, Kobi and Helen Margetts, 'Evaluating the Persuasive Influence of Political Microtargeting with Large Language Models, PNAS' (2024) 121(24) *Political Sciences*, e2403116121. https://doi.org/10.1073/pnas.2403116121.

Hallinan, Dara and others, 'Legal Neuroexceptionalism: Framing a Concept' (2023) 14(2) *European Journal of Law and Technology*. www.ejlt.org/index.php/ejlt/article/view/902 (accessed 8 January 2025).

Hallinan, Dara and others, 'Neurodata and Neuroprivacy: Data Protection Outdated?' (2014) 12(1) *Surveillance & Society*, 55–72. doi: 10.24908/ss.v12i1.4500.

Häuselmann, Andreas, 'Fit for purpose? Affective Computing meets EU data protection law' (2021) 11(3) *International Data Privacy Law*, 245–256. https://doi.org/10.1093/idpl/ipab008.

Häuselmann, Andreas and Bart Custers, 'Substantive fairness in the GDPR: Fairness Elements for Article 5.1a GDPR' (2024) 52(105942) *Computer Law & Security Review*. https://doi.org/10.1016/j.clsr.2024.105942.

Häuselmann, Andreas and others, 'EU law and emotion data' (11th International Conference on Affective Computing and Intelligent Interaction ACII, Cambridge, MA, USA, 2023), 1–8. doi: 10.1109/ACII59096.2023.10388181.

Helberger, Natali and others, 'Choice Architectures in the Digital Economy: Towards a New Understanding of Digital Vulnerability' (2022) 45 *Journal of Consumer Policy*, 175–200. https://doi.org/10.1007/s10603-021-09500-5.

Helberger, Natali and others, 'Digital Fairness for Consumers' BEUC (2024). www.beuc.eu/sites/default/files/publications/BEUC-X-2024-032_Digital_fairness_for_consumers_Report.pdf (accessed 8 January 2025).

Helberger, Natali and others, 'EU Consumer Protection 2.0: Structural Asymmetries in Digital Consumer Markets' A joint report from research conducted under the EUCP2.0 project. BEUC (2021). www.beuc.eu/sites/default/files/publications/beuc-x-2021-018_eu_consumer_protection_2.0.pdf (accessed 8 January 2025).

Helberger, Natali and others, 'EU Consumer Protection 2.0: The Regulatory Gap: Consumer Protection in the Digital Economy. Addendum to the report "Structural asymmetries in digital consumer markets"' BEUC (2021). www.beuc.eu/sites/default/files/publications/beuc-x-2021-116_the_regulatory_gap-consumer_protection_in_the_digital_economy.pdf (accessed 8 January 2025).

Helberger, Natali and others, 'Towards Unfair Political Practices Law: Learning Lessons from the Regulation of Unfair Commercial Practices for Online Political Advertising' (2021) 12(3) *Journal of Intellectual Property, Information Technology and E-Commerce Law* JIPITEC, 273–296.

Hofmann, Franz and Benjamin Raue (eds), *Digital Services Act. Gesetz über digitale Dienste* (Nomos 2023).

Hupont, Isabelle and others, 'Measuring and Fostering Diversity in Affective Computing Research' (2024) 15(01) *IEEE Transactions on Affective Computing*, 63–78. doi: 10.1109/TAFFC.2023.3244041.

ICO, Biometrics: Insight, version 1.0 (2022). https://ico.org.uk/media/4021972/biometrics-insight-report.pdf (accessed 8 January 2025).

ICO, Data protection and monitoring workers. https://ico.org.uk/for-organisations/uk-gdpr-guidance-and-resources/employment/monitoring-workers/data-protection-and-monitoring-workers/ (accessed 8 January 2025).

ICO, Employment practices and data protection: Monitoring workers. Data protection and monitoring workers. https://ico.org.uk/for-organisations/uk-gdpr-guidance-and-resources/employment/monitoring-workers/data-protection-and-monitoring-workers/#dp4 (accessed 8 January 2025).

ICO, ICO tech futures: Neurotechnology. (version 01 June 2023). https://ico.org.uk/about-the-ico/research-reports-impact-and-evaluation/research-and-reports/technology-and-innovation/ico-tech-futures-neurotechnology/ (accessed 8 January 2025).

ICO, Information Commissioner's Opinion: The use of live facial recognition technology in public places 18 June 2021, https://ico.org.uk/media/2619985/ico-opinion-the-use-of-lfr-in-public-places-20210618.pdf (accessed 8 January 2025).

ICO, Investigation into the use of data analytics in political campaigns. A report to Parliament (6 November 2018). https://ico.org.uk/media/action-weve-taken/2260271/investigation-into-the-use-of-data-analytics-in-political-campaigns-final-20181105.pdf (accessed 30 January 2025).

ICO, Key data protection concepts, What is special category biometric data? https://ico.org.uk/for-organisations/uk-gdpr-guidance-and-resources/lawful-basis/biometric-data-guidance-biometric-recognition/key-data-protection-concepts/#whatisspecial (accessed 8 January 2025).

Ienca, Marcello, 'On Neurorights' (24 September 2021) *Frontiers in Human Neuroscience*, https://doi.org/10.3389/fnhum.2021.701258.

Ienca, Marcello and Gianclaudio Malgieri, 'Mental Data Protection and the GDPR' (2022) 9(1) *Journal of Law and the Biosciences*. https://doi.org/10.1093/jlb/lsac006.

Ienca, Marcello and Roberto Andorno, 'Towards New Human Rights in the Age of Neuroscience and Neurotechnology' (2017) 13(5) *Life Sciences, Society and Policy*. https://doi.org/10.1186/s40504-017-0050-1.

Indra, Spiecker gen. Döhmann and others (eds), *General Data Protection Regulation. Article-by-Article Commentary* (Nomos 2023), https://doi.org/10.5771/9783845276984.

Interim report of the Special Rapporteur on freedom of religion or belief, Ahmed Shaheed: 'Freedom of thought' published on 05 October 2021 (A/76/380), 3 www.ohchr.org/en/documents/thematic-reports/a76380-interim-report-special-rapporteur-freedom-religion-or-belief (accessed 8 January 2025).

Iwaya, Leonardo Horn and others, 'On the Privacy of Mental Health Apps' (2023) 28(2) *Empir Software Engineering*. https://doi.org/10.1007/s10664-022-10236-0.

Jasserand, Catherine A., 'Avoiding Terminological Confusion between the Notions of "Biometrics" and "Biometric Data": An Investigation into the Meanings of the Terms from a European Data Protection and a Scientific Perspective' (2016) 6(1) *International Data Privacy Law*, 63–76. https://doi.org/10.1093/idpl/ipv020.

Jasserand, Catherine A, 'Legal Nature of Biometric Data: From "Generic" Personal Data to Sensitive Data' (2016) 3 *European Data Protection Law Review*, 297–311. https://doi.org/10.21552/EDPL/2016/3/6.

Kelly-Lyth, Aislinn, 'Algorithmic Discrimination at Work' (2023) 14(2) *European Labour Law Journal*, 152–171. https://doi.org/10.1177/20319525231167300.

Kindt, Els J, *Privacy and Data Protection Issues of Biometric Applications. A Comparative Legal Analysis* (Springer 2013).

Kramer, Adam DI and others, 'Experimental Evidence of Massive-Scale Emotional Contagion through Social Networks' (2014) *Proceedings of the National Academy of Sciences (PNAS)*. https://doi.org/10.1073/pnas.1320040111.

Kröger, Jacob Leon and others, 'Privacy Implications of Voice and Speech Analysis – Information Disclosure by Inference' In M. Friedewald and others (eds), *Privacy and Identity Management. Data for Better Living: AI and Privacy*. Privacy and Identity 2019. IFIP Advances in Information and Communication Technology, vol 576. (Springer 2020). https://doi.org/10.1007/978-3-030-42504-3_16.

Kuner, Christopher and others (eds), *The EU General Data Protection Regulation (GDPR), A Commentary* (Print publication date: 2020. Published to Oxford Scholarship Online 2021). https://doi.org/10.1093/oso/9780198826491.001.0001.

Landsec, London's iconic Piccadilly Lights are switched back on (Press Release 26 October 2017). https://landsec.com/media/press-releases/2017/londons-iconic-piccadilly-lights-are-switched-back (accessed 24 January 2025).

Laux, Johann and others, 'Neutralizing Online Behavioural Advertising: Algorithmic Targeting with Market Power as an Unfair Commercial Practice' (2021) 58(3) *Common Market Law Review*, 719–750. https://doi.org/10.54648/cola2021048 (accessed 8 January 2025).

Le Mau, Tuan and others, 'Professional Actors Demonstrate Variability, Not Stereotypical Expressions, When Portraying Emotional States in Photographs' (2021) 12 (Article no. 5037) *Nature Communications*. https://doi.org/10.1038/s41467-021-25352-6.

Leiser, Mark, 'Psychological Patterns and Article 5 of the AI Act' (2024) 1(1) *Journal of AI Law and Regulation*, 5–23. https://doi.org/10.21552/aire/2024/1/4.

Levine, Alexandra S, 'Suicide hotline shares data with for-profit spinoff, raising ethical questions' *Politico* (28 January 2022) www.politico.com/news/2022/01/28/suicide-hotline-silicon-valley-privacy-debates-00002617 (accessed 8 January 2025).

Li, Wenkai and Paul Quinn, 'The European Health Data Space: An Expanded Right to Data Portability?' (2024) 52(105913) *Computer Law & Security Review*. https://doi.org/10.1016/j.clsr.2023.105913.

Ligthart, Sjors, 'Freedom of Thought in Europe: Do Advances in 'Brain-Reading' Technology Call for Revision?' (2020) 7(1) *Journal of Law and the Biosciences*. https://doi.org/10.1093/jlb/lsaa048.

Ligthart, Sjors and others, 'Minding Rights: Mapping Ethical and Legal Foundations of "Neurorights"' (2023) 32(4) *Cambridge Quarterly of Healthcare Ethics*, 461–481. https://doi.org/10.1017/S0963180123000245.

Ligthart, Sjors and others (eds), *Neurolaw. Advances in Neuroscience, Justice & Security* (Springer 2021).

Ligthart, Sjors and others, 'Rethinking the Right to Freedom of Thought: A Multidisciplinary Analysis' (2022) 22(4) *Human Rights Law Review*. https://doi.org/10.1093/hrlr/ngac028.

López-Silva, Pablo and Luca Valera (eds), *Protecting the Mind. Challenges in Law, Neuroprotection, and Neurorights* (Springer 2022)

Lynskey, Orla, *The Foundations of EU Data Protection Law* (Oxford University Press 2015).

Malgieri, Gianclaudio, 'The Concept of Fairness in the GDPR: A Linguistic and Contextual Interpretation', *ACM Proceedings of the 2020 Conference on Fairness, Accountability, and Transparency* (27 January 2020), 154–166. https://doi.org/10.1145/3351095.3372868.

Malgieri, Gianclaudio, *Vulnerability and Data Protection Law* (Oxford, 2023; online ed., Oxford Academic, 19 December 2019) https://doi.org/10.1177/1461444820924631.

Malgieri, Gianclaudio and Giovanni Comandé, 'Sensitive-by-Distance: Quasi-Health Data in the Algorithmic Era' (2017), 26(3) *Information & Communications Technology Law*, 229–249. doi: 10.1080/13600834.2017.1335468.

Malgieri, Gianclaudio and Jędrzej Niklas, 'Vulnerable Data Subjects' (2020) 37(105415) *Computer Law & Security Review*. https://doi.org/10.1016/j.clsr.2020.105415.

Mantelero, Alessandro, 'Fundamental rights impact assessments in the DSA', *Verfassungsblog* (1.11.2022). https://verfassungsblog.de/dsa-impact-assessment/ (accessed 8 January 2025).

Mantelero, Alessandro, 'Human Rights Impact Assessment and AI' In *Beyond Data. Human Rights, Ethical and Social Impact Assessment in AI*, Information Technology and Law Series, vol 36. (T.M.C. Asser Press 2022). https://doi.org/10.1007/978-94-6265-531-7_2.

Mantelero, Alessandro, 'The Future of Consumer Data Protection in the E.U. Re-Thinking the "Notice and Consent" Paradigm in the New Era of Predictive Analytics' (2014) 30(6) *Computer Law & Security Review*. https://doi.org/10.1016/j.clsr.2014.09.004.

Mantelero, Alessandro, 'The Fundamental Rights Impact Assessment (FRIA) in the AI Act: Roots, Legal Obligations and Key Elements for a Model Template' (2024) 54 *Computer Law & Security Review*, 106020. https://doi.org/10.1016/j.clsr.2024.106020.

Marda, Vidushi, 'Not Just Privacy: The Dangers of Emotion Recognition Technology' (14 August 2024) https://casi.sas.upenn.edu/iit/vidushimarda (accessed 8 January 2025).

Market Research Future, 'Global Digital Mental Health Market Overview' (2024). www.marketresearchfuture.com/reports/digital-mental-health-market-11062 (accessed 8 January 2025).

Martini, Mario and Christiane Wendehorst (eds), *KI-VO. Künstliche Intelligenz-Verordnung* (C.H. Beck 2024).

Martini, Mario and others, 'Dark Patterns' (2021) 01 *Zeitschrift für Digitalisierung und Recht*.

Mashrur, FR and others, 'BCI-Based Consumers' Choice Prediction from EEG Signals: An Intelligent Neuromarketing Framework' (2022) 16(861270) *Frontiers in Human Neuroscience* doi: 10.3389/fnhum.2022.861270.

Maslen, Hannah and others, 'The Regulation of Cognitive Enhancement Devices: Extending the Medical Model' (2014) 1(1) *Journal of Law and the Biosciences*, 68–93. https://doi.org/10.1093/jlb/lst003.

McStay, Andrew and L Urquhart, '"This Time with Feeling?" Assessing EU Data Governance Implications of Out of Home Appraisal Based Emotional AI' (2019) 24 *First Monday* 10 https://doi.org/10.5210/fm.v24i10.9457.

MDCG, Guidance notes for manufacturers of class I medical devices, 2019–15 rev.1 (December 2019, July 2020 rev.1). https://health.ec.europa.eu/document/download/349a2d4c-ea2a-4279-861c-7c063bc077e4_en?filename=md_guidance-manufacturers_en.pdf (accessed 8 January 2025).

MDCG, Manual on borderline and classification for medical devices under Regulation (EU) 2017/745 on medical devices and Regulation (EU) 2017/746 on in vitro diagnostic medical devices, Version 3 – September 2023, https://health.ec.europa.eu/document/download/71a87df8-5ca1-4555-b453-b65bdf8de909_en?filename=md_borderline_manual_en.pdf (accessed 8 January 2025).

Meredith, Sam, 'Facebook-Cambridge Analytica: A timeline of the data hijacking scandal' CNBC (10 April 2018) www.cnbc.com/2018/04/10/facebook-cambridge-analytica-a-timeline-of-the-data-hijacking-scandal.html (accessed 8 January 2025).

Merrill, Jeremy B and Will Oremus, 'Five points for anger, one for a "like": How Facebook's formula fostered rage and misinformation', *Washington Post* (26 October 2021). www.washingtonpost.com/technology/2021/10/26/facebook-angry-emoji-algorithm/ (accessed 8 January 2025).

Ministère de l'Enseignement supérieur et de la Recherche, Charte de développement responsable des neurotechnologies (17 November 2022). www.enseignementsup-recherche.gouv.fr/fr/charte-de-developpement-responsable-des-neurotechnologies-87964 (accessed 8 January 2025).

Moreu Carbonell, Elisa, 'The Regulation of Neuro-Rights' (2021) 2(2) *European Review of Digital Administration & Law – Erdal*, 149–162. https://doi.org/10.53136/979125994752914.

Mozilla, 'Top Mental Health and Prayer Apps Fail Spectacularly at Privacy, Security' (2022) https://foundation.mozilla.org/en/blog/top-mental-health-and-prayer-apps-fail-spectacularly-at-privacy-security/ (accessed 8 January 2025).

Muhl, Ekaterina and Roberto Andorno, 'Neurosurveillance in the Workplace: Do Employers Have the Right to Monitor Employees' Minds?' *Frontiers in Human Dynamics*, 19 September 2023, Sec. Digital Impacts, 5–2023. https://doi.org/10.3389/fhumd.2023.1245619.

Murdoch, Jim *Protecting the right to freedom of thought, conscience and religion under the European Convention on Human Right* (Council of Europe Human Rights Handbook 2012).

Nam, Chang S. and others (eds), *Brain–Computer Interfaces Handbook. Technological and Theoretical Advances* (CRC Press 2018).

Nandakumar, K and AK Jain, 'Soft Biometrics'. In S. Z. Li and A. K. Jain (eds), *Encyclopedia of Biometrics* (Springer, 2009), 1235–1239. https://doi.org/10.1007/978-0-387-73003-5_225.

Neuwirth, Rostam J, 'Prohibited Artificial Intelligence Practices in the Proposed EU Artificial Intelligence Act (AIA)' (2023) 48(105798) *Computer Law & Security Review*, https://doi.org/10.1016/j.clsr.2023.105798.

Neuwirth, Rostam J, *The EU Artificial Intelligence Act: Regulating Subliminal AI Systems* (Routledge 2023).

Norwegian Data Protection Authority, Urgent and Provisional Measures – Meta (14. Jul 2023) www.datatilsynet.no/contentassets/36ad4a92100943439df9a8a3a7015c19/urgent-and-provisional-measures--meta_redacted.pdf (accessed 8 January 2025).

Novelli, Claudio and others, 'Generative AI in EU Law: Liability, Privacy, Intellectual Property, and Cybersecurity' (2024) 55 *Computer Law & Security Review*, 106066. https://doi.org/10.1016/j.clsr.2024.106066.

Noyb, 'noyb files GDPR complaint against Meta over "Pay or Okay"' (28 November 2023). https://noyb.eu/en/noyb-files-gdpr-complaint-against-meta-over-pay-or-okay (accessed 8 January 2025).

OECD, Consumer vulnerability in the digital age, OECD Digital Economy Papers, No. 355. OECD Publishing, (2023). https://doi.org/10.1787/4d013cc5-en.

OECD, Guidelines on the Protection of Privacy and Transborder Flows of Personal Data (OECD Publishing 2002). https://doi.org/10.1787/9789264196391-en.

OECD, Neurotechnology Toolkit to support policymakers in implementing the OECD Recommendation on Responsible Innovation in Neurotechnology (2024).

OECD, Recommendation of the Council on Responsible Innovation in Neurotechnology (2019) https://legalinstruments.oecd.org/en/instruments/OECD-LEGAL-0457 (accessed 8 January 2025).

Office of the Data Protection Ombudsman, Administrative fine imposed on psychotherapy centre Vastaamo for data protection violations (2021) https://tietosuoja.fi/en/-/administrative-fine-imposed-on-psychotherapy-centre-vastaamo-for-data-protection-violations (accessed 8 January 2025).

Onitiu, Daria and others, 'How AI Challenges the Medical Device Regulation: Patient Safety, Benefits, and Intended Uses' (2024) lsae007 *Journal of Law and the Biosciences*. https://doi.org/10.1093/jlb/lsae007.

Open letter to EU AI Act negotiators: Do not trade away our rights! (8 December 2023). https://edri.org/wp-content/uploads/2023/12/Open-letter-to-EU-AI-Act-negotiators_Do-not-trade-away-our-rights-8-December-2023.pdf (accessed 8 January 2025).

Paal, Boris and Daniel Pauly (eds), *Datenschutz-Grundverordnung Bundesdatenschutzgesetz: DS-GVO BDSG* (3rd ed. C.H. Beck 2021).

Panopytkon Foundation, 'Algorithms of trauma: New case study shows that Facebook doesn't give users real control over disturbing surveillance ads' (28/09/2021), https://en.panoptykon.org/algorithms-of-trauma (accessed 8 January 2025).

Panopytkon Foundation, 'Anxious about your health? Facebook won't let you forget' (7/12/2023). https://en.panoptykon.org/algorithms-of-trauma-2-anxious-about-health (accessed 20 June 2024).

Picard, Rosalind W, *Affective Computing* (MIT Press 2000).

Picozza, Eugenio (ed), *Neurolaw: An Introduction* (Springer 2016).

Prassl, Jeremias, *Humans as a Service. The Promise and Perils of Work in the Gig Economy* (OUP 2018)

Privacy International, 'Your mental health for sale' (2019) https://privacyinternational.org/node/3193 (accessed 8 January 2025).

Purdy, Mark and others, 'The Risks of AI to Interpret Human Emotions', *Harvard Business Review* (18 November 2019) https://hbr.org/2019/11/the-risks-of-using-ai-to-interpret-human-emotions (accessed 8 January 2025).

Purtova, Nadehzda, 'The Law of Everything. Broad Concept of Personal Data and Future of EU Data Protection Law' (2018) 10 *Law, Innovation and Technology*, 40–81. https://doi.org/10.1080/17579961.2018.1452176.

Quinn, Paul and Giancarlo Malgieri, 'The Difficulty of Defining Sensitive Data – The Concept of Sensitive Data in the EU Data Protection Framework' (2021) 22 *German Law Journal*, 1583–1612. doi:10.1017/glj.2021.79.

Rai, Sunny and others, 'Key Language Markers of Depression on Social Media Depend on Race', *Proceedings of the National Academy of Sciences* (26 March 2024). https://doi.org/10.1073/pnas.231983712.

Rainey, Stephen and others, 'Is the European Data Protection Regulation Sufficient to Deal with Emerging Data Concerns Relating to Neurotechnology?' (2020) 7(1) *Journal of Law and the Biosciences*, 1–19. doi:10.1093/jlb/lsaa051.

Ralston, William, 'They Told Their Therapists Everything. Hackers Leaked It All' *Wired* (4 May 2021) www.wired.com/story/vastaamo-psychotherapy-patients-hack-data-breach/ (accessed 8 January 2025).

Report on the novelties of the Audiovisual Media Services Directive (AVMSD) and its relevance for national legislative transposition (2023). www.osce.org/files/f/documents/a/1/539114_0.pdf (accessed 8 January 2025).

Report on the Public Consultation for the European Democracy Action Plan (EDAP), (2 December 2020). https://commission.europa.eu/system/files/2020-12/report_edap_public_consultation_final.pdf (accessed 8 January 2025).

Rhue, Lauren, 'Racial Influence on Automated Perceptions of Emotions' (2018) https://papers.ssrn.com/sol3/papers.cfm?abstract_id=3281765 (accessed 8 January 2025).

Riefa, Christine, 'Protecting Vulnerable Consumers in the Digital Single Market' (2022) 33 *European Business Law Review*, 607–634. https://doi.org/10.54648/eulr2022028.

Rigby, Sandra and others, 'Implementation of the Australian National Safety and Quality Digital Mental Health Standards' (2024) 32(4) *Australasian Psychiatry*, 314–318. doi: 10.1177/10398562241246488.

Robertson, Claire E and others, 'Negativity Drives Online News Consumption' (2023) 7 *Nature Human Behaviour*, 812–822. https://doi.org/10.1038/s41562-023-01538-4.

Ruohonen, Jukka, 'A Review of Product Safety Regulations in the European Union' (2022) 3 *International Cybersecurity Law Review*, 345–366. https://doi.org/10.1365/s43439-022-00057-8.

Sartor, Giovanni and others, 'Regulating targeted and behavioural advertising in digital services: How to ensure users' informed consent'. Study requested by the European Parliament's Committee on Legal Affairs (JURI committee) (2021). www.europarl.europa.eu/thinktank/en/document/IPOL_STU(2021)694680 (accessed 8 January 2025).

Sententia, Wyre, 'Neuroethical Considerations: Cognitive Liberty and Converging Technologies for Improving Human Cognition' (2004) 1013 *Annals of the New York Academy of Sciences*, 221–228. doi: 10.1196/annals.1305.014.

Simitis, Spiros, 'Reconsidering the Premises of Labour Law: Prolegomena to an EU Regulation on the Protection of Employees' Personal Data' (1999) 5(1) *European Law Journal*, 45–62.

Solove, Daniel J, 'Data Is What Data Does: Regulating Risk, Based on Harm and Risk Instead of Sensitive Data' (2024) 118 4 *Northwestern University Law Review*, 1081–1138.

Solove, Daniel J, 'Murky Consent: An Approach to the Fictions of Consent in Privacy Law' (2024) 104(593) *Boston Law Review*, 593. www.bu.edu/bulawreview/files/2024/04/SOLOVE.pdf (accessed 8 January 2025).

Spranger, Tade Matthias (ed.), *International Neurolaw. A Comparative Analysis* (Springer 2012).

Steindl, Elisabeth, 'Consumer Neuro Devices within EU Product Safety Law: Are We Prepared for Big Tech Ante Portas?' (2024) 52, *Computer, Law & Security Review*, 105945. https://doi.org/10.1016/j.clsr.2024.105945.

Steindl, Elisabeth, 'Does the European Data Protection Framework Adequately Protect our Emotions?', (2022) 8 (2) *European Data Protection Law Review*, 311–319. https://doi.org/10.21552/edpl/2022/2/20.

Steindl, Elisabeth, 'Safeguarding Privacy and Efficacy in E-mental Health: Policy Options in the EU and Australia' (2023) 13(3) *International Data Privacy Law*, 207–224. https://doi.org/10.1093/idpl/ipad009.

Stribling, Gordon, 'Mental Health Chatbot Gains Medical Device Status in World First', *Health Tech World* (17 January 2023). www.htworld.co.uk/news/mental-health-chatbot-gains-medical-device-status-in-world-first/ (accessed 8 January 2025).

Taka, Anni-Mara, 'A Deep Dive into Dynamic Data Flows, Wearable Devices, and the Concept of Health Data' (2023), 13(2) *International Data Privacy Law*, 124–140. https://doi.org/10.1093/idpl/ipad007.

Taylor, JS and others, 'Neuropsychologists and Neurolawyers' (1991) 5(293) *Neuropsychology*. https://doi.org/10.1037/0894-4105.5.4.293.

Taylor, Paul M, *Freedom of Religion: UN and European Human Rights Law and Practice* (Cambridge University Press 2005), 115. doi: 10.1017/CBO9780511616129.

Teo, Sue Anne, 'How to Think about Freedom of Thought (and Opinion) in the Age of AI' (2024) 53 *Computer Law & Security Review*. https://doi.org/10.1016/j.clsr.2024.105969.

Tidy, Joey, 'Hacker jailed for blackmailing therapy patients' (BBC 1 May 2024). www.bbc.com/news/articles/c97zndooq7mo (accessed 8 January 2025).

Tzanou, Maria, 'The GDPR and (Big) Health Data. Assessing the EU Legislator's Choices' In Maria Tzanou (ed), *Health Data Privacy under the GDPR. Big Data Challenges and Regulatory Responses* (Routledge 2020).

UN Committee on the Rights of the Child, General comment No. 25 (2021) on children's rights in relation to the digital environment https://digitallibrary.un.org/record/3906061 (accessed 8 January 2025).

UN Human Rights Council Advisory Committee, 'Impact, opportunities and challenges of neurotechnology with regard to the promotion and protection of all human rights' (A/HRC/57/61) (2024). https://documents.un.org/doc/undoc/gen/g24/133/28/pdf/g2413328.pdf. 20 January 2025.

UN, Our Common Agenda – Report of the Secretary-General (2021). www.un.org/en/content/common-agenda-report/assets/pdf/Common_Agenda_Report_English.pdf (accessed 8 January 2025).

Unesco, Ethical issues of neurotechnology: Report, adopted in December 2021 (2022), https://doi.org/10.54678/QNKB6229.

Unesco, First draft of a Recommendation on the Ethics of Neurotechnology (revised version): Working document as of 27 August 2024, SHS/BIO/AHEG-Neuro-2/2024/1 https://unesdoc.unesco.org/ark:/48223/pf0000391074 (accessed 14 January 2025).

Unesco, Outcome Document of the First Meeting of the AHEG First Draft of a Recommendation on the Ethics of Neurotechnology (First Version), SHS/BIO/AHEG-Neuro/2024/1 (9 May 2024). https://unesdoc.unesco.org/ark:/48223/pf0000389768?posInSet=1&queryId=cfc56e24-7a88-4b19-90e7-63bcfc4e556b (accessed 4 May 2025).

Unesco, Draft Text of the Recommendation on the Ethics of Neurotechnology, SHS/IGM-NEURO/2025/MAY/3 (9 April 2025). https://unesdoc.unesco.org/ark:/48223/pf0000393395 (accessed 19 June 2025).

Unesco, The risks and challenges of neurotechnologies for human rights (2023), https://doi.org/10.54678/POGS7778.

Valcke, Peggy and others, 'Constitutional Challenges in the Emotional AI Era' In H-W. Micklitz and others (eds), *Constitutional Challenges in the Algorithmic Society* (Cambridge University Press 2021), 57–77.

Van Drunen, Max Zeno and others, 'The Beginning of EU Political Advertising Law: Unifying Democratic Visions through the Internal Market' (2022) 30(2) *International Journal of Law and Information Technology*, 181–199. https://doi.org/10.1093/ijlit/eaac017.

Veale, Michael and Frederik Zuiderveen Borgesius, 'Demystifying the Draft EU Artificial Intelligence Act – Analysing the Good, the Bad, and the Unclear Elements of the Proposed Approach' (2021) 22(4) *Computer Law Review International*, 97–112. https://doi.org/10.9785/cri-2021-220402.

Veale, Michael and others, 'Fortifying the Algorithmic Management Provisions in the Proposed Platform Work Directive' (2023) 14(2) *European Labour Law Journal*, 308–332. https://doi.org/10.1177/20319525231167983.

Vemou, Konstantina and others, 'TechDispatch – Facial emotion recognition', EDPS TechDispatch 2021-1. https://doi.org/10.2804/519064.

Verhoef, Tessa and Eduard Fosch-Villaronga, 'Towards affective computing that works for everyone', 2023 11th International Conference on Affective Computing and Intelligent Interaction (ACII), Cambridge, MA, USA, 2023, 1–8. doi: 10.1109/ACII59096.2023.10388169.

VUB Brussels Privacy Hub, More than 150 university professors from all over Europe and beyond are calling on the European institutions to include a fundamental rights impact assessment in the future regulation on artificial intelligence (12 September 2023). https://brusselsprivacyhub.com/2023/09/12/brussels-privacy-hub-and-other-academic-institutions-ask-to-approve-a-fundamental-rights-impact-assessment-in-the-eu-artificial-intelligence-act/ (accessed 8 January 2025).

Wachter, Sandra, 'Affinity Profiling and Discrimination by Association in Online Behavioural Advertising' (2020) 35(2) *Berkeley Technology Law Journal*, 369–430. https://doi.org/10.15779/Z38JS9H82M.

Wachter, Sandra, 'Limitations and Loopholes in the EU AI Act and AI Liability Directives: What This Means for the European Union, the United States, and Beyond' (2024) 26(3) *Yale Journal of Law & Technology*, 671–718.

Wachter, Sandra and Brent Mittelstadt, 'A Right to Reasonable Inferences: Re-thinking Data Protection Law in the Age of Big Data and AI' (2019) 2019(2) *Columbia Business Law Review*, 494–620.

Waterson, Jim, '"Show This to Everyone": UK Political ads Move Away from Microtargeting', *The Guardian* (31 May 2024). www.theguardian.com/politics/article/2024/may/31/show-this-to-everyone-uk-political-ads-move-away-from-microtargeting (accessed 8 January 2025).

Wendehorst, Christiane, 'The Proposal for an Artificial Intelligence Act COM(2021)206 from a Consumer Policy Perspective (2021)'. www.sozialministerium.at/dam/sozialministeriumat/Anlagen/Themen/Konsumentenschutz/Konsumentenpolitik/The-Proposal-for-an-Artificial-Intelligence-Act-COM2021-206-from-a-Consumer-Policy-Perspective_dec2021__pdfUA.pdf (accessed 8 January 2025).

Wendehorst, Christiane and Yannic Duller, 'Biometric Recognition and Behavioural Detection. Assessing the ethical aspects of biometric recognition and behavioural detection techniques with a focus on their current and future use in public spaces'. Study requested by the European Parliament's Committee on Legal Affairs and Petitions' (JURI and PETI committees) (2021). www.europarl.europa.eu/RegData/etudes/STUD/2021/696968/IPOL_STU(2021)696968_EN.pdf (accessed 8 January 2025).

WHO, Mental health: Concepts in mental health (17 June 2022) www.who.int/news-room/fact-sheets/detail/mental-health-strengthening-our-response (accessed 8 January 2025).

WHO, 'World mental health report: Transforming mental health for all' (2022). www.who.int/publications/i/item/9789240049338 (accessed 30 January 2025).

Witley, Skye, 'Brain-Scanning Technology Spurs State Moves on Neural Privacy' (13 February 2024). https://news.bloomberglaw.com/privacy-and-data-security/brain-scanning-technology-spurs-state-moves-on-neural-privacy (accessed 8 January 2025).

Wolfangel, Eva, 'Wenn Hacker mit Gesundheits-Apps besonders leichtes Spiel haben' *Die Zeit* (9 May 2023) www.zeit.de/digital/datenschutz/2023-05/gesundheitsapp-datenschutz-depression-edupression-sicherheitsluecke (accessed 8 January 2025).

Wolff, Heinrich Amadeus and others (eds), *Datenschutzrecht, Beck'scher Online-Kommentar* (48th ed. C.H. Beck 2024).

World Economic Forum and Deloitte, 'Global Governance Toolkit for Digital Mental Health: Building Trust in Disruptive Technology for Mental Health', White Paper (2021). www.weforum.org/publications/global-governance-toolkit-for-digital-mental-health/ (accessed 8 January 2025).

Yue Liu, Nancy, *Bio-Privacy: Privacy Regulations and the Challenge of Biometrics* (1st ed. Routledge 2011). https://doi.org/10.4324/9780203804087.

Zanfir, Gabriela, 'Forgetting About Consent. Why The Focus Should Be On "Suitable Safeguards" in Data Protection Law' In Serge Gutwirth and others (eds), *Reloading Data Protection: Multidisciplinary Insights and Contemporary Challenges* (Springer 2014) https://doi.org/10.1007/978-94-007-7540-4_12 (accessed 8 January 2025).

Zard, Lex and Alan M. Sears, 'Targeted Advertising and Consumer Protection Law in the European Union' (2023) 56(3) *Vanderbilt Journal of Transnational Law*.

Zarsky, Tal Z, 'Incompatible: The GDPR in the Age of Big Data' (2017) 47(4) *Seton Hall Law Review*, Article 2. https://scholarship.shu.edu/shlr/vol47/iss4/2 (accessed 30 January).

Zenner, Kai, 'A Law for Foundation Models: The EU AI Act Can Improve Regulation for Fairer Competition', *OECD.AI Policy Observer* (23 July 2023). https://oecd.ai/en/wonk/foundation-models-eu-ai-act-fairer-competition (accessed 8 January 2025).

Zuiderveen Borgesius, Frederik J, 'Personal Data Processing for Behavioural Targeting: Which Legal Basis?' (2015) 5(3) *International Data Privacy Law*, 163–176. https://doi.org/10.1093/idpl/ipv011.

Zuiderveen Borgesius, Frederik J and others, 'Online Political Microtargeting: Promises and Threats for Democracy' (2018) 14(1) *Utrecht Law Review*, 82–96. https://doi.org/10.18352/ulr.420.

LEGAL ACTS

Amendments adopted by the European Parliament on 14 June 2023 on the proposal for a regulation of the European Parliament and of the Council on laying down harmonised rules on artificial intelligence (Artificial Intelligence Act) and amending certain Union legislative acts (COM(2021)0206 – C9-0146/2021–2021/0106(COD)).

Charter of Fundamental Rights of the European Union 2012/C 326/02.

Consolidated versions of the Treaty on European Union and the Treaty on the Functioning of the European Union 2012/C 326/01.

Council Directive 93/42/EEC of 14 June 1993 concerning medical devices, OJ 1993 L 169.

Council of Europe Convention for the Protection of Individuals with regard to Automatic Processing of Personal Data, European Treaty Series No. 108 (1981).

Directive (EU) 2018/1808 of the European Parliament and of the Council of 14 November 2018 amending Directive 2010/13/EU on the coordination of certain provisions laid down by law, regulation or administrative action in Member States concerning the provision of audiovisual media services (Audiovisual Media Services Directive) in view of changing market realities. OJ L 303/69.

Directive (EU) 2024/2831 of the European Parliament and of the Council of 23 October 2024 on improving working conditions in platform work, OJ L, 2024/2831.

Directive 2001/95/EC of the European Parliament and of the Council of 3 December 2001 on general product safety, OJ 2001 L 11.

Directive 2010/13/EU on the coordination of certain provisions laid down by law, regulation or administrative action in Member States concerning the provision of audiovisual media services (Audiovisual Media Services Directive). OJ L 95/1.

Proposal for a Regulation of the European Parliament and of the Council concerning the respect for private life and the protection of personal data in electronic communications and repealing Directive 2002/58/EC (Regulation on Privacy and Electronic Communications) COM/2017/010 final – 2017/03 (COD).

Proposal for a Regulation of the European Parliament and of the Council laying down harmonized rules on Artificial Intelligence (Artificial Intelligence Act) and amending certain Union legislative Acts. (COM/2021/206 final).

Proposal for a Regulation of the European Parliament and of the Council laying down harmonised rules on artificial intelligence (Artificial Intelligence Act) and amending certain Union legislative acts – General approach. Institutional File 2021/0106(COD).

Proposal for a Regulation of the European Parliament and of the Council on the European Health Data Space (COM/2022/197 final).

Regulation (EU) 2016/679 of the European Parliament and of the Council of 27 April 2016 on the protection of natural persons with regard to the processing of personal data and on the free movement of such data, and repealing Directive 95/46/EC (General Data Protection Regulation), OJ 2016 L 119/1.

Regulation (EU) 2017/745 of the European Parliament and of the Council of 5 April 2017 on medical devices, amending Directive 2001/83/EC, Regulation (EC) No 178/2002 and Regulation (EC) No 1223/2009 and repealing Council Directives 90/385/EEC and 93/42/EEC, OJ 2017 L117/1.

Regulation (EU) 2022/2065 of the European Parliament and of the Council of 19 October 2022 on a Single Market For Digital Services and amending Directive 2000/31/EC (Digital Services Act). OJ L 277/1.

Regulation (EU) 2023/988 of the European Parliament and of the Council of 10 May 2023 on general product safety, amending Regulation (EU) No 1025/2012 of the European Parliament and of the Council and Directive (EU) 2020/1828 of the European Parliament and the Council, and repealing Directive 2001/95/EC of the European Parliament and of the Council and Council Directive 87/357/EEC. OJ L 135.

Regulation (EU) 2024/1689 of the European Parliament and of the Council of 13 June 2024 laying down harmonised rules on artificial intelligence and amending Regulations (EC) No 300/2008, (EU) No 167/2013, (EU) No 168/2013, (EU) 2018/858, (EU) 2018/1139 and (EU) 2019/2144 and Directives 2014/90/EU, (EU) 2016/797 and (EU) 2020/1828 (Artificial Intelligence Act) OJ L.

Regulation (EU) 2024/900 of the European Parliament and of the Council of 13 March 2024 on the transparency and targeting of political advertising. OJ L 2024/900.

Regulation (EU) 2025/327 of the European Parliament and of the Council of 11 February 2025 on the European Health Data Space and amending Directive 2011/24/EU and Regulation (EU) 2024/284. OJ L.

CASE LAW

CJEU Case C-101/01 *Bodil Lindqvist* [2003].

CJEU Case C–184/20 *OT v Vyriausioji tarnybinės etikos komisija* [2022].

CJEU Case C-219/11 *Brain Products GmbH v BioSemi VOF* [2012].

CJEU Case C-252/21 *Meta Platforms Inc and Others v Bundeskartellamt* [2023].

CJEU Case C-291/12 *Michael Schwarz v Stadt Bochum:* Opinion of Advocate General Megozzi delivered on 13 June 2013 Case C-291/12 *Michael Schwarz v Stadt Bochum.*

CJEU Case C-446/21 *Maximilian Schrems v Meta Platforms Ireland Ltd, formerly Facebook Ireland Ltd* [2024].

CJEU Case C-667/21 *ZQ versus Medizinischer Dienst der Krankenversicherung Nordrhein, Körperschaft des öffentlichen Rechts* [2023].

ECtHR, Case *Bărbulescu v Romania* (Application no. 61496/08), 5 September 2017.

ECtHR, Case *Niemietz v Germany* (Application no. 13710/88), 16 December 1992.

Index

addictive design, 147
advertising
  behavioural, 90, 138
  commercial, 89
  contextual, 90
  conversational, 90
  display, 89
  emotion-based, 91
  keyword, 90
  political, 119, 141, 146
  segmented, 90
  targeted, 89, 135, 138, 150
algorithmic management, 181
Amazon, 169
approach
  purpose-based, 36, 46, 76
  technology-based, 75–76
  use case-based, 3
Artificial Intelligence Act, 39, 80, 149, 185
assessment of the working capacity, 173
Audiovisual Media Services Directive, 116
Australia, 63, 79
automated monitoring, 181
automated processing, 33, 37, 105, 183
average consumer, 110

balancing test, 100, 102
Bărbulescu v Romania, 167
BEUC, 68, 87, 107, 112, 147
binary concept, 13, 65, 139
biometrics, 17, 20, 27, 162
  authentication, 22, 24
  categorisation, 22, 26, 54
  data, 17, 41, 45
  dilemma, 17, 41, 44
  biometric data, special category, 17, 29
  identification, 22
  identification, remote, 54
  identification, unique, 19, 41
  multimodal, 21
  segregation, 22, 26
  soft, 20
  verification, 22
  weak, 20
blacklist, 109, 113, 131, 183, 189
bossware, 159
brain data, 20, 64, 87
Brain Products GmbH v BioSemi VOF, 75
Brain–Computer Interface, 5

Cambridge Analytica, 120, 127
ChatGPT, 21, 40
classification, 13, 54, 70, 77, 81
commercial practice, 150
  aggressive, 111, 113, 141
  unfair, 140
complementing governance instruments, 69
conditioned exemption, 79, 82
confirmshaming, 115
conformity assessment, 48, 81
consent, 92, 102, 165, 181
  explicit, 67, 87, 123, 165
consumer BCI, 74
consumer health market, 64
consumer protection, 133, 145
consumer protection law, 106
content moderation, 140
co-regulatory instruments, 69, 79

dark patterns, 114, 148
data concerning health, 60
data manifestly made public, 123
Data Protection Directive, 13, 30
data revealing political opinions, 122
data sharing, 68, 87
deceptive design patterns, 116
detection system, 26–27, 139
Digital Markets Act, 133

digital mental health, 59
Digital Services Act, 49, 57, 129, 133
Directive on Equal Treatment in the Access to and Supply of Goods and Services, 177
Directive on Safety and Health of Workers, 175
discrimination, 30, 34, 121, 176
Display Screen Equipment Directive, 175

efficacy, 59, 70, 77
e-mental health, 59
emotion recognition system, 35, 37, 41, 187
emotion technology, 9
emotional contagion, 97, 142, 157
emotional stirring/steering, 115
emotional targeting, 91
employment, 158
Employment Equality Directive, 177
enforcement, 69, 176
equality law, 176
European Health Data Space, 68, 82

Facebook, 96, 120–121, 142, 149
fairness, 171
forum internum, 32
freedom of assembly and of association, 170
freedom of choice or conduct, 112
freedom of expression and information, 99, 128
freedom of thought, 32
fundamental rights impact assessment, 49

Gender Equality Directive, 178
General Data Protection Regulation (GDPR), 13, 60, 91, 122, 160
  certification, 69, 79
  code of conduct, 69
General Product Safety Directive, 70
General Product Safety Regulation, 70
general-purpose AI, 40, 55
  model, 55
  model with systemic risk, 57
  system, 56
generative AI, 40, 55
group privacy, 26, 41

illegal content, 140, 145
incentives, 80
inferences, 65
  sensitive, 66
information fatigue, 136, 143
inner sanctum, 33
input data, 123, 131, 137, 184
intended medical purpose, 73

labour law, 161
labour platforms, digital, 180

legal basis, 92
legitimate activity by a not-for-profit body, 123
legitimate interest, 92, 99, 166
lifestyle device, 73

manipulation, 101, 108, 117, 121, 132, 153
material distortion, 155
Maximilian Schrems v Meta Platforms Ireland Ltd, 104
medical device, 63, 71
Medical Device Coordination Group, 74
Medical Devices Directive, 72, 75
Medical Devices Regulation (MDR), 70
  certification, 70
mental health, 59, 73
Meta, 102
Meta Platforms Inc and Others v Bundeskartellamt, 102, 125
mind data, 13, 15, 29, 31, 36
Mind Datafying Technologies, 1, 11
momentary processing, 27
monitoring, 158, 162, 167
  practice, 159, 183

neurodiscrimination, 177, 179
neurodiversity, 179
neurolaw, 6
neuroright, 1, 9
neurosurveillance, 172
neurotechnology, 5, 35
Niemietz v Germany, 167

online platform, 135
opening clause, 160–161
output data, 123, 131, 137, 184

Panoptykon Foundation, 143, 146
people analytics, 159
performance of a contract, 92
personalisation of content, 95, 98, 103, 107, 141, 146
physical states, 45, 184, 187
Piccadilly Circus, 26
Platform Work Directive, 54, 180
political microtargeting, 120, 131
political practice, 119, 150
power imbalance, 34, 103, 111, 160, 171, 182, 186
product safety law, 40, 70
profile
  consumer, 90, 100
  political, 120
  predictive, 91
  psychographic, 113, 131
  voter, 120
profiling, 49, 105, 127, 170

Racial Equality Directive, 177
raw sensor data, 65
recommender system, 142, 145–146, 157
recruitment, 161, 164, 183, 185

sensitive data, 13
special category data, concept of, 30, 32
substantial public interest, 123
sui generis special category, 29, 35, 38
surveillance, 114, 158, 163, 172
systemic risk, 57, 144

technique
  biometric, 17, 43
  deceptive, 152
  manipulative, 152–153
  subliminal, 117, 152, 154
tracking, 90
transactional decision, 108, 112
transparency, 163, 167, 170
Transparency and Targeting of Political Advertising Regulation, 128

undue influence, 111
Unfair Commercial Practices Directive, 106, 127, 155
user expectation, 94, 96, 102

Vastaamo, 68
vignette, 3
vital interest, 173
VLOPs, 134, 136, 143
vulnerability, 102, 109, 147

well-being, 59, 73
  device, 73, 83
wellness application, 83

For EU product safety concerns, contact us at Calle de José Abascal, 56–1°, 28003 Madrid, Spain or eugpsr@cambridge.org.

www.ingramcontent.com/pod-product-compliance
Lightning Source LLC
LaVergne TN
LVHW011813200926
848484LV00005B/1177